THE CRUCIFIXION *of* MARY MAGDALENE

The Historical Tradition of the First Apostle and the Ancient Church's Campaign to Suppress It

RICHARD J. HOOPER

SANCTUARY PUBLICATIONS

The Crucifixion of Mary Magdalene: The Historical Tradition of the First Apostle and the Ancient Church's Campaign to Suppress it

Cover and book design: Jane Perini, Thunder Mountain Design & Communications
Original pen and ink, J. Rogers, painting by Susun Lovit

Published by Sanctuary Publications, P.O. Box 20697, Sedona, AZ 86351

ISBN 0974699543
Library of Congress Control Number: 2005935319

For my wife, Sharon,
my guide, my mirror, and my life—
without whose support and encouragement
this book could not have been written.

This book is also dedicated to my sisters:
all of the women of the world who continue
to suffer oppression at the hands of men.
May you, like Mary, one day become free.

TABLE OF CONTENTS

"Ignorance is the Mother of All Evil."

– The Gospel of Philip

Author's Note

The following three narratives which serve as the preface to this work are dramatizations of probable and actual people and events. The first is a fictional account, based on historical facts, that chronicles the fourth century interment of the sacred Gnostic Christian texts now known as the *Nag Hammadi Library*. The narrative also proposes a fictitious scenario to account for the original disappearance of *The Gospel According to Mary* (Magdalene), and how it may have become separated from the *Library*, as modern scholars believe it was.

The second narrative is a dramatization of the actual events that took place in 1896 when an ancient codex (now known as Papyrus Berolinensis 8502.1, or the Berlin Codex) was discovered in an antiquities market in Cairo, Egypt. One of the four works contained in this codex turned out to be a previously unknown Gospel, and the only Gospel ever attributed to a female disciple of Jesus: *The Gospel of Mary*. Only the name of the antiquities dealer has been invented.

The third narrative chronicles the actual events surrounding the discovery of the Nag Hammadi codices, in Egypt, in 1945. The content of these ancient texts has forced scholars to entirely rethink the origins of Christianity.

CHENOBOSKIA, EGYPT, 385 C.E.

A scorpion burrowing its way out of the hot sand beyond the opening of the cave was the only witness to Sansnos' despair. The red crosses painted everywhere on the walls of stone did not console the monk in this time of trial. Now a cell for hermits, the cave itself had long since been plundered of its treasures. Nothing at all—save for empty air and rock—remained of the tombs that had at one time been the burial grounds of the sixth dynasty. The mummies of Pepi I and II were long gone, along with their retinue and their gold.

Two millennia had passed since the Pharaohs had occupied these caves, and Sansnos reflected on the fact that humanity was no better off now then it had been then. Those who turned their backs on the Light still ruled, and the innocent still died. But what else could one expect from the realm of matter?

The hour of dismissal from that realm would soon be at hand for Sansnos, and the monk was only too willing to cast off the worthless shell that was his body. A fraction of fear still remained, it was true, and Sansnos plunged deep within himself in order to discover its hiding place. Fear, like flesh, was the prison of the soul. The Savior had taught this, and so had Mary, the Blessed One.[1]

Fear, this monk knew, would steal away eternal life by robbing the soul of its destiny. But like every other emotion and the passion of the flesh, fear—Sansnos recognized—was nothing more than a projection of the mind. Like death itself, it was an illusion manifested by the perceiver. The monk knew that he must keep his mind focused on the All, with which he was one. In order to remain in this consciousness, Sansnos repeated a passage from the *Gospel of Eve* over and over again in his mind: "I am identical with thee, and thou art identical with me; wherever thou art, there am I, for I am sown in all things; wherever thou wilt thou reapest me; but in reaping me it is thyself that thou reapest."[2]

Sansnos focused his attention of the Light within—his divine Self. He knew that he must remain in this pure, bright place at the moment of death in order for his soul to be liberated from the bonds of matter and return to the source of Light itself. But as pleasant as this thought was, even this Sansnos had to brush aside in order to complete his immediate mission. At present he had to concentrate on the task at hand: the burial of the beloved books of his community—the sacred scriptures that had guided him since his youth. The books must not fall into the hands of those without gnosis, for they would surely destroy them.

Sansnos wondered if perhaps this place of dry earth would become the graveyard for his faith. Even if this was to be, perhaps the books would live on. Most importantly, they must not be found by the ignorant ones—those who lacked eyes to see and ears to hear.

Sansnos' community had entrusted him with the sacred duty of preserving the teachings of the Savior, but letting go of the books he so loved was an enormously difficult task. Even now, the monk looked lovingly upon the hand-tooled, leather-bound book in his hands. It was Sansnos' favorite book because, along with other works, it included a Gospel with one hundred and fourteen secret teachings of Jesus which Judas Thomas, Jesus' twin, had written down.[3]

As a youth, Sansnos had watched the process of translating this text from the original Greek into his own language, which was Coptic.[4] As a boy, Sansnos had gathered papyrus from the nearby Nile, and learned the art of processing it into long sheets of writing material. These sheets would then be cut into separate pages and bound together. *Such an improvement over scrolls*, Sansnos thought. The scribe could write text on both sides of the papyrus instead of just one.[5]

As a young adult, Sansnos had been put in charge of the monastery's cattle, so the monk thought it only natural to learn how to tan and tool leather.[6] The leather cover of the book Sansnos now held in his hands was one that he himself had tooled into a series of crosses that stood out in relief. And although he loved this collection of manuscripts dearly, the monk reminded himself that only the teachings they contained had any real value—and he had long since committed most of those to memory.

The monk held no illusions; it was highly doubtful that he or any members of his community would ever retrieve these books. In all likelihood his people would all be dead by nightfall.[7] All that Sansnos could hope for was enough time to complete his mission. If he was very fortunate, he might even have enough time to return to the monastery where he could die in the loving arms of his brothers and sisters.

Sansnos' thoughts turned to Hatibi, and he hoped and prayed that she would remain safe on her journey. Her mission, Sansnos knew, was every bit as important as his own, since she was carrying the remainder of their community's books to the monastery at Achmim—some sixty seven miles north along the Nile. There, hopefully, Hatibi would find sanctuary for their books somewhere among the extensive monastery graves.[8]

Sansnos had insisted that Hatibi remain in Achmim after she had completed her task. It was not likely that the Roman soldiers would raid the Pachomian monastery at Achmim because it did not generally harbor those whom the Catholic Church considered heretical. The monastery at Chenoboskia was another matter altogether. The Pachomian monks here were tolerant of the form of Christianity practiced by Sansnos, Hatibi and dozens of others. The orthodox monks at the monastery had even allowed the Gnostic Christians to keep their scriptures in the monastery library—at least, until today.

The orthodox patriarchs in Alexandria and Rome showed no such tolerance, however. The tide had turned in orthodoxy's favor ever since Epiphanius and Athanasius had become so bold as to insist that heresy had to be rooted out once and for all.

Decades earlier, when Sansnos had been a child, Athanasius, Archbishop of Alexandria, had written an Easter letter condemning the form of Christianity Sansnos adhered to. Theodore—then leader of the Pachomian monasteries—even established that letter as a monastic rule of order, and yet he had made no move to actually expel monks like Sansnos.

There had been an empire-wide respite from Constantine's persecution during the brief reign of Julian. But Julian was dead, and Theodosius' decree against heretics was now in effect. Word had reached Sansnos' community just the previous night that Catholic soldiers at the Roman garrison at Diospolis Parva—just across the Nile—were preparing to raid the monastery at Chenoboskia. There they were sure to find and burn all heretical books along with their adherents.

Forewarned, Sansnos and Hatibi had managed to spirit all of their community's sacred scripture from the monastery library during the previous night. Just before dawn they had also liberated two mules that were tied up outside the adjacent cattle pen. The pack mules were necessary because Sansnos was afraid of hiding all the books in one place. Better to use the mules and take some of the manuscripts somewhere else entirely. The council had all agreed that Sansnos would inter half of the books in the surrounding hills, and Hatibi would take the rest to be buried in the Pachomian monastery graveyards of Achmim.

Neither Sansnos nor Hatibi could have managed their burdens without the mules. While Sansnos' own journey was a short one, it had been necessary to transport thirteen books, a two-foot-tall earthenware pot in which to hide the books, a small digging tool, and bitumen—an asphalt-like mortar—which would be used to seal the top of the pot. Hatibi was carrying only manuscripts, but they were heavy and her journey would be long.

Sansnos reflected upon all of this as he left the coolness of the cave to resume his digging outside. Just as the sun was touching the horizon, Sansnos' job was finished. The holy scriptures of the Pachomian-Gnostic Christians were now safely buried beneath the dry soil of an ancient empire, and there they would be preserved for the next sixteen hundred years.[9]

CAIRO, EGYPT, 1896

Abdullah Zayd was a clever man, or so he had convinced himself over the years. As a dealer of old manuscripts, Abdullah's business was reasonably lucrative due to the fact that he was not overly stringent in the way he interpreted the laws governing Egyptian antiquities. In Abdullah's opinion, the laws having to do with the acquisition, possession and sale of ancient relics and manuscripts were oppressive. After all, a man had to eat! At any rate, Abdullah believed that all the laws demanded interpretation, and one's interpretation should sometimes be very liberal.

As far as Abdullah was concerned, the spoils of war might belong to Allah, but everything else that did not specifically belong to some living person should be available to anyone on a first-come, first-serve basis. Certainly this rule applied to ancient artifacts that he himself had discovered . . . or at least had acquired as a result of his time-honed negotiation skills. It should not be his problem if others had not versed themselves well on the value of Egyptian artifacts.

Abdullah reasoned that if one put in the personal effort to unearth, or acquire, something from the distant past, one should be allowed to keep said item and do with it as he wished. Obviously, the original owners of these items no longer had any need of them, and the museums already had too much. It was stupid to just leave such treasures undisturbed beneath the soil, or wherever else they were hidden. What good could they do anyone there?

As the natural consequence of such opinions, Abdullah had a disdain for professional archaeologists. How could these people be so arrogant and self-righteous? What made their profession any more ethical, or legal, than his own? Did they not dig in the soil just like he did? Did they not rob graves just like he did? So what if they gave everything they found to museums? The museums had so many artifacts they couldn't even display most of them. Beautiful things wound up in drawers, cabinets, closets or storerooms, all of it filed away under a silly system of numerical codes. How could the public enjoy them there? This was craziness.

Because of all the inequities of the law, and because Abdullah had the good sense that Allah had given him, he had long ago established what he considered to be a simple, firm and fair policy regarding the acquisition and dispensation of relics, artifacts, antiquities, and whatever else one might choose to call the detritus of history—finders keepers. One could then choose to sell an item, keep it for oneself or, Allah forbid, hand it over to the vultures of academia. Hah! The last option was a laugh. A man had to eat!

Abdullah Zayd's thoughts were interrupted by the dong-dong of a camel bell hanging around the door knob of his front door. Instantly, his scowl turned into an enormous and gracious smile as he welcomed the infidel who had just entered his shop.

Abdullah loved infidels, even if Allah did not. They were, after all, his best customers. Being stupid, these infidels rarely argued over price—and even when they did, Abdullah knew how to get the better of them. And Abdullah especially liked the infidel that stood in front of him now: Dr. Carl Reinhardt, a scholar from Germany whom the antiquities dealer had not seen for over a year. Abdullah had missed the good doctor, particularly because he had been saving something very special for him.

After Abdullah Zayd had served tea, and after a pleasant but meaningless conversation, the antiquities dealer told Dr. Reinhardt about his recent acquisition, and then went into a back room to fetch it. Returning to the front of the shop, and moving the tea service to one side, Abdullah laid the manuscripts on the table in front of Reinhardt.

It did not take but a moment for Reinhardt to recognize that the manuscripts must be very ancient. The pages, after all, were not parchment, but papyrus. Clearly the letters on the pages were from the Greek alphabet, but when he was unable to form them into words—he was well versed in ancient Greek—he correctly surmised that the manuscripts were written in Coptic—the ancient language of Egyptian Christians.

Reinhardt asked about the provenance of the codex he had before him. Where had it come from? Abdullah hesitated for only a moment before remarking that he had purchased it from a peasant who had told him that he had found it in a wall niche of a house. Reinhardt did not reply, but he knew perfectly well that this could not have been the case. If this very old book had been residing in the open air for many centuries, it would be nothing but a pile of dust by now. Reinhardt suspected that Abdullah was making up a story to cover up the fact that he had come by the codex illegally.

Even though Reinhardt could not read the manuscripts, and even though he had no way of determining the provenance, he still purchased the work from Abdullah after some obligatory haggling. One day in the not too distant future, the Egyptian government would cease letting such prizes leave Egyptian soil. But Dr. Carl Reinhardt was in the right place at the right time, so he was able to return to Berlin with a treasure beyond his imagining.

After arriving back in Berlin, Reinhardt gave the manuscript to the Egyptian Museum where it was examined by an Egyptologist by the name of Carl Schmidt. Schmidt confirmed that the text was indeed in Coptic and that the papyrus pages were, indeed, very ancient.

In discussing the issue of provenance with Schmidt, Dr. Reinhardt happened to mention that Abdullah Zayd's hometown was Achmim, an ancient village along the Nile, north of Nag Hammadi, that had once been the site of a Pachomian monastery. This being the case, Carl Schmidt speculated that the manuscript could have been found in the graveyards of Achmim, or else someplace nearby.

Upon further examination and translation of the codex, Schmidt discovered that this ancient book of papyrus was actually four different "lost" works: the *Act of Peter*, The *Sophia* (or "Wisdom") *of Jesus Christ*, *The Apocryphon* (or "Secret Book") *of John* and—most incredible of all—a previously unknown Gospel attributed to Mary Magdalene! Still, it was what the Gospel claimed that was its most shocking feature. In this Gospel, Mary Magdalene was not just one of Jesus' disciples, she was his most spiritually worthy disciple and recipient of his most secret teachings.

It was obvious to both Reinhardt and Schmidt that if such a claim about Mary were proven to be true, then the history of early Christianity would have to be rewritten! As it was, however, this long-held secret about Mary Magdalene was neglected for yet another century.[10]

NAG HAMMADI, EGYPT, 1945

Muhammad 'Ali al-Samman had only one thing on his mind today, and that was vengeance. Hate clouded all of his thoughts as he, his brother Khalifah, and a few of their friends set out from their home at al-Qasron on camelback. The band of men first crossed the Nile, and then the railroad tracks beside it.

The Nazis, under the command of Rommel, had laid these tracks not so many years ago. The German army had used them during their temporary occupation of the northernmost part of the African continent. Given Hitler's penchant for finding, and seizing, Christian artifacts all over the world, it was fortunate that the Gestapo had no knowledge of what lay buried in the Egyptian soil not so far away from these very tracks. Now the infidel Nazis were only a bad memory, but Muhammad knew that one's enemies were endless.

As the small band of men crossed over the tracks, they became acutely aware of entering enemy territory, but the enemy was no longer the Germans. The enemy was now the Hawwaris—a clan which had produced the murderer of Muhammad's father. At the moment, these murderous cowards were hiding behind the well-protected walls of Hamrah Dum, but their time would come. Muhammad swore this to Allah. Coming so close to this town, Muhammad's heart seared with hate. With his brothers, he would avenge his father's death. That was a certainty, but Muhammad regretted that today would not be the day.

Muhammad turned his camel and signaled his brother and his friends toward the southeast flank of the Jabal al-Tarif, a mountainous area slightly north of Hamrah Dum. It was a wondrous area, really—pockmarked with hundreds of caves, caves that he and his younger brother, Abu al-Majd, had explored many times during happier days before the blood feud.

As a youth, Muhammad had been told by his father about the caves, how they were used as burial sites for the ancient Egyptians more than four thousand years before. Muhammad's father also told him the strange legend about Christian monks who had also once used these caves to hide from other Christians. One could not understand the ways of infidels.

But here it was, a fine day in December, and Muhammad had come with his brothers and friends, not to enjoy themselves, not even to plot against the Hawwaris, but to work. For the Jabal al-Tarif, itself, produced *sabakh*, and sabakh was a fine soil that Muhammad's clan had used to fertilize their crops for generations.

Muhammad knew that if he and the other men did not return with the valuable sabakh, his mother, 'Umm-Ahmad, would be furious. And no one wanted that. So today the group of men had to take great care not to be discovered by their enemy. There would be time enough for killing later.

The camels ventured up the slope of the hills until finally pulled to a halt. The seven men dismounted, brought out their picks and mattocks and got right to work. It was no more than an hour after the men had begun to dig that Khalifah, Muhammad's fifteen-year-old brother yelled down the hill, "Come and see." Muhammad did not like to waste time, but he climbed up to where Abu was working to see what the problem was.

Khalifah had been using his pick, digging around a very large boulder.

"I hit on something solid that wasn't rock, so I started to dig around it. Look, see, it is some kind of pot." Muhammad sighed, but bent down to take a closer look. It certainly seemed that it was, indeed, some kind of pot. It was reddish in color, with four small handles around the top. Once it was standing, Muhammad thought, it would be about two feet tall. The color of the pot was not like the color of the surrounding hills. That is why it stood out.

Muhammad used his hands to remove more dirt from around the object. "I don't know what it is, Abu, but we should be careful. It could be some exploding device left by the Germans." As the brothers continued to remove more dirt, however, they both soon became convinced that the object was just some pot after all.

Then Khalifah said, "Perhaps it is something of value, Muhammad. What do you think?" Khalifah's older brother merely made a grunting sound and continued pawing at the dirt until he had outlined the certain shape.

"Just an old pot, Khalifah," Muhammad stated to the boy who was now looking disappointed. "Still, it might be something interesting. Call the others." Abu obeyed, yelling down the hill. Soon, several men joined Muhammad and Khalifah who dug with their hands around the earthenware vessel. Within minutes they were able to pull the object from its earthly tomb.

Setting it upright, Muhammad saw that the top of the pot was entirely sealed by some substance. *Probably bitumen*, he thought. Muhammad and Khalifah tried removing the seal, but it would not budge. "Break it," Khalifah encouraged his older brother.

"I don't think so, Khalifah. It might contain jinn. Who knows what would happen then?" Jinn, all the men knew, were evil spirits, the kind only fools would tempt.

"Oh, Muhammad," teased Khalifah. "Are you afraid of a jar? You are too superstitious."

"Perhaps," Muhammad replied. "But who knows? One should be careful. It looks to me like this pot has been here a very long time."

"Muhammad," another of the men spoke up. "It might contain gold! What if it were to contain gold, and we didn't look? We could all be rich!" The others eagerly nodded their agreement.

"Muhammad stood there looking at the red earthenware vessel, considering it for some moments. It might be dangerous to break the pot. But, then again, what if it *did* contain something valuable? In the end, his curiosity won out. Muhammad reached for his pick, looked at the others and said, "Alright, I will break it. But if anything bad happens, don't say I didn't warn you."

The men stood back as Muhammad took a wide swing with his pick, and as metal hit clay, the pot broke into a dozen shards. The men stared at the contents. No jinn—at least none that they could actually see. That was good. But there was no gold either. All that was in the pot was a bunch of . . . what? Some old books of some kind.

Trying not to look too disappointed, the men dusted off thirteen leather-bound volumes in all. Held together by the overlapping leather covers were pages of papyrus—the men knew what ancient papyrus looked like—with some kind of writing on them. But none of the men could read a word of whatever was written on the papyrus. The letters were in some language they had never seen before.

All the men by now, except Muhammad, were looking discouraged. They had hoped for gold, or at least *something* of value. Instead, the contents of the pot were obviously worthless. Just a bunch of old books. The look on Muhammad's face, however, was not one of discouragement: it was anger. He was mad mostly at himself for wasting all this time on nothing.

Muhammad put all the books in a pile, then ordered the men back to work. For the next several hours the men dug for sabakh, their dreams of wealth dashed by a single blow of a pick.

As the sun eventually began to dip its fiery head beyond the ridges, the men shoveled their piles of sabakh onto large pieces of dry burlap that they had brought along for this purpose. After several shovels full, they made the burlap into bags by tying off the corners, so that the precious soil would not shake loose on the way back to their village.

Each of the men took their respective bags and tied them to thongs that hung from the camel saddles. Other bags they tied, two by two, to the ends of long pieces of rope which they then flung over the beasts of burden. Finally they were finished, but Muhammad motioned to the others to follow him up the hill. When they arrived at the pile of old books—if you could call them that—Muhammad started to hand the leather-bound scraps to each of the workers. But, to a man, they all refused to take them. It could only mean bad luck. Even to hold them. Maybe the books themselves were possessed by jinn. Who could say? Better to leave them alone.

This turn of events only made Muhammad angrier still. He stared at the other men, but said nothing. Finally he walked back down the hill, took his last remaining length of burlap, and climbed back up where they were. He piled all thirteen books onto the fabric, then tied the burlap into a bag. Next, he angrily flung the bag over his shoulder and stomped down the hill without saying a single word to the rest of the group.

The men and their camels arrived back home just as twilight was turning into darkness. After unloading the camels and dumping their bags of sabakh on the ground in front of Muhammad's house, the friends left for their own dwellings, and Muhammad and his brother entered their own home. Hopefully their mother had prepared something delicious to eat tonight, for they were not in a good mood. Especially Muhammad.

The next morning, Muhammad went outside to the pile of bags. He grabbed the one full of old books, untied it, and shook them out onto the ground. Then he picked them up and stacked them against the house, after which he went off to the village for the day.

That night, before any of her sons had returned home, 'Umm-Ahmad was about to start dinner until she noticed she had run out of straw to start the fire. She went outside looking for kindling, and happened to notice the pile of old books by the side of the house. She grabbed a handful of the papyrus pages and took them inside where she crumpled them up and then set them on fire inside the oven.

This same day in the village, Muhammad had run into his old friend Raghib, who taught history at the local school. Muhammad told his friend about his discovery from the prior day, and Raghib said, "Ah, dear friend, this sounds interesting. I should like very much to take a look at these books. They could be worth something, you know. Perhaps they are very old. Who knows? Perhaps they are of some importance to *someone*, yes?"

Muhammad had no idea, but he told his friend that he would save the old books until he could come take a look at them. When Muhammad returned home that evening he saw that quite a few pages of one of the books were missing. Figuring that his mother had used them for kindling, he removed the books to a safe hiding place.

Life went on as usual in the village for the next several weeks, and Muhammad forgot all about the leather-bound pages. He had much more important matters to take care of—like killing his father's murderer. His father, 'Ali, had been killed only because he had performed his duties as a night watchman. He had killed an intruder who happened to be one of the Hawara tribe. In an act of revenge, Ali was murdered just an hour later, beginning a blood feud that would not end for some time.

Day and night, Muhammad and his brothers plotted while they sharpened their working tools into acceptable weapons. One day a friend came by to tell the brothers that he had seen Ahmed Isma'il, their father's murderer, close to town. Muhammad and his brothers immediately got up, took their tools—now weapons—and rushed to town.

After several frantic hours of searching, the brothers found their father's killer, Ahmad Isma'il, asleep alongside a road. Muhammad and his brothers immediately attacked the sleeping murderer with their sharpened mattocks and hacked him to death. Then, as the ultimate act of blood vengeance, the brothers ripped the murderer's heart from his chest and ate it raw. Finishing their work, the brothers left to return home. They would tell their mother what they had done, and she would be very proud of them.

Yet the killing did not end. A long time later, Ahmad's son avenged his own father's death by sneaking into town when an Ali family funeral procession was taking place, and shot up the crowd—killing several people and wounding Muhammad Ali' himself.

From here, the drama that surrounded the 13 codices of Nag Hammadi—found not far from the ancient site of Chenoboskia—continued to unfold as if it were an Indiana Jones movie—and sometimes the Keystone Kops. The collection of 52 manuscripts, or tractates, at one point became separated, and disappeared in various directions. Individual parts were bought, sold, seized, stolen and smuggled. Manuscripts fell into the hands of shady merchants, a one-eyed outlaw, the Coptic Museum of Cairo, and the Jung Institute in Zurich.

More deaths and tragedies took place among those who came in contact with the codices, and some began to wonder if the "curse of Jesus" (found near the end of the Secret Book of John from Codex II) might not have taken effect: "And the Savior presented these things to him that he might write them down and keep them secure. And he said to him, 'Cursed be everyone who will exchange these things for a gift or for food or for drink or for clothing or for any other such thing."[11]

Introduction

I f human beings valued truth above all else, we would be able to define the word "history" very simply as "facts about the past." In reality, the definition of "history" remains equivocal. My diction- ary, for instance, defines "history" as "the branch of knowledge dealing with past events."[1] Therefore, history is open to interpretation.

Sometimes facts are unknown and the historian writes an approxi- mation. Sometimes those facts are discovered much later, and history is revised. But the reverse holds true as well; history is sometimes revised in order to hide the facts. And wherever cultures clash and wars are fought, history is written by the victor.

In antiquity many of those who wrote stories about historical events considered what actually happened, historically, to be far less important than the religious and cosmological meaning of those events. Historical fact was readily and commonly subordinated to faith, and in many cases, mythology took the place of history.

What was "true" about a myth had little to do with events which ac- tually took place, and everything to do with the interpretation of those events. Indeed, historical facts often got in the way of meaning, and had to be altered in order to fit the message.

Given the multiple layers of early Christian mythology that were superimposed over the story of the historical Jesus in the Gospels of the New Testament, the task of modern scholars and historians has been to deconstruct the myths in an attempt to discover the historical facts that lay behind them. Their job is a difficult one for many reasons, and their work is further complicated by having to address contemporary myths that are based on people's misunderstanding and misinterpretation of the original ones.

Certainly no other historical figure has been more mythologized, misunderstood and maligned than Jesus' disciple, Mary of Magdala. Negative rumors and innuendos about Mary have circulated for many centuries and have led to the common perception that Mary had been a wanton woman, a penitent sinner, who was saved by Jesus. Most people—including most Christians—who hold such beliefs about Mary no doubt assume that this is how Mary is represented in the canonical Gospels of the New Testament. Yet this is not true at all.

There is not a single reference in the Gospels of *Matthew, Mark, Luke* or *John* to suggest that Mary was a sinner saved by Jesus, much less a prostitute. The image of Mary as a penitent sinner and prostitute actually comes from a sermon given by Pope Gregory the Great in 597 C.E. in which he conflated the persons of Mary Magdalene, Mary of Bethany, and Luke's "sinful woman" who washed Jesus' feet with her tears and dried them with her hair.[2] Yet it matters little that Gregory's Mary was entirely fictional. The innuendos about Mary that resulted from his sermon have persisted in the form of rumors to the present day.

If rumors and myths are self-perpetuating, they can also be self-replicating. Based on the original fiction that Mary Magdalene had been a lusty woman, mythologists of the modern era have further complicated this image of Mary by suggesting that Mary Magdalene must have been married to Jesus. Once again, it does not seem to matter that there is not a shred of historical evidence to support such an idea: this is how Mary Magdalene is often portrayed in modern books and movies.

These two images of Mary have been repeated so many times—throughout history, and especially in our modern media—that many people simply assume that they must be factual. Certainly for media sensationalists, the real facts about Mary only serve to get in the way of who they *want* Mary to be.

In spite of these ancient and modern misconceptions, the actual historical record about Mary Magdalene reveals a woman who could not have been more different from the Mary of popular imagination. The canonical Gospels—although their authors attempted to obscure Mary's true impor-

> *...for media sensationalists, the real facts about Mary only serve to get in the way of who they want Mary to be.*

tance—represent the Magdalene as Jesus' most faithful disciple. She was a witness to his crucifixion and, in three out of the four canonical Gospels,[3] the first disciple to receive an appearance of Jesus after his death. She was also the first disciple to be commissioned as an apostle.[4]

There exists, also, a second historical tradition of Mary Magdalene that can be found in another group of ancient scriptures often referred to as the "Gnostic" Gospels. These texts include *The Gospel According to Mary* (Magdalene), *The Gospel According to Philip*, *The Gospel According to Thomas*, *Dialogue of the Savior*, *The Sophia of Jesus Christ*, *The Pistis Sophia*, and *The (first) Apocalypse of James*. All of these works have been rediscovered in modern times, and all but *The Gospel of Mary* and the *Pistis Sophia* were discovered at Nag Hammadi.

This group of ancient sacred texts often represents Mary Magdalene as a disciple especially favored by Jesus for her spiritual maturity, as a leader and teacher in her own right. Virtually all accounts about Mary in the texts of both Orthodox and Gnostic Christian traditions agree on one thing: *Mary Magdalene was a holy woman, not a penitent sinner.*

In spite of how Mary was represented in all of these texts, a number of early patriarchs of the Church—including the evangelists who wrote the canonical Gospels—often ignored, and sometimes even altered, the historical record about Mary in order to have her serve their political and theological ends. Ultimately, Mary Magdalene became subordinate to the male apostles—both in the Gospels and thereafter. When the political and theological need arose to suppress Mary's tradition even further, she became a great sinner who had been redeemed by Jesus.

Given the patriarchal nature of all Semitic religions—Judaism, Christianity and Islam—it should not be entirely surprising that all of the false rumors and innuendos about Mary Magdalene throughout the ages have been the work of men. Beginning with the apostle Paul, who was strangely silent about Mary Magdalene as a witness to the resurrection, to the author of Luke's Gospel, who invented Mary's "seven demons," to Simon Peter, who was Mary's mythological/historical arch-rival, to the sixth-century pope, Gregory, who reinvented Mary as a prostitute and penitent sinner, slanders against Mary have always been the work of men.

> *Given the patriarchal nature of all Semitic religions...it should not be entirely surprising that all of the false rumors and innuendos about Mary Magdalene throughout the ages have been the work of men.*

We might expect today—in an enlightened society and age—that Mary would be treated differently by men. Yet the opposite has been the case. Producers of movies like *The Last Temptation of Christ* and *The Passion of the Christ*—which continue to portray Mary as a seductive femme fatale—are men. The authors of such books as *Holy Blood, Holy Grail* and *The Da Vinci Code* are also men. Mary continues to be, even today, the subject of male prurient interest.

Elizabeth Moltmann-Wendel in her book, *The Women around Jesus*, pointed out back in 1982 that the "portrait of Mary Magdalene, constructed by men, served to kindle male fantasies."[5] While this is true, Susan Haskins in *Mary Magdalene in Myth and Metaphor* reminds us that Moltmann-Wendel's own work only served to kindle *female* fantasies.[6] When it comes to the subject of Mary Magdalene, fantasy has always been the order of the day.

Aside from the obvious commercial benefits of representing Mary Magdalene as Jesus' "significant other," I sense a more subtle male bias at work in such portrayals. The underlying message of all fictional movies and books in which Mary appears is that the Magdalene was important only because of her *relationship* to Jesus. She matters only because she was saved ... by a man, and because she then *supported* this man. No consideration is ever given to the possibility that Mary was important because of who *she* was and because of what *she* did. History, however, is quite clear on this subject. Haskins has pointed out that among Biblical women, Mary Magdalene stands out as a woman "undefined by a designation attaching her to some male as wife, mother or daughter; and she is the only one to be identified by her place of birth."[7]

Certainly Mary Magdalene did not become history's most misunderstood and maligned woman by accident. While rumor and innuendo have kept the myths about her alive for many centuries, the original campaign to slander Mary was quite intentional and purposeful, and is the subject of this work.

Yet Mary's story is not Mary's alone. In the ancient Church, the various attacks on the tradition of Mary had less to do with her personally than they did with the perceived need to subordinate all women to the authority of men. Mary, like the mythical Eve in the Garden of Eden, became Everywoman. The slanders against her were aimed at all women.

It is important to recognize that the story of Jesus was written by men. Until very recently the story of Jesus has also always been *interpreted* by men. For almost two thousand years women have been denied access to the very story in which—we will soon discover—they played a critical role.

Not long before I graduated from seminary in 1970, our school admitted its very first female student. Our seminary, in fact, was the first Lutheran seminary in the United States to do so. Prior to this time, women had not only been barred from entering the ministry, they had also been denied a theological education, and the possibility of earning a PhD in the fields of Biblical studies and Church history. This, of course, meant that virtually all New Testament scholars had been men. Until just a few decades ago, the canonical literature of the New Testament and the history of early Christianity had been studied and interpreted exclusively by men!

Although the Church fathers' position on women in the Roman Catholic Church remains unchanged, in most Protestant denominations there are now women in academia as well as in the ministry. Consider, for a moment, what this implies. Since women do not think just like men, because women often notice things that men do not, and because women often interpret *facts* differently from men, the original Christian message, and all of Christian history, is now open to reinterpretation!

Ultimately what all this means is that much of the work, and many of the conclusions, of (male) Biblical scholars over the past two centuries is now being reconsidered by women. Nowhere is this more evident than in the study of "Gnostic" Christianity. Some of today's best female scholars have chosen this particular field of studies to specialize in. They have done so, perhaps, because this early branch of Christianity often supported women as leaders and teachers, and because its theology never eliminated the idea of the divine feminine.

When I was in college during the early '60s, one of the textbooks for my philosophy of religion major was *The Gnostic Religion* by Hans Jonas.[8] At the time, Jonas' observations about this ancient religion were considered to be the last word on the subject. In recent years, however, women scholars such as Elaine Pagels and Karen King—who have done extensive work on such texts as *The Gospel of Mary* and *The Gospel of Thomas*—have revised much of academia's thinking about Gnosticism in general, and so-called Gnostic Christianity in particular.

The work of such women has been long overdue. My brother, who is still a Lutheran pastor, pointed out to me recently that when Elaine Pagels' seminal work, *The Gnostic Gospels*, was first published in the 70's, academia paid little attention to it for the simple reason that it was written by a woman. Times have changed. At a keynote address given at a meeting of the Jesus Seminar a few years ago, Elaine Pagels had the rapt attention of the many male scholars present. She received a standing ovation for her presentation.

At an even more recent convocation of the same body, Karen King—who had just published *The Gospel of Mary of Magdala*—held the audience of scholars and lay associates spellbound for a full eight hours. The research these women are doing is extremely important and impressive, and the reader will find that I pay particular attention to what these women have to say. Two other female scholars I take

> *...women scholars are continually proving this to be the case by teasing out important evidence from ancient texts that men have either ignored, missed or just didn't think was important.*

very seriously in this work on Mary Magdalene are Ann Graham Brock (*Mary Magdalene, the First Apostle—The Struggle for Authority*) and Antoinette Clark Wire (*The Corinthian Women Prophets*).

Even though it has taken me a long time to realize it, it now seems clear to me that an academic club made up exclusively of male scholars never stood a chance of giving the world a clear and unbiased history of what took place during the first few centuries of the Christian era. In fact, women scholars are continually proving this to be the case by teasing out important evidence from ancient texts that men have either ignored, missed or just didn't think was important.

The more I read the work of women scholars the more I have become convinced that the patriarchal mind-set throughout the history of Christianity has distorted—not only our view of early Christianity—but of the historical Jesus as well. How could it be otherwise? Jesus did not travel with just men, but also with women. His disciples were not only men, but women as well—and not a few of them either. This is a particularly important observation, I think, because it was not at all a common activity for first-century women to follow a Palestinian rabbi. Susan Haskins points out that while women sometimes assisted rabbis financially, they rarely traveled with them as disciples.[9]

Ironically, we only know that women played a significant role in the life and ministry of Jesus because the male evangelists who wrote the Gospels of *Matthew, Mark, Luke* and *John* reported that this was the case—albeit begrudgingly. It is not a small thing, either, that these men revealed this little "footnote" to Christian history right at the most critical part of their narratives: that is, the telling of events that took place during and just after the crucifixion of Jesus. These events involved women exclusively.

Consider this: women were the only witnesses to the crucifixion of Jesus.[10] Women were the only witnesses to the Easter event—whatever that event might have been. Most of the evangelists that wrote the Gospels also tell us that a woman—and perhaps other women as well—was the first disciple to receive an appearance of the risen Jesus. And most telling of all: the male disciples of Jesus only adopted a resurrection faith *after* they received the testimony of women. I will argue throughout this work that the earliest tradition about the resurrection of Jesus was a matriarchal tradition, and that early patriarchs did everything in their power to obscure that fact.

> *If we are to understand what happened to Mary Magdalene, we will first have to come to terms with the times, cultures, and religious traditions in which women were often dismissed as irrelevant and, worse, sinful impediments to the spiritual life of men.*

Whereas the male evangelists did their best to minimize the importance of women everywhere else in their Gospels, they were apparently compelled to admit that women not only played the most critical role in Christianity's myth of origin (the crucifixion and resurrection of Jesus), but the only role. Why did the patriarchs of orthodoxy find the need to suppress the historical tradition of Mary Magdalene? Here is our first clue.

In our attempt to find the Mary Magdalene of history, as well as her historical tradition, we will be investigating a period in history in which few men were enlightened in their treatment of women, a time when nearly all men felt quite certain that they were altogether superior to women. If we are to understand what happened to Mary Magdalene, we will first have to come to terms with the times, cultures, and religious traditions in which women were often dismissed as irrelevant and, worse, sinful impediments to the spiritual life of men. Jesus was one of the few Jewish men of his age to take a different view on this subject, but many of those who ultimately founded a religion in his name paid little or no attention to that fact.

In attempting (successfully) to eliminate the concepts of the goddess and the divine feminine in orthodox Christianity, the earliest patriarchs launched a campaign to minimize the importance of Jesus' female disciples, and one disciple in particular: Mary Magdalene. Certainly it was a great embarrassment to many early Church fathers that a woman had played the central role in the origin of their faith.

But the tradition of Mary Magdalene came under attack for other reasons as well. As early as the end of the first century, Mary Magdalene came to be associated with a form of Christian faith that the fathers of Orthodoxy considered to be heretical. That Mary was revered by these heretical Christians only helped to seal her fate. For the sake of the orthodox Church, Mary Magdalene had to be sacrificed.

There were, then, a variety of factors that contributed to the perceived need of the early Church to suppress the historical tradition of Mary Magdalene. Obviously, its campaign was enormously successful, and it has hidden the truth about Mary from us for almost two thousand years. Fortunately the light of reason eventually prevails, and it is my hope that this present work will contribute to a new campaign—under way in many quarters—that will restore the original Mary Magdalene to her rightful place in history.

In the course of accomplishing this task, we will examine all of the ancient texts in which Mary Magdalene appears. We will attempt to determine how and why Mary's reputation was tarnished and by whom. We will meet friends of Mary and also her enemies: Christians who revered Mary, and Christians who hoped to erase all traces of her.

To find the original Mary we must return to source material in which the Magdalene appears—that is, the canonical Gospels of the New

Testament, apocryphal works, and the so-called "Gnostic" Gospels. The canonical tradition about Mary will be studied in detail in chapters nine through twelve, but we will begin with less familiar material—literature, in fact, that has been lost to us until recently. Here we will discover what I call "the second tradition of Mary," a tradition that honored Mary Magdalene as "the Blessed One,"[11] a visionary and teacher who was Jesus' most worthy disciple,[12] a woman who "always walked with the Lord,"[13] "a woman who understood completely"[14] and who—in myth and metaphor—was sometimes viewed as the spiritual consort of the Christ and the embodiment of Sophia, or Divine Wisdom.

It should not be surprising that those Christians who regarded Mary Magdalene as a teacher and a holy woman were themselves maligned, persecuted and crucified for the sake of a single, literalistic version of Christianity that tolerated no diversity. Even so, "heretical" Christians survived for almost three centuries before being eradicated by force during the fourth and fifth centuries.

Prior to the fourth century when Constantine—the first Christian emperor—took power, heterodox Christians existed in such numbers that they represented virtually half of all Christendom, threatening to overwhelm orthodox Christianity altogether. The fact that they were ultimately defeated, however, does not mean that their message was not important, or that their religion should not have prevailed.

While the adherents to Gnostic forms of Christianity were branded as heretics—along with numerous other Christian movements—they certainly did not see themselves as anything other than Christians. Heresy is in the mind of the beholder, of course, so it should not be surprising that these believers regarded *themselves* to be the true representatives of Christ on Earth. At the very least, they believed that they had the right to exist, the right to tell their own story, and the right to call themselves followers of Jesus.

While liberal New Testament scholars are now willing to give these ancient Christians their voices back, such an attitude is far from universal. Many modern Christians would argue that "true" Christianity prevailed and heresy was defeated because that was God's will. In a review of one of Elaine Pagels' early works on Gnostic Christianity, the Catholic historian and New Testament scholar, Raymond Brown, called her topic, "the rubbish of the second century," adding that it was still "rubbish."[15]

Even so, more and more scholars and theologians are beginning to agree with the German New Testament scholar, Gerd Lüdemann, who states, "The heretics of the second century, men and women, are at least as close to Jesus as the orthodox, and must be welcomed back into the Church."[16] There is, then, some cause for hope that some day Christianity might develop a heart big enough to embrace all those who in ancient times claimed to follow the teachings of the man from Galilee.

For their part, Gnostic Christians were able to honor Mary Magdalene because their cosmology allowed for both God the Father, and God the Mother. Like ancient Taoists, these Christians believed that all of reality is ordered into pairs of opposites: male and female, good and evil, night and day, war and peace, love and hate, light and dark—and that one half of the pair could not exist without the other. Male cannot exist apart from female. And if humanity was created in the image of God, these Christians would have argued, then God must have both masculine and feminine attributes.

Christians who held such beliefs often used anthropomorphic terminology and gender metaphors to express the workings of the cosmos, but ultimately believed that God was pure spirit and was, therefore, genderless. They reasoned that the true God—often referred to as the All—like the Tao (made up of yin and yang), incorporated the totality of all opposites. Like Buddhists and Hindus, many of these Christians also taught that duality was an illusion, a result of human consciousness that was itself divided.

If the All was genderless, these Christians reasoned, the ideal state of human existence was one of spiritual androgyny. If one truly wanted to see God, it was necessary to first reunite the masculine and feminine sides of one's own nature. Karen King states that those Christians who used *The Gospel According to Mary* believed that, "in order to conform as far as possible to the divine Image, one must abandon the distinctions of the flesh, including sex and gender."[17]

These Marian Christians, like most of their spiritual cousins, valued celibacy over sex and marriage. Conserving the life force and directing it toward the work of seeking gnosis, or self-knowledge, led to a victory over the passions of the flesh, and ultimately liberated the soul from the material body, allowing it to return to the Source from which it came.

Mary Magdalene, in a vision, describes the last stage of the ascent of the soul:

> What binds me has been slain, and what surrounds me has been destroyed, and my desire has been brought to an end, and ignorance has died ... I was set loose from ... the chain of forgetfulness which exists in time. From this hour on ... I will receive rest in silence.[18]

Once the seeker, freed from the delusion of the senses, ceases to recognize any distinction between this and that, all of reality is recognized for what it really is: God. At this point the individual soul no longer perceives itself to be separate from the divine Image. God and the Self are one:

> I am identical with thee, and thou art identical with me; wherever thou art, there am I, for I am sown in all things; wherever thou wilt thou reapest me; but in reaping me it is thyself that thou reapest.[19]

Any modern Christian will have no trouble seeing why these teachings were considered heretical by the early fathers of the Church. They sound to us very much like philosophical ideas expressed by Hindus and Buddhists, not Christians. And yet in *The Gospel According to Thomas* these words are attributed to Jesus himself:

> I am the Light which is above everything. I am the All. All came forth from me, and all returns to me. Split the wood, I am there. Lift the rock and you will find Me.[20]

The patriarchs of orthodoxy could not abide such mystical ideas, and continuously railed against them in their writings. Words alone, however, did not prevail in winning over the hearts and minds of many early Christians who understood the teachings of Jesus in a mystical sense. In the end, Christian "heresy" had to be eliminated by force.

The purge of heretics during the fourth and fifth centuries was successful to the point that literally hundreds of early Christian Gospels, epistles, apocalypses and apocryphons (hidden books) simply disappeared, most of them forever. Prior to the fourth century, orthodox heresiologists such as Tertullian, Irenaeus, Clement of Alexandria and Epiphanius wrote lengthy condemnations of heresy in which they sometimes mentioned—even quoted from—various heretical texts. As a consequence, modern scholars have long known that various scriptures once existed, but knew little about their contents, or whether the beliefs of the Christians who wrote them were fairly represented in the writings of the orthodox Church fathers. Then came the discovery of *The Gospel of Mary* and the unearthing of the *Nag Hammadi Library*.

IN SUMMARY:

♦ No Gospel in the New Testament represents Mary Magdalene as a prostitute or penitent sinner. Such slanders against Mary were created by later patriarchs of the orthodox Church in an effort to subordinate women.

♦ The canonical Gospels represent Mary Magdalene as Jesus' most faithful disciple, and first witness to his resurrection. In the "Gnostic" Gospels, Mary is consistently represented as a leader, teacher and spiritual adept.

♦ Mary Magdalene was an important historical figure in her own right, not just because of her relationship to Jesus.

♦ The story of Mary Magdalene is also the story of women's classic struggle to gain positions of leadership and authority in a male-dominated world.

I. Voices from the Past

I t was years after the discovery at Nag Hammadi that all of the pieces of the 13 codices were brought back together again. In the end, all of the manuscripts came safely to rest in the Coptic Museum in Cairo, Egypt. But more years would pass before scholars were allowed to examine and translate the documents. As a result, the first complete text of the Nag Hammadi Library in English did not become available until 1977.

Often, resurrecting the shards of history that have remained hidden for centuries—even millennia—confirm what we have long believed to be true about a culture, a religion, or a historical person. Other discoveries, however, are so unexpected that they compel academics to rewrite the history books and force the rest of us to modify our opinions, even our belief systems. The discovery at Nag Hammadi in 1945 was just such an event.

Archeology has never unearthed the cross that Jesus died on, or the tomb in which he was buried—in spite of claims to the contrary. What archeology *has* produced in modern times, though not by design or intention, are numerous—formerly unknown—texts. These are the holy scriptures that were written by early Christians who were once thought of as heretics, and whose history has been obscured for more than sixteen centuries. Among the recovered works are ancient gospels that preserve an early Christian tradition about Mary Magdalene that—were it to be shown to be historically accurate—might well force scholars to revise many of their assumptions about the origin of the Christian faith.

In fact, as scholars continue to study the newly discovered texts, many of them are beginning to think about early Christianity in radically new ways. No longer is it possible, for instance, to maintain that early Christianity was a single, original faith that only later fell prey to schism and heresy. Indeed, two of the founders of what later became known as "Gnostic" Christianity—Simon Magus and Nicolaus the deacon—actually appear in the New Testament itself.[1]

What is becoming increasingly clear to scholars is that Christians such as these were part of the evolution of Christianity almost from the beginning. What scholars are now beginning to admit is that the version of Christianity that has been passed down to us through the centuries was just one of the *original* forms of the faith.[2]

> No longer is it possible to maintain that early Christianity was a single, original, faith that only later fell prey to schism and heresy.

As we become more informed on this subject, we begin to realize just how truly diverse early Christianity really was. This knowledge makes it much more difficult to use words like "orthodox" and "heretic" to define and categorize the various schools of early Christian faith. Such words were, and are, theological judgments, not historical descriptions. As such, they belong to another era and to a worldview that is no longer valid for most of us at the beginning of the third millennia.

Elaine Pagels probably speaks for many scholars today when she relates that her greatest challenge in studying Christian origins has been to "unlearn what I thought I knew, and to shed presuppositions I had taken for granted."[3] It is also useful to note Karen King's objection to the use of the term "Gnostic." She rightly points out that this term was largely invented by modern scholars, and that these ancient people saw themselves simply as Christians, without any qualification.[4]

In addition to being prejudicial, the term "Gnostic" is often used incorrectly. More often than not, it is used arbitrarily when referring to various early Christian movements which happened to have held some beliefs in common with various traditional schools of Gnosticism that had no relationship to Christianity. Technically, to qualify as being "Gnostic," a sect would have to believe—at a minimum—that God was entirely alien to creation, that creation was the product of an evil demi-god and, accordingly, that the material world was itself inherently evil. These are characteristics that scholars call "radical dualism."

Elaine Pagels, Karen King, and many other scholars have pointed out that works such as *The Gospel According to Thomas* and *The Gospel According to Mary* entirely lack these qualifying characteristics. Many such texts seem to share more in common with monistic philosophies of Hinduism than they do with the true dualism of orthodox Christianity which—like Judaism and Islam—have always held that God and *His* creation are, and always will be, separate realities.[5]

THE NATURE OF THE TEXTS

The discovery at Nag Hammadi in 1945 proved to be unique for two additional reasons. Many of the individual tractates were of works not previously known to exist, and many of the manuscripts were *complete* versions of the text. Most early Christian documents which have been recovered over the years only exist in fragmentary form. The most complete version of the *Gospel According to Mary*, for instance, represents less than half of the original work.[6] Two additional, much smaller, fragments of *Mary* (Papyrus Rylands 463 and Papyrus Oxyrhynchus 3525) have also been recovered, but they do not provide us with any new material.[7]

Even the earliest versions of the canonical books of the New Testament are extant only in fragmentary form. The New Testament as we have it today was, quite literally, patched together using bits and pieces.

No complete manuscript of any book in the New Testament can be dated earlier that 200 C.E.[8] The New Testament exists today only because literally thousands of fragments of the individual books survived history.[9]

Quite the opposite situation holds true for those works deemed heretical by the early Church. Scholars have long suspected that many early Christian documents disappeared during the fourth and fifth centuries as a result of the Roman emperor Constantine's efforts to "banish, persecute, imprison and execute" Christians who refused the Catholic faith.[10]

Although the extant corpus of early Christian literature is quite large (including, in addition to the canonical books of the New Testament, hundreds of apocryphal works) the vast *majority* of early Christian literature did *not* survive history. Christoph Markschies believes that 85% of all first- and second-century Christian documents are now entirely lost to us, and this estimate applies only to those works scholars already know about.[11]

RECOVERY OF THE LOST TRADITION OF MARY MAGDALENE

Because the early orthodox heresiologists regularly mentioned titles of various "heretical" scriptures in their written condemnations of them, it is a mystery why the names of many of the documents found at Nag Hammadi do not appear in those works. It is equally hard to understand why such men would have been silent about a gospel attributed to a woman disciple of Jesus.

These Christian apologists cannot have been unaware of the existence of these works simply because they were used by *Egyptian* Christians. The Egyptian city of Alexandria was one of the great learning centers of the ancient world, and it was also the official seat of power for Christian orthodoxy in the East. Alexandria produced some of the Church's most famous ante-Nicene fathers: Clement of Alexandria, and his famous pupil Origen, Dionysius of Alexandria, and Alexander of Alexandria. Tertullian—certainly the most caustic of all the early heresiologists—wrote from Carthage, a city which, like Alexandria, was located in North Africa.[12]

The only Church father who made reference to a work in which Mary Magdalene appeared was Epiphanius who—writing during the latter part of the fourth century—quoted from a book he called *The Questions of Mary*. According to Epiphanius, *Questions* was actually composed of two different texts: *The Great Questions of Mary*, and a supposed forgery known as *The Little Questions of Mary*. Epiphanius says nothing of Mary herself, but claimed that the text represented Jesus as a revealer of obscene practices.[13]

Discovery of the *Pistis Sophia*:

Some scholars in the past have theorized that the lost *Questions of Mary* may have been the work known as the *Pistis Sophia* (Faith Wisdom). Also known as the Askew Codex, the *Pistis Sophia* first came to light in 1772 when it was discovered in a London bookstore by Dr. A. Askew, an English physician and book collector. There is no record as to how this manuscript came to be in the bookstore, so the actual date of its discovery, as well as its provenance, is unknown.[14] The only reason for associating this text with the lost *Questions of Mary* is the fact that out of the forty-six questions asked of Jesus in this manuscript, thirty-nine of those are put into the mouth of Mary Magdalene.[15]

Written in Coptic, the *Pistis Sophia* is in four parts—not all of which are considered to have been part of the original work. Parts one through three of Codex Askewianus have been dated to the second half of the third century, while part four was written somewhat earlier.[16]

The *Pistis Sophia* is a revelation dialogue between the Savior and certain of his disciples, none of whom has a more prominent position than Mary Magdalene. One of several works that promote Mary as being spiritually superior to all of the male disciples, the *Pistis Sophia* has Jesus say of her,

> You blessed one in whom I will perfect in all mysteries of the height; speak to me openly, you whose heart is raised to the kingdom of heaven more than all of your brothers.[17]

By sheer virtue of her many questions, Mary Magdalene is far and away the most prominent figure in this work, second only to Jesus himself. Other disciples who play small roles include Thomas, Andrew, Bartholomew, Peter, John, Simon the Canaanite, Philip and Salome.

While the *Pistis Sophia* has much in common with the other revelation dialogues discussed below, it also has a number of unique features. Like all the revelation dialogue Gospels, this dialogue takes place after Jesus' resurrection. But the *Pistis Sophia* additionally makes the claim that the resurrected Jesus remained and discoursed with his disciples *for eleven years.*[18]

One unusual theme that runs throughout this work is that of magic, mainly in the form of sacred names and incantations.[19] The *Pistis Sophia* also makes it very clear that those who wrote and read it believed in reincarnation.[20] Additionally, this text makes reference to the battle for apostolic authority in the early Church by making Simon Peter and Mary Magdalene adversaries—a subject that will be discussed later.

Peter, in this text, is unhappy because Mary Magdalene is dominating the dialogue. She is asking many more questions and making many more statements than all of the other disciples combined. Peter complains to Jesus, "My Lord, we are not able to suffer this woman who takes the opportunity from us, and does not allow any one of us to speak, but she speaks many times."[21] At another point, Peter complains about both Mary *and* Salome, "Let these women cease to question, that we may also question."[22]

Mary Magdalene tells Jesus that she feels justified in her contributions, but is intimidated by Peter: "My Lord, my mind is understanding at all times that I should come forward at any time and give the interpretation of the words she (Pistis Sophia) spoke, but I am afraid of Peter for he threatens me and hates our race."[23]

This same theme of rivalry (and of Peter's misogynistic attitude) between Peter and Mary is also found in *The Gospel of Thomas*,[24] and in *The Gospel of Mary*.[25]

Discovery of *The Gospel According to Mary*:

An even more sensational text involving Mary Magdalene came to light more than a century after the discovery of the *Pistis Sophia*. In 1896, Dr. Carl Reinhardt, a German scholar traveling in Egypt, purchased a codex from an antiquities dealer in Cairo. Reinhardt recognized that he was looking at an ancient manuscript, but since he could not read the text he had no idea of the manuscript's contents, much less any idea of when the document had been written.

Reinhardt queried the antiquities dealer about the provenance of the manuscript, and was told that a peasant had found it in a niche in a wall of a house. It may have occurred to the German academic at this point that the dealer was not being entirely honest. The codex happened to be in excellent condition, and had it actually rested in the open air of a wall niche for many centuries, it would have been little more than a pile of dust.[26]

Reinhardt may have suspected that the dealer had come by the codex illegally, but he purchased the manuscript anyway and took it back to Berlin where he placed it with the Egyptian Museum which, in turn, catalogued it as Codex Berolinensis 8502, known more commonly as the Berlin Codex. Carl Schmidt, an Egyptologist at the museum, became the next person to lay hands on the codex. When Reinhardt told Schmidt that the Egyptian antiquities dealer had come from Achmim in central Egypt—the former site of a fifth-century Pachomian monastery—Schmidt speculated that the Codex had possibly been discovered in one of the local graveyards of Achmim, or perhaps somewhere else in the city.[27]

Schmidt set about to translate the text of the codex into German and, ultimately, to publish it. But this was not to be. All manner of unfortunate circumstances conspired against publication, including the destruction of its first press run, two world wars, and Schmidt's own death. It was not until 1955 that the first German translation of the codex was published—some sixty years after its discovery.[28]

The Berlin Codex turned out to contain not just one, but four separate texts: the *Act of Peter, The Apocryphon of John, The Sophia of Jesus*

Christ, and *The Gospel According to Mary* (Magdalene). While the discovery of all of these works was exciting, a Gospel attributed to a female disciple of Jesus came as a complete surprise to Christian academia.

> *Not only is Mary's Gospel unique because it is attributed to a woman, it is also unusual in that it highlights the struggle for apostolic authority in the early Church.*

The first English translation of *The Gospel According to Mary* was not published for another two decades, and the first scholarly analysis of Mary's Gospel (that of Karen King's) was not published until 2003.[29] Long before the world learned of Mary's Gospel, two more (but extremely fragmentary) manuscripts of this Gospel were discovered during excavation of the ancient town of Oxyrhynchus, along the Nile in Northern Egypt. Whereas the four manuscripts of the Berlin Codex were written in Coptic and date to the fifth century,[30] the Papyrus Rylands 463 and Papyrus Oxyrhynchus 3525 fragments of *Mary* found at Oxyrhynchus were written in Greek, and date to the third century. The Gospel itself was probably composed sometime during the second century,[31] and Karen King believes that it may have been written as early as 125 C.E.[32]

The Gospel According to Mary, however, was not the only manuscript in the Berlin Codex to refer to Mary Magdalene. *The Sophia of Jesus Christ*—a Christianized version of a first-century work known as *Eugnostos the Blessed*—also mentions Mary. This same work was also discovered at Nag Hammadi in 1945.[33]

All four works contained in the Berlin Codex have been significant for the study of early Christianity, but no text more so than *The Gospel According to Mary*. Not only is Mary's Gospel unique because it is attributed to a woman, it is also unusual in that it highlights the struggle for apostolic authority in the early Church. Other works bearing the tradition of Mary Magdalene hint of this struggle, but Mary's Gospel addresses it directly.[34]

Although *The Gospel According to Mary* has been available to academics for some time, most scholars have only recently begun to address the central issue of this Gospel: the early struggle for apostolic authority that pitted male apostles against female apostles. No doubt academia has been slow to recognize the importance of gender issues in the early Church simply because New Testament scholarship has heretofore been the exclusive domain of men.

Study on *The Gospel According to Mary* also languished for many years because scholars had a hard time categorizing it. Specialists in Gnostic Christianity focused on such texts, but generalists in the field of New Testament studies tended to view Mary's Gospel as just one more "Gnostic" or "heretical" work that had no relationship to the evolution of "legitimate" Christianity. During the 1980s, this attitude slowly began to shift as a result of Elaine Pagel's ground-breaking work, *The Gnostic Gospels*. Pagels insisted that many gospels, long considered "Gnostic," needed to be reviewed in an entirely new light. Karen King's seminal work on *The Gospel of Mary* has given this argument considerable support.

As to the contents of *The Gospel of Mary*, there are a number of important themes. The first six pages of this Gospel are missing, and the extant manuscript begins with the Savior discoursing on the nature of matter (all matter returns to its source of origin), and the nature of sin (sin does not exist in reality, but is the by-product of disharmony within the individual due to passions of the flesh).

At this point the Savior bids farewell to his disciples and instructs them that from this moment on they should seek, and then follow, the infallible teacher that abides within every human soul. He also tells them that, as apostles, they should not lay down ecclesiastical laws as "the lawgiver" (the orthodox Church) does. As his disciples and apostles they are merely to follow his teachings and preach the ever-present kingdom of God—called here the Son of Man, or Child of True Humanity.

Once Jesus disappears, Mary Magdalene takes his place by comforting the grieving disciples and encouraging their faith. The other disciples

23

are afraid that if they go out and preach the gospel, they will wind up like Jesus. Mary alone is unafraid. Because of Mary's lack of fear, she presents herself as a living example of Jesus' teachings. She is therefore able to support and comfort the other disciples.

Peter then asks Mary to share the teachings she has received from Jesus when they were not present. Mary agrees to this and begins by sharing a vision in which Jesus had appeared to her and complimented her for her ability to focus on him without wavering. Mary then asks Jesus about the nature of visions.

At this point pages 11-14 are missing, and the text picks up again in the middle of a treatise on the ascent of the soul after death. After Mary finishes her teachings, she falls silent. Peter and his brother, Andrew, then express outrage at Mary's words. They consider the teachings related by Mary to be strange and do not believe that Jesus would have actually taught such things.

Peter, in effect, calls Mary a liar, and then expresses jealousy by wondering aloud whether Jesus would have favored her, a woman, with his secret teachings. Mary begins to weep, and the disciple Levi comes to her defense, redresses Peter for his hot temper, and states clearly that Jesus favored Mary as a disciple because she was the most spiritually advanced of all his students. Levi finally calms the men down, repeats Jesus' final instructions to them, and the group goes forth to teach and preach.

We will give more attention to the various sections of Mary's Gospel as we proceed, but this synopsis will at least give the reader a basic idea of the contents of this work.

The Sophia of Jesus Christ:

While *The Sophia of Jesus Christ* was discovered, along with *The Gospel of Mary*, as part of the Berlin Codex, it was also found among the manuscripts of Nag Hammadi. The *Sophia* is another revelation dialogue, and may have been composed as early as the second half of the first century C.E.[35]

As with all of the newly discovered works in which Mary Magdalene appears, Mary's role in this text makes her an important disciple with few peers. Mary is one of just five disciples (along with Philip, Matthew, Thomas and Bartholomew) who pose questions to Jesus.

The fact that Mary repeatedly asks questions of Jesus in all of these dialogue Gospels indicates that she was recognized by their authors as a teacher in her own right, since only teachers were allowed to ask questions in this type of literature.[36] In every case as well, Mary is represented as an intimate of Jesus. Such a relationship indicates that Mary was perceived as having apostolic authority. At the end

> *The Sophia of Jesus Christ is the first known text to make the specific claim that Jesus had seven female disciples as well as twelve who were male.*

of the *Sophia*, Jesus makes this point clear by stating to the male disciples *and* Mary, "I have given you authority over all things as Sons of Light."[37] As an apostle of Christ, Mary had the authority to speak for Jesus as much as any man.

The Sophia of Jesus Christ is the first known text to make the specific claim that Jesus had *seven female disciples* as well as twelve who were male. The *Sophia* promotes the concept of the divine feminine, which is here represented as Sophia, or Wisdom— the "Mother of the Universe." Sophia is the consort of "Immortal Androgynous Man," and was manifested by the Great Invisible Spirit, the First Existent Unbegotten Father, Lord of the Universe.[38]

Dialogue of the Savior:

This work, also found at Nag Hammadi, was written sometime during the second century, perhaps close to the end of the first century.[39] Again, this is a revelation dialogue and, again, Mary is one of just a few disciples who are allowed to ask questions of Jesus. Matthew and Judas (not Iscariot) are the only other named disciples.

Mary, in *Dialogue of the Savior*, is clearly a teacher figure who makes profound statements, as well as asks questions. As in the *Pistis Sophia*, Jesus approves of everything Mary says. The author of this work states of Mary, "She uttered this as a woman who understood completely,"[40] At another point Jesus says of Mary, "You make clear the abundance of the revealer."[41]

Mary's unwavering spiritual strength is revealed in statements like, "There is but one saying I will [speak] to the Lord concerning the mystery of truth: In this have we taken our stand, and to the cosmic are we transparent."[42]

The theme of a weeping Mary plays out again in this text, and is here posed as a question to Jesus: "Mary said, behold! Whence [do I] bear the body [while I] weep, and whence while…," and the rest of her question is lost. But Jesus replies, as the Buddha would, by stating that suffering is due to our attachment to the body. Let go of this attachment, Jesus says, and "the mind laughs."[43]

Yet Jesus also understands that suffering is not without purpose, and should not be avoided since "If one does not stand in the darkness, he will not be able to see the light."

As always, the answer to all questions can be found within one's own self. Self-knowledge—the understanding that the individual soul is actually part of the All—leads to individual enlightenment. "[Strive]," Jesus says, "to save that [which] can follow [you] (treasures of the spirit), and seek it out, and to speak from within it, so that, as you seek it out, [everything] might be in harmony with you! For I [say] to you, truly, the living God [is] (in you) [and you] [are] in him."[44]

The Gospel According to Philip:

Philip is not a gospel in the technical sense of the term. It is, rather, a sermon delivered by its author—an adherent of the Valentinian school of "Gnostic" Christianity. The Coptic text is a translation of a Greek original, which was written as late as the second half of the third century.[45] Besides the infamous "kiss" passage which we will treat at length in Chapter VI, Philip states that Mary Magdalene was one of three women who always walked with the Lord, the other two being Mary, Jesus' mother, and her sister. Karen King believes, however, that since the passage that follows this one in the text ("His sister and his mother and his companion were each a Mary") refers to only one Mary. The author meant to imply that Mary Magdalene embodied all of these feminine qualities and was, therefore, mother and sister and companion to Jesus.[46]

Jesus' preference for Mary over the male disciples is, as in *The Gospel of Mary*, due to the fact that she understands what he is teaching while his other disciples do not. Mary is the chosen one because she recognized "the Light" the moment it came into her presence.

Mary, in *Philip*, is also compared to Wisdom (Sophia) who is "the mother [of the] angels."

The Gospel According to Philip contains a number of profound teachings that have parallels in Eastern philosophy, and I quote just a few:

> Light and darkness, life and death, right and left are brothers of one another. They are inseparable. Because of this neither are the good good, nor the evil evil, nor is life life, nor death death. For this reason each one will dissolve into its earliest origin. But those that are exalted above the world (the spirit within) are indissoluble, eternal.
>
> Fear not the flesh nor love it. If you fear it, it will gain mastery over you. If you love it, it will swallow and paralyze you.
>
> If one receives the power of the cross...the power the apostles called the 'right and the left'...this person is no longer a Christian but a Christ.
>
> I came to make [the things below] like the things [above, and the things] outside like those [inside. I came to unite] them in the place.

The (First) Apocalypse of James:

Because of its many Jewish references, *James* was probably written no later than the second half of the second century. The James who is

27

referred to in this text is not James, the disciple and brother of John, but Jesus' brother, James the Just, who was leader of the first "church" in Jerusalem. James was an immensely important figure in the early Jesus movement, and I will have a good deal more to say about him later.

The Apocalypse of James, like *The Sophia of Jesus Christ*, also refers to Jesus having seven women as disciples, about whom the author states: "I also am amazed how [powerless] vessels have become strong by a perception which is in them." In other words, these women had the innate ability to perceive spiritual truth. Jesus tells James to especially encourage four women: Salome, Mariam (Mary Magdalene), [Martha and Arsinoe...].[47] More than this, Jesus indicates that James should turn to these women for instruction![48]

The Gospel According to Thomas:

A Gospel attributed to Thomas the Twin (of Jesus) was previously known to scholars through the discovery of three separate fragments at Oxyrhynchus in 1897. One fragment is but a single leaf, written in Greek, and known as POxy 1. Two other finds consisted of a single fragment from a papyrus scroll (POxy 654) and six small fragments from yet another scroll (POxy 655). These also are in Greek. *The Gospel of Thomas* discovered at Nag Hammadi in 1945 (from Codex II) contained, surprisingly, the *entire* text of *Thomas*, and was written in Coptic.[49]

Of all of the manuscripts discovered at Nag Hammadi, *The Gospel of Thomas* is by far the most important and well known. Some scholars now generally refer to *Thomas* as the *fifth* Gospel, and there are several good reasons for this.

First, some of the sayings attributed to Jesus in *The Gospel of Thomas* parallel sayings found in the canonical Gospels. This, in itself, is not startling. What *is* startling is that some of the *Thomasian* versions have been shown to be *older*—that is, more original—than the versions we find in the *New Testament*.[50] If there was little difference between the parallel sayings, this probably wouldn't matter. But there are substantial differences in meaning between the Thomasian version of a saying and the version that appears in the canonical Gospels.

Such comparisons of parallel sayings have provided direct evidence that *the authors of the canonical Gospels reworked Jesus' teachings to fit their own Christian theology*! As Helmut Koester states: "Moreover a number of studies have shown that in many cases a saying or parable, as it appears in *The Gospel of Thomas*, is preserved in a form that is more original than any of its canonical parallels. This means that the tradition of sayings preserved in *The Gospel of Thomas* pre-dates the canonical Gospels..."[51]

Secondly, there are sayings attributed to Jesus in *Thomas* (that scholars now feel certain can be traced to the *historical* Jesus) that *do not* appear in any of the canonical Gospels. Nor do they appear anywhere else in Christian literature. These formerly unknown sayings of Jesus—along with his sayings that have parallels in the canonical literature—represent Jesus as a teacher of a theology that is substantially different from the one promoted by the canonical Gospels. *Thomas'* Jesus is quite clearly not the Jesus promoted by orthodox Christianity.

Scholars believe that there are at least two layers of *Thomas*, one that was written as early as 50 C.E., and a second layer added around the end of the first century. This makes *Thomas*—or at least part of it—the *earliest known extant Gospel*. The only other source of Jesus' sayings shown to have been in writing as early as 50 C.E. is *The Gospel of Q*, otherwise known as the *Synoptic Sayings Source*. Scholars believe that Q ("Q" stands for the first letter of the German word, "quell," which means "source") was once a written "sayings" Gospel similar to *Thomas*—but now can only be found

These formerly unknown sayings of Jesus—along with his sayings that have parallels in the canonical literature—represent Jesus as a teacher of a theology that is substantially different from the one promoted by the canonical Gospels.

embedded in the Gospels of *Matthew* and *Luke*. Like *Thomas*, the original "*Q*" was redacted, and scholars identify three layers, which they designate as Q^1, Q^2 and Q^3—Q^1 being the earliest layer.

Neither "Q^1" nor *The Gospel of Thomas* represent Jesus as an apocalyptic preacher who believed the world was about to end. Neither is there any evidence in these earliest of all gospels that Jesus' disciples viewed him as the Messiah, much less the son of God. Most startling, both gospels are entirely uninterested in the death and resurrection of Jesus! Helmut Koester believes that, "Both documents presuppose that Jesus' significance lay in his words, and in his words alone."[52]

Thomas, unlike the canonical Gospels, is not a narrative Gospel. There are no stories about what Jesus did in *Thomas*, just a collection of 114 of his sayings (called "logia"). While disciples sometimes ask questions of Jesus in *Thomas*, most of Jesus' teachings are merely prefaced by the words, "Jesus said." Written collections of Jesus' teachings—devoid of story line—represent the most primitive form of gospel construction and are, therefore, closest to the historical Jesus.

Mary Magdalene, in *Thomas*, plays the same role as she does in the other dialogue Gospels, but in Thomas she asks just one question. The only other reference to her is in logion 114, which is the last logion in the work. The format of this one logion is unusual and problematic, and some scholars believe it was added at a later date. Logion 114 has Peter asking Jesus to make Mary leave their group (of *apostles*) because "women are not worthy of life." We will deal with this statement in Chapter III, on the battle for apostolic authority in the early Church, and again in Chapter VII on Peter.

We can see from these few examples that Mary Magdalene was held in exceptionally high regard by those Christians who opposed Christian "orthodoxy." But we have to ask whether or not this "second" tradition about Mary Magdalene has any connection to the tradition found in the canonical Gospels. Is the Mary Magdalene of the canonical Gospels the same Mary who is Jesus' most spiritually worthy disciple? Do any of these texts have any *historical* value?

It is impossible to answer such questions until we gain more insight into the early history of the Jesus movement and the early history of what many scholars today refer to as the Christ cult—the movement which eventually became orthodox Christianity. Neither can we answer these questions without first spending time with those figures who surrounded Mary and those Christians who later wrote about her.

As we proceed we need to keep in mind that early Christianity was in a constant process of evolution over a period of several centuries, and that disagreements about who Jesus was, and what his life meant, were part of an ongoing debate right from the very beginning. As Karen King points out, "There was no pure doctrine stemming from Jesus that later generations merely fixed in creedal form."[53] The meaning of Jesus' teachings and his life was a matter of interpretation, and interpretations varied widely.

As for those who followed Jesus, and who taught in his name, the question was simply this: who had the authority to speak for him? Who were his authorized representatives? Who were legitimate, and who were false apostles?

The issues that resulted from asking these questions are debated in virtually every early Christian document. "All early texts without exception show evidence of being shaped in the forges of those controversies. In the first centuries, the appeal to apostolic genealogy, to Scripture, to revelation and ecstasy, or to a rule of faith did not settle matters since groups made such appeals to support diverse positions."[54]

The Corpus of Marian Literature:

It is now evident to the reader that Mary Magdalene appears in many early Christian texts, yet not all of these texts offer valid historical information about her. However, even those documents that are wholly mythological in nature still make a valuable contribution to our understanding of early Christianity in that they tell us how various early Christian groups viewed the importance of Mary.

Such texts also provide us with an understanding of how the tradition

...Mary Magdalene appears in many early Christian texts, yet not all of these texts offer valid historical information about Mary.

of Mary was used and manipulated, and how and why her tradition became a casualty in the early struggle for apostolic authority. Ultimately, "Mary had become a figure to whom some Christians appealed in order to defend and promote their views of the meaning of Jesus' teachings, the basis of leadership and the roles of women."[55]

All of the works in which Mary appears ultimately share the same point of view: Mary Magdalene was an important disciple of Jesus who became a central figure in the foundation of Christianity. Obviously, the Mary Magdalene of early Christian history bears no resemblance to the woman of later fantasy, fiction and prurient interest.

All of the documents which contribute to what I call the historical tradition of Mary were written prior to the end of the third century. Fictive romances and legends about Mary that developed during the fourth century and much later are not part of this tradition and can contribute nothing to the study of the historical Mary. For our purposes, the legitimate corpus of Marian literature—or texts that bear on this subject—include:

Canonical Gospels:

> *The Gospel According to Mark*
> *The Gospel According to Matthew*
> *The Gospel According to Luke*
> *The Gospel According to John*

Apocryphal Literature:

> *The Gospel According to Peter*
> *The Epistula Apostolorum*

So-called "Gnostic" Christian Literature:

The Gospel According to Mary
The Gospel According to Thomas
The Gospel According to Philip
Dialogue of the Savior
The Pistis Sophia
The Sophia of Jesus Christ
The (first) Apocalypse of James
The Manichean Coptic Psalm-book II

Works in which Mary has been replaced, or her story altered:

The Acts of Pilate and the *Gospel of Nicodemus*
The Greek and Coptic *Acts of Philip*
The *Acta Thaddaei, Diatessaron, Quaestiones et responsiones ad Orthodoxos, Didascalia Apostulorum,* and the Coptic *Book of the Resurrection of Jesus Christ*
Works attributed to the disciple, Bartholomew

With these texts, the historical tradition of Mary Magdalene comes to an end. However, from the fourth century through the rest of the Middle Ages, numerous other legends and pious fictions about Mary Magdalene were invented by Christian occultists looking to make a quick buck. "Relics" of Mary Magdalene were "discovered" (including her hair, and skeleton!), and a cult of Mary was even founded in Vezelay, France.

Such fictions having to do with Mary Magdalene have provided modern "new age" occultists with "historical evidence" that Mary Magdalene (among other things) was married to Jesus. The reader, however, needs to understand that such material—provocative as it is—has no place in a serious study of this subject. Medieval mythology about Mary has no relationship to the historical tradition of Mary Magdalene—even though most of that tradition is mythological as well.

When the first Jewish/Roman war ended in 70 C.E., the original Jesus movement—those men and women who had known Jesus personally—disappeared forever, and Christianity took its place.[56] Many of the new Christians were Gentiles who were also influenced by Greek philosophy, as well as the Greek and Roman mystery religions. The worldview of these Christians was quite different from that of the Jews who had known Jesus in the flesh.

These second generation believers could not agree on who Jesus was. Was he a man or a god? Was he really human, or did he come down from heaven as a divine being? Was his resurrection a spiritual, or a physical, event?

Since these men and women had not walked with Jesus, they also could not agree as to what he had taught. They often transformed his teachings, putting them into different contexts and giving them new meanings. Often they went even further by inventing new sayings and teachings, and then attributed those teachings to Jesus.[57]

Although the transformation was gradual, ultimately such Christians transformed a Jewish holy man and religious reformer into the Christ, the Savior of humanity, and the Son of God. But even then these Christians could not even agree on what those terms meant.

Virtually all early Christians mythologized Jesus, but one group of mythologists insisted that their myths were superior to all others, and represented the only true form of Christian faith. In order to prevail over Christians who did not share their convictions, they "burned the books of their rivals, destroyed their churches, broke into pieces their stone monuments... (The) Christian destruction of the ancient records and literature, sometimes dramatic as when bishops led mobs to burn libraries as at Alexandria, in the main (was) not dramatic but routine clerical activity of destruction going on for centuries, did succeed in preventing humanity from ever successfully reconstructing what the others were like."[58]

IN SUMMARY:

♦ The discovery of *The Gospel According to Mary*, as well as the discovery of many other early Christian works at Nag Hammadi, Egypt, finally allows early Christians who were considered heretics to tell their own story.

♦ "Gnostic" is a prejudicial term invented by modern scholars to categorize certain early Christians.

♦ The vast majority of early Christian scripture did not survive history.

♦ *The Gospel of Mary* and a number of other recently discovered texts contain a tradition about Mary Magdalene that is not found in the canonical Gospels of the New Testament.

♦ This literature represents Mary as a spiritual adept, teacher and leader.

♦ All of the literature that offers insight into the historical tradition of Mary Magdalene was written prior to the end of the third century.

II. Spiritual Authority and the Status of Women in the Early Church

THE FIRST ATTACKS ON MARY MAGDALENE

In his first letter to the congregants of his church in Corinth, the apostle Paul named those persons to whom the risen Jesus had appeared (15:5-8). His list included "Cephas" (Simon Peter), "the twelve," "five-hundred brethren at one time," "James" (Jesus' brother) and, finally, himself. Oddly, Paul's list did not include the name of Mary Magdalene. Since three out of four canonical Gospels claim that Mary Magdalene was the first person to see the risen Jesus[1], how do we explain Paul's silence?

Many scholars have argued over the years that perhaps Paul didn't mention Mary because he knew nothing about her. And he knew nothing about her because she was part of the empty tomb story which had yet to be *invented*. I believe this assessment is entirely incorrect for numerous reasons—all of which will be discussed later.

The reader will notice, first, that there are *no* women's names on Paul's list. One way to explain Paul's silence on Mary Magdalene is to simply note the apostle's inherent patriarchal bias. And Paul was not alone in that bias. Few men in Paul's time mentioned women in their letters.

This bias is particularly evident in Paul's first letter to the Corinthians. His rather vicious, anti-feminist rhetoric in this letter has caused many readers to believe that Paul was truly a misogynist at heart. But Paul's reasons for attacking the women of Corinth were far more complex.

> ...the first patriarch of orthodox Christianity was also the first Christian of record to purposely turn his back on the woman from Magdala.

The Corinthian women, as it turns out, were a special case. They posed specific problems for Paul that women in his other churches did not. Among other things, they were overtly challenging his authority over them, his right to be called an apostle, and even his doctrine of the resurrection. So Paul had good reason not to stir up the hornet's nest any further by mentioning the name of a well-known and highly regarded female apostle.

In chapter V, I will argue that Paul not only knew of the existence of Mary Magdalene, he *intentionally* left her name off his list of resurrection witnesses as part of his overall strategy for dealing with the women of Corinth. While the supporting evidence will come later, I believe that the first patriarch of orthodox Christianity was also the first Christian of record to purposely turn his back on the woman from Magdala.

Some 40 to 60 years after Paul wrote to the Corinthians, a disciple of a disciple of Paul's—the author of *The Gospel According to Luke*—decided to take a more direct approach in denying Mary Magdalene her rightful place in Christian history. And since the historical record did not serve his ends to that effect, the author of Luke simply rewrote the history.

It is generally accepted in scholarly circles that while the historical Luke was a disciple of Paul's, the actual author of Luke's Gospel was a later Gentile convert to a Lukan community.[2] There is also general agreement that the Gospel attributed to Luke was written sometime near the end of the first century.[3] Some scholars, however, are now proposing a date as late as 120 C.E.[4]

Given the date of composition, it is obvious that the Christian evangelist who wrote Luke's Gospel was not attacking a contemporary historical figure. The historical Mary had long since passed on. Luke was attacking Mary's reputation, and her enduring popularity—perhaps even a school of teaching founded in her name. Whatever the reasons, Luke's attack clearly shows that some orthodox Christian patriarchs at the beginning of the second century still felt threatened by the tradition of Mary Magdalene.

Unlike Paul, Luke could not simply ignore Mary Magdalene. The legend of Mary and the empty tomb was, in Luke's time, well-known Christian lore. In order to diminish Mary's importance, Luke's challenge was to rewrite her story, and revise her biography to whatever degree necessary.

To this end, Luke left no stone unturned. Since the story of Mary in the other canonical Gospels began with her witnessing the death of Jesus, Luke removed her from the crucifixion scene altogether by deleting her name from the text (23:49). And while Luke is the only canonical author to mention Mary Magdalene outside the context of the passion/resurrection narrative (8:1-3), he mentioned her only for the purpose of challenging her prominence and relieving her of her apostolic credentials.

While Mark stated (15:41) that Mary Magdalene had been a disciple who had followed Jesus in Galilee, and had "ministered to *him*," Luke wrote (8:3) that Mary "had provided for *them*"—that is, the male disciples. Luke attempted to diminish Mary's importance by changing her proximity to Jesus, and by making her a supporter—not of Jesus—but of his disciples.

Next, Luke raised doubts about Mary's credibility by challenging her mental capacity.[5] In 8:2 Luke identifies Mary Magdalene as a disciple "out of whom seven 'daimonia' (or demons) went." In Luke's time, "demonic possession" was seen as an affliction roughly equivalent to what we consider mental illness today—although such spirits could be "wicked." By claiming that Mary had once been possessed by "daimonia," Luke was intimating that she had not always been in full possession of her mental faculties.

If Mary had a history of mental illness, then she (or, rather, her historical tradition) should not be taken seriously. Neither should a former demoniac be trusted with any important role. In his empty tomb narrative (24:8-11), Luke is alone among Gospel authors in withholding a commissioning story about Mary. There is no young man, no angel, no Jesus who officially commissions Mary to "go and tell" the others that he had risen. And when Mary and the other women go and tell the male disciples of their experiences anyway, the men—according to Luke—refused to believe them.

To sum up Luke's case: Since Mary had once been crazy, she could not have been a reliable witness to the life, death and resurrection of Jesus. If she had not been a reliable witness, then she had no apostolic credentials. If she had no apostolic credentials, then she had no authority to speak in Jesus' name. And if Mary had no authority to speak for Jesus, then the tradition founded in her name was illegitimate.

We can give Luke an A for effort, but all of his ploys are transparent and lack veracity. Luke stands alone in reporting Mary's "daimonia,"[6] so we can be certain that it is Luke's testimony that is not credible. Mary's "demons" were Luke's invention. As Karen King puts it, Luke's description of Mary as a former demoniac was "an attempt to conceal her prominence rather than ... a report of historical facts."[7]

THE STATUS OF WOMEN IN CHRISTIAN ORTHODOXY

Mary Magdalene and all of her sisters were born into a time and culture that clearly defined, and formally established, the roles of both men and women, as well as husbands and wives. Wives were often treated as a man's property. The Mosaic Law relating to adultery actually had nothing to do with sexual indiscretion and everything to do with property rights.[8]

The most famous attack on women in the New Testament is found in Paul's first letter to his Church in Corinth in which he insisted that women in that church were to veil themselves and remain silent during church services. Apparently the Corinthian women were preaching and prophesying in church, and Paul wanted an immediate end to this unseemly behavior.

Paul went one step further in his demands by insisting that if women had any questions about anything during church services, they were to wait and ask their husbands at home.[9] The women of Corinth apparently failed to take Paul's message to heart because Clement, bishop of Rome during the early part of the second century, had to write to the women of this same church that they were to "remain in the rule of subjection" to their husbands.[10]

Things got worse for women in the orthodox Church as time went on. Whereas in early Christian communities, women and men sat together during worship services, the later Church adopted the Jewish synagogue custom of segregating men and women. By the end of the second century, women were no longer even allowed to *attend* church services! If the message was not clear enough, the Church's hierarchy also ordered that any women in any church who took on positions of leadership were to be branded as heretics.[11]

The early Church appealed to Paul in constructing its policy on women, but Paul's authority was limited. Even though Paul's theology makes up virtually half of all orthodox Christian doctrine, Paul had never met Jesus, nor had he been commissioned as an apostle by any of Jesus' disciples. For a policy on women to be fully credible, the Church had to appeal to Jesus himself.

According to the Church's interpretation of the Gospel narratives, only men were part of Jesus' inner circle, and only men had been commissioned by him as apostles.[12] As we will soon discover, however, the evangelists who wrote the canonical Gospels left clues that suggest that not only had Mary Magdalene been an apostle, she was the *first* apostle. Various early Church fathers pointed this out, but such insights fell on deaf ears.

When one actually examines the scriptural evidence for gender bias,

> *...the Church used the mythical Eve as the whipping girl for humanity's fall from grace, and thereby made every woman on Earth—for all time—guilty of her crimes by association. In some orthodox circles Mary Magdalene—once she had been reinvented as a sinner—became the new Eve, undoing Eve's defiance of God by her ultimate faith in, and devotion to, Jesus Christ.*

however, it becomes clear that the Church's case against women has always been quite weak. Paul's anti-feminist rhetoric in *I Corinthians*, for instance, was specific to the women of Corinth. None of Paul's other letters exhibit such hostility toward women. This is not to say that Paul was a feminist. Like most men of his day, Paul believed that to maintain good order in society—and in his churches—women should be subordinate to men.[13]

When we read other letters written by Paul, however, we do not find rhetoric that is necessarily demeaning to women. In fact, some of Paul's allies and fellow missionaries were women, and Paul even considered one woman, Junia, to be an apostle.[14] Even so, Paul's successors used his letter to the women at Corinth to support their own gender bias. The following passage from *I Timothy*—a letter falsely attributed to Paul—makes this very clear:

> Let a woman learn in silence with all submissiveness. I permit no woman to teach or to have authority over men; she is to keep silent. For Adam was formed first, then Eve; and Adam was not deceived, but the woman was deceived and became a transgressor. Yet woman will be saved through bearing children, if she continues in faith and love and holiness, with modesty.[15]

The "sin of Eve" is a topic we will deal with more completely in Chapter IV, and it is an important topic since the Church used the mythical Eve as the whipping girl for humanity's fall from grace, and thereby made every woman on Earth—for all time—guilty of her crimes by association. In some orthodox circles Mary Magdalene—once she had been reinvented as a sinner—became the new Eve, undoing Eve's defiance of God by her ultimate faith in, and devotion to, Jesus Christ.[16]

The Church's doctrine of original sin (which necessitated a Savior from sin in the person of Jesus the Christ) was based on the *Genesis* creation story in which Eve disobeyed God by eating fruit from a forbidden tree, and then compounded her sin by "tricking" Adam into eating it as well. The patriarchs of orthodoxy insisted on the innocence of Adam, and placed the entire blame for the human condition on Eve. Inasmuch as Eve represented all women in the minds of many Church fathers, it was completely clear to them that: 1) women were rebellious; 2) women could not be trusted; and 3) women were temptresses. Gender discrimination, therefore, was both justified and necessary!

The second notable element of Timothy's statement is that women's redemption could only be achieved through bearing children. Since God in the *Genesis* creation myth had condemned all women to the pain of childbearing, giving birth amounted to an act of penance.

Timothy's statement on childbearing as penance for original sin also served the Church's purpose of discouraging the popular practice of celibacy among women during a time of persecution when Christian women—as well as men—were being martyred in large numbers.

During the earliest years of Christianity, women—like those in Corinth—followed Jesus in taking up an ascetic lifestyle which encouraged celibacy. Those elements within the Church that promoted the opposite lifestyle of home and family saw such women as renegades. Since these women lived outside the household structure, they were also beyond the reach of patriarchal authority.[17] Nevertheless, women in large numbers were adopting the practice of celibacy to increase their spiritual powers and predispose themselves to communion with God.[18]

The practice of celibacy was especially favored by Christian women outside the orthodox communion, so *I Timothy* 2:11-15 was also a thinly veiled attack on those Christians (such as those who stood behind *The*

Gospel of Mary) who rejected the concept of original sin, and did not make women scapegoats for men's weaknesses.

RADICAL FEMINISM IN CORINTH

Let us now return to Paul and his first letter to the Corinthians. If Paul was not an outright misogynist—and I think his other letters show that he was not—then we need to understand what was behind his heavy-handed treatment of the women in his church at Corinth. Why did Paul particularly wish to silence these specific women? When we discover the answer to that question, I believe that we will also find the reason for Paul's silence on Mary Magdalene as a witness to the resurrection.

As much grief as they caused him, women were not the only problem for Paul in Corinth. Paul had serious issues with the entire congregation. To hear Paul tell it, the members of his church were unruly in all respects. Paul especially accused the congregation of being arrogant, and believed that such arrogance had led to rebellion. Even worse, Paul considered many in the congregation to be heading in the direction of heresy by rejecting the gospel he had preached to them from the beginning.

In his first letter to this congregation, Paul laid out all of his grievances point by point, and then informed the church that he was sending his co-worker, Timothy, to "remind" the congregation of his "ways in Christ." One way or another, Paul intended to lay down the law. If the congregation refused to listen to Timothy, Paul threatened, he would return to Corinth himself. "Some of you are arrogant, as though I were not coming to you … What do you wish? Shall I come to you with a rod, or with love in the spirit of gentleness?"[19]

In Paul's mind, his discipline of this congregation was long overdue. Paul's long list of accusations against these Christians included dissention, unspiritual behavior, jealousy, strife, judgementalism, slander, immorality, drunkenness, complacency, boasting, heresy and litigiousness. One gets the distinct impression in reading Paul's letter that he had never fully converted this congregation to his gospel in the first place.

Paul's anger seems based around this very fact. Corinth, after all, was a Greek city in the empire of Rome. Its philosophy was Greek and the Greek and Roman mysteries had a strong influence on all of its citizens. Initially, this was an advantage for Paul. He preached a gospel about the risen Christ, and the Corinthians were entirely familiar with—and amenable to—myths about dying and resurrected gods. But Paul expected the Corinthians to limit their enthusiasm for such myths to the one he had constructed around Jesus. Certainly this was the message Paul had originally brought and argued in the Jewish synagogue in Corinth.[20]

Some of Paul's problems with these new Christians can be traced to the normal behavior of those belonging to the institutional traditions of that city and to its cultic rituals.[21] But Paul faced a bigger problem: the congregation at Corinth had been infected with Gnostic thinking. Paul's issues around the Corinthians use of ecstatic gifts (prophesying in the spirit, and speaking in tongues), and their non-acceptance of his doctrine of resurrection, can be directly traced to Gnostic influence.[22]

Due to all these factors, the Corinthians were apparently rejecting, or at least questioning, much of Paul's gospel. As a result, Paul considered these Christians "men of the flesh" and "babes in Christ" who could not yet tolerate "solid (spiritual) food."[23]

While Paul addressed his letter to the entire congregation at Corinth, and whereas many of the men of the congregation were among the malefactors, in three different places in his letter Paul singles out women (as a group) for censure. Paul believed, among other things, that the women were publicly challenging his authority over this church by refusing to be silent and submissive. At home these same women had withdrawn from sexual relations with their husbands.[24] Worst of all, the women were rejecting Paul's theology.

Paul had no choice but to lay down the law. His new rules were simple and direct: 1) Married women must henceforth give up their newly adopted vows of celibacy;[25] 2) Women must submit to men, and express their submissiveness by veiling their hair, especially when using their gift of prophecy;[26] 3) Women must remain silent in church;[27] and 4) Those women who did not fall into line would be excommunicated.[28]

Paul's demand that women be silent was not an arbitrary one, nor did it have only to do with patriarchal authority. Paul's real purpose for wanting to silence the Corinthian women has to be understood within the context of other issues.

By examining both the text and the context of each group of anti-feminist statements in Paul's letter, it becomes possible to understand Paul's true motives for wanting to subordinate and silence the Corinthian women.

It is no accident that Paul's insistence on women's silence in the body of his letter is sandwiched between his reflections on two other very important topics. Paul's demand for women's silence *immediately follows* a list of rules Paul hoped would bring order to the chaotic Corinthian practice of speaking in tongues and prophesying. And the demand for silence *immediately proceeds* Paul's address on his doctrine of resurrection, a doctrine many of the Corinthians had apparently abandoned—especially the women. Worse still, the Corinthians did not even accept Paul as a resurrection witness.[29]

Understanding the context of Paul's other rules regarding women is equally important in understanding what Paul's real issues were. By examining both the text and the context of each group of anti-feminist statements in Paul's letter, it becomes possible to understand Paul's true motives for wanting to subordinate and silence the Corinthian women. Antoinette Clark Wire highlights the main issues Paul had with these women:

1) In order to enhance their spiritual powers, women were withdrawing from sexual relations with their husbands, and this was causing disharmony in the church.[30]

2) By refusing the veil, the Corinthian women were stating, in effect, that they were no longer willing to accept subservient roles in the church.[31]

3) The women were entering altered states of consciousness during church services, and these states compelled them to prophecy in the moment.[32]

4) The women no longer believed Paul's theology about the general resurrection of the dead at the end of time.[33]

5) The women—whether they intended to do so or not—were setting
themselves up as an alternative authority to Paul.[34]

We might add to this list the observation that the men of the Corinthian congregation were either listening to, or agreeing with, the women. At
the very least, men had failed to silence them. Paul calls for the women's
silencing in the hope that the men would enforce his policies, even if the
women ignored him.

> As in all the churches of the saints, the women should
> keep silence in the churches. For they are not permitted to
> speak, but should be subordinate, as even the Law says. If there
> is anything they desire to know, let them ask their husbands
> at home. For it is shameful for a woman to speak in church.
> What! Did the word of God originate with you, or are you the
> only ones it has reached?[35]

The last sentence is the key to the entire paragraph, and the real
reason Paul wished to silence the women. The women were not just
challenging Paul's gospel as their spiritual authority. As visionaries they
had set themselves up as an *alternative* authority, and were preaching
an alternative gospel as a result. These women had so much confidence
in their own ability to receive spiritual truth directly from God that they
apparently saw no need for Paul to return to Corinth—ever.[36]

That attitude, of course, was entirely unacceptable to Paul. As far as
Paul was concerned, his vision of the risen Christ was unique, his gospel
was unique, and his continuing visions in which he communicated with
God were unique. Paul believed that he was special and that no one else on
earth would ever again experience the risen Christ. Women were incapable
of having such visions in any case.

The Corinthian women disagreed with Paul. Their continued visions enhanced their reputations and status in the community, and that ability posed a major threat to Paul's continued leadership of the congregation.[37] Paul, after all, was the founder of the Corinthian Church, and saw himself as its spiritual father. Paul's gospel—received directly from God—was his gift to the Corinthian congregation, and now it was being rejected. Paul could not accept this turn of events. Above all else, this apostle of Christ needed to be needed. Paul directly challenged the women's authority:

> If anyone thinks that he is a prophet, or spiritual, he should acknowledge that what I am writing to you is a command of the Lord. If anyone does recognize this, he is not recognized.[38]

It is unclear just what Paul meant by writing "a command of the Lord," since there is nothing in the teachings of the historical Jesus that would support his position. But the rest of Paul's statement is clear enough. The women were having visions and prophesying, and the men, ostensibly, were finding nothing objectionable about the women's behavior. This attitude did not sit well with Paul, so he threatened that anyone who didn't abide by *his* command would be ignored or excommunicated.

Later we will discover that the underlying reason for the rebellion at Corinth was the influence of outside agitators or, as Paul put it, "false apostles." Other sorts of Christian apostles were visiting the Corinthian congregation in Paul's absence, and their influence was being felt. The gospel other Christians had brought to Corinth was not the same gospel as that being preached by Paul.[39]

In Chapter V we will discuss the theology that influenced the Corinthian women, as well as the nature of their spiritual gifts. Additionally, we will see how those issues were directly related to Paul's silence on Mary Magdalene. Here it is important simply to demonstrate that as early as twenty-five years after the death of Jesus, some Christian women were actively rejecting patriarchal authority as the sole norm for the leadership of Christian communities. In spite of all that Paul taught and wrote, some Christian women were making themselves heard. And some Christian men were listening to what they had to say.

THE STATUS OF WOMEN IN *THE GOSPEL ACCORDING TO MARY*

While Paul (and the patriarchal tradition that followed him) denied the Corinthian women the right to interpret the Christian message for themselves, the Christians who stood behind *The Gospel According to Mary* took the exact opposite position. Written during the early part of the second century,[40] the Gospel attributed to Mary Magdalene addresses the issue of women's right to become leaders and teachers in the Church.

The dialogue in this Gospel begins after Jesus' crucifixion, and it is the risen Jesus who is giving his final teachings and instructions to his disciples. When Jesus departs for the last time, Mary Magdalene effectively takes over his role as teacher, and her first task is to comfort the disciples who are grieving. With Jesus no longer among them, the male disciples have lost their backbone and are full of fear and doubt. In particular, they are concerned that if they do as Jesus asked—go forth and preach the gospel of the inner kingdom of God—they will meet the same end as he did.

Only Mary Magdalene is unafraid of the consequences of following Jesus' mission. She is the only one among the disciples who has the strength to both encourage and comfort the others:

[Then Mary stood up and greeted] them; she tenderly kissed [them all, and said, "Brothers and sisters, do not weep, do not be dis]tressed nor be in doubt. [For his grace will be w]ith you sheltering you. Rather [we should] praise his [great]ness, for he has united us and [made (us)] true human beings." [When Ma]ry [said these things] she turned their mind to[ward the good and they began to debat]e about the sayings of the Savior.[41]

49

Because Mary is a visionary like Jesus, and because she is fearless like Jesus, she is uniquely qualified to take on the role of community teacher and leader—a role denied women in the orthodox Church. But her most important qualification, certainly, is her innate ability to understand the full meaning of Jesus' teachings.

For the author of this Gospel, Mary Magdalene represents those Christians who had attained gnosis, or inner knowledge. Because of their spiritual maturity, they alone are qualified to teach Jesus' true message. Karen King points out that by representing the other disciples as being consumed with grief and reluctant to go forth and teach, the author was implying that they (orthodox Christians) had not truly understood Jesus' message.[42]

> *Because Mary is a visionary like Jesus, and because she is fearless like Jesus, she is uniquely qualified to take on the role of community teacher and leader – a role denied women in the orthodox Church.*

Mary is represented as Jesus' successor, not because she was a woman, but in spite of the fact that she was a woman. The point is clear: it is spiritual maturity, not gender, that qualifies one to be a true apostle of Christ. For this author, to base apostolic succession on gender was simply wrong headed.

After Mary comforts the other disciples, Peter pulls it together enough to ask Mary to teach them what the Savior had taught her in private. The implication here is that Mary had been a recipient of Jesus' secret teachings, while Peter (who represents both patriarchy and orthodoxy) and the others had not.

> Sister, we know that the Savior loved you more than all other women. Tell us the words of the Savior that you remember, the things which you know that we don't because we haven't heard them.[43]

At first, it might seem that Peter is asking Mary only for what she had heard Jesus say when he and the other disciples had been somewhere else. But Mary's response makes it clear that the issue is Jesus' secret teachings—secret in the sense that they were reserved only for those who had the capacity to understand them. Mary responds:

> I will teach you about what is hidden from you.[44]

Mary then shares a vision in which she had seen Jesus, asked a question and was given an answer. But when Mary concludes, Peter's brother, Andrew, accuses her of lying:

> Say what you will about the things she has said, but I do not believe that the S[a]vior said these things, f[or] indeed these teachings are strange ideas.

Andrew's complaint has to do with the strangeness of Mary's teaching, and the implication is that orthodox Christians reject all teachings they can't comprehend. Peter, however, is more concerned about the fact that the teachings couldn't have come from Jesus because they were given to a woman:

> Did he, then, speak with a woman in private without our knowing about it? Are we to turn around and listen to her? Did he choose her over us?

Mary is crushed by Peter and Andrew's rebukes and begins to weep. It is clear to her that Peter and Andrew think she is lying. Mary responds,

> My brother Peter, what are you imagining? Do you think that I have thought up these things by myself in my heart or that I am telling lies about the Savior?[45]

The author is making the point that true Christians do not base their theological ideas on some external philosophical system, or on the ideas of another teacher, or on the ideas that arise in one's own mind. They base their understanding—just as the orthodox claim they do—on Jesus' actual teachings. They may interpret those teachings differently, but this is because they understand them at a deeper level of awareness.

The next person to enter the conversation is the disciple, Levi, who comes to Mary's defense:

> "Peter, you have always been a wrathful person. Now I see you contending against the woman like the Adversaries. For if the Savior made her worthy, who are you then to reject her? Assuredly the Savior's knowledge of her is completely reliable. That is why he loved her more than us."[46]

Levi compares Peter to the "adversaries," those in the orthodox Church who are theologically contentious over every issue. Levi points out that Peter is often irrational and contentious himself, and reminds him that his attitude and opinions are not supported by Jesus, who completely understood and approved of Mary.

Levi, according to *The Gospels of Mark* and *Luke*, was a former tax collector who left his livelihood in order to follow Jesus. But Levi was generally not considered one of "the twelve" in the canonical Gospels. The author seems to be suggesting that even though Levi and Mary stood outside the apostolic tradition represented by "the twelve," their understanding of Jesus' teachings had been superior to those disciples—since only Mary and Levi worked toward unity and harmony in the group.[47]

The author of *Mary* is arguing that the right of apostolic succession should not be based arbitrarily on any person or group, but on the ability of a person to understand Jesus' teachings correctly. And if this was so, then one's gender made no difference at all. A true apostle was one who understood Jesus' teachings, and then put those teachings into practice. Moreover, the author argues, if some women were more spiritually advanced then men, those women should be preferred over men as community leaders and teachers. Legitimate authority, in other words, should be based solely on spiritual maturity.[48]

The author of *Mary* is making his or her case against the orthodox Church which believes, wrongly, that:

1) All heterodox teachings are strange, therefore invalid. They should be rejected without consideration.

2) Jesus did not teach in secret, but if he had, he would have taught men, not women.

3) Jesus' principal disciples were men, not women.

4) Women could not possibly be more spiritually advanced than men.

As Christian orthodoxy evolved, Paul's position on the women of Corinth was taken out of context and codified. Whereas Paul argued against a specific community of women, the Church decided that his words applied to all women. *The Gospel According to Mary*, then, represents the alternative Christian point of view, and shows that this issue was far from settled within the larger Christian community.

MARY'S HISTORICAL TRADITION AND APOSTOLIC AUTHORITY

Aside from Paul's statements about women, orthodox patriarchs of the Church denied women equality and authority based on the Gospel tradition which held that Jesus' core group of disciples ("the twelve") had consisted only of men. Even more to the point, the risen Christ had commissioned these men—and only these men—as apostles. Men alone, according to this argument, were given the command to go forth and preach to all nations.

If we look at the evidence behind this argument with a more critical eye, however, it soon becomes evident that the Gospel basis for excluding women as teachers and leaders is not as strong as it appears to be. The story of the risen Christ commissioning the male disciples to "go forth," for instance, can only be found in *The Gospel According to Matthew*. The original ending (16:8) of the earliest narrative Gospel (*Mark*) not only lacks a patriarchal commissioning story, *it doesn't even allow for Jesus appearing to the male disciples after the resurrection!*[49]

More complexity is added to the commissioning story by Luke, who states that Jesus commanded the male disciples *not* to go forth, but to "stay in the city" (Jerusalem) until they were "clothed with power from on high." That such power eventually did come to the men is implied here by Luke (and made manifest in his Pentecost story in *Acts* 2:1-47), but Luke's Gospel itself lacks a specific commissioning story.

The Gospel According to John also lacks a commissioning story involving male disciples. Three out of four canonical Gospels, then, say nothing about Jesus commissioning men as apostles. In fact, three out of four Gospels actually report that the first apostles of the risen Jesus were women!

Mark 16:7, *Matthew* 28:7-8 and *John* 20:17 all state that Mary Magdalene, either alone or with other women, was commissioned to "go and tell" what she had seen and heard. Such was the function of an apostle. The English word, apostle, comes from the Greek, "apostolos" and means "one who is sent out," a "delegate" or "representative." In the *New Testament*, the word carries the additional meaning of an honored believer who had a special function.

As surprising as this may seem to most Christians, if one reads the resurrection narratives in all four canonical Gospels in the original Greek, and without the usual patriarchal bias, it becomes quite clear that the women who followed Jesus were the first disciples to be commissioned as apostles. If the female disciples were first to have some kind of experience of the risen Jesus, and if they were first to receive the commission to "go and tell," then this observation gives rise to an interesting question: Did Christianity begin as a matriarchal tradition?

...three out of four Gospels actually report that the first apostles of the risen Jesus were women!

We will give a good deal of attention to this question in subsequent chapters.

IN SUMMARY:

♦ Attacks against Mary Magdalene and her historical tradition began very early in Christian history, and were aimed at subordinating women to the patriarchal tradition of the orthodox Church.

♦ Paul's first letter to his church in Corinth contains rhetoric that was aimed at silencing the women of that church and discounting their spiritual gifts. The Church used Paul's statements on women, along with similar statements found in *I Timothy*, to build its case against women.

♦ Various Christian movements, such as the one which stood behind *The Gospel According to Mary*, challenged patriarchalism and proposed an alternative tradition in which women had the right to become leaders and teachers.

♦ According to the canonical Gospels of the New Testament, the first apostles of Christianity were women, not men.

III. The Suppressed Tradition of Mary

MARY AS APOSTULA APOSTOLORUM

We have learned so far that only Matthew's Gospel (80-90 C.E.) specifically argued that the risen Jesus commissioned only his male disciples as apostles. That the other Gospels are vague on this point suggests the possibility that not all early apostolic traditions were based on a patriarchal model. Even though Paul argued against the women of Corinth, for example, he referred to at least one woman, Junia, as an apostle.[1]

The most impressive argument against the Church's claim that all of the apostles were men, however, can be found in the resurrection narratives themselves. Even though each of the evangelists attempted to obscure the apostolic tradition of Mary to one degree or another, they did not altogether succeed. A careful reading of the various resurrection accounts will, I believe, reveal that the earliest apostolic commission was granted to a woman—Mary Magdalene—not to *any* of the male disciples of Jesus.

Although many Christians may not be aware of it, the tradition of Mary Magdalene as the first apostle goes back to ancient times. Church leaders throughout Christian history have often referred to Mary Magdalene as the apostula apostolorum, the apostle *to* the apostles!

The Greek word, apostolos, means "one chosen and sent with a special commission as the fully authorized representative of the sender."[2] Due to theological and political necessity, the male evangelists took pains to obfuscate Mary's true status in early Christianity. It is easy to read the canonical Gospel accounts of the resurrection of Jesus and still miss one of the story's main elements: the commissioning of Mary Magdalene—not as an apostle to the world at large, but as an apostle to the *other* apostles. The author of *The Gospel of John* is even more specific in stating that Mary was commissioned to go to the *male* disciples of Jesus![3]

> Church leaders throughout Christian history have often referred to Mary Magdalene as the apostula apostolorum, the apostle to the apostles!

Once we begin to accept Mary's apostolic claim as standard Gospel tradition, then all of the references to Mary as leader, teacher and comforter *of men* in extra-canonical literature (such as *The Gospel of Mary*) no longer seem new or out of place. These claims for Mary were solidly based on canonical tradition.

Mary Magdalene was first given the honorific of "apostola apostolorum" by Hippolytus, Bishop of Rome during the early part of the third century.[4] Hippolytus—like others before and after him—noted that Mary's commission was inherent in the words: "Go and tell."

As an apostle, Mary was more than a messenger, however. She was not just sent to deliver a message that Jesus had risen, she was sent to *convince* the other disciples that Jesus had transcended death. This is an important distinction since first-century Jewish men routinely ignored and belittled the testimony of women. If the male disciples eventually came to believe in the risen Jesus as a result of Mary's testimony, then that turn of events would have been highly unusual (and embarrassing to the early Church fathers). Even so, we will discover that this transference of faith was neither automatic nor immediate.

Since the names of other women who accompany Mary Magdalene change from Gospel to Gospel, it seems likely that the evangelists did not know who had been with Mary at the crucifixion and on Easter morning—or if there *were* any other women. The evangelists may have invented the other women for one of two purposes: to diminish the importance of Mary, or to add credibility to the story. On balance, I think the second possibility is more likely since Mary Magdalene's name—in every case—appears before the names of other women. Whatever the case, we can be certain that Mary Magdalene played *the* central role in the earliest tradition about the passion and resurrection of Jesus.

If we look at each Gospel account of the resurrection of Jesus carefully, we will realize that Mary Magdalene meets all the criteria for being an apostle: She is someone who was chosen. She is given a special commission. And she has the authorization of the sender. That authorization comes either from a heavenly messenger, or from Jesus himself. Mary's credentials couldn't be better.

In the earliest narrative Gospel, *Mark*, Mary is commissioned to "go and tell his disciples" by a "young man" dressed in a white robe. The story in *Matthew* is considerably more interesting because the evangelist recorded not one, but two, commissioning stories. In *Matthew* 28:7, Mary is commissioned by an angel, then in 28:10 she is commissioned by Jesus himself (as in *The Gospel of John*).

Ann Brock and other scholars see two separate Marian traditions at work in *Matthew's* two commissioning stories. She points out that *Matthew's* "angelophany" parallels *Mark's* account, and his "Christophany" parallels *The Gospel of John's* account in 20:17.[5]

Of the four canonical authors, Luke stands alone in denying Mary a specific apostolic commission from either an angel or from Jesus. As we will discover later, this slight was probably intentional. Like Paul in *I Corinthians*, the author of *Luke* had an anti-feminist agenda, and he expressed it wherever possible by diminishing Mary Magdalene's importance in the Christian myth of origin.

The internal evidence of the canonical Gospels, then, confirms this much about Mary Magdalene: Many early Christians considered Mary Magdalene to have been an apostle. They also believed that her crucifixion/resurrection tradition was the earliest and primary one. Finally, these texts also make it clear that the later patriarchs of orthodoxy had no scriptural grounds for denying Mary the status of an apostle.

THE CANONICAL WITNESS TO THE MARIAN TRADITION

If we are at all familiar with the Gospel resurrection stories, we might wonder why it was so important for Mary, and possibly other women, to *go and tell* the male disciples about their extraordinary experiences. Didn't Jesus appear to the male disciples directly? Why the need for a "middle woman"? The real purpose of Mary's testimony, therefore, is not immediately apparent.

If we pay close attention to the sequence of events in each Gospel, however, we might notice one very important detail: *in no version of the resurrection story do men experience the risen Jesus until after Mary (and possibly other women) tells them of her experience.* What does this discovery tell us? Simply this: The male disciples of Jesus did not come to faith in the risen Jesus on their own!

In some way or another, the later resurrection faith of men had been dependent on the initial experience of women! Mary was the apostola apostolorum, apostle to the apostles, because she bore witness to all that had happened to Jesus, and then *encouraged faith* in the hearts of the male disciples.

Mark's Gospel (14:50) tells us—in spite of the insertion of a story about Peter remaining in Jerusalem long enough to deny Jesus three times after he was arrested—that "*all* (male disciples) forsook him, and fled."[6] Mark further tells us that they all fled back *to Galilee*.[7] The male disciples, in other words, had no idea whatsoever about what had happened to Jesus after he was arrested, although they must have feared the worst.

The men were probably consumed with guilt and shame over having deserted Jesus, and were experiencing grief over their loss. Most likely these men were having doubts about what to do next, and considered returning to their crops, their woodsheds and their fishing nets. At this point, the male disciples believed that the grand experiment was over. It died with Jesus.

What series of events turned all this around? What led to the birth of Christianity in the first place? The answer is as shocking as it is obvious: If Mary Magdalene and the other women had not returned to Galilee to inform the men of Jesus' crucifixion and resurrection, Christianity would never have been born. This statement sounds rather simplistic, and yet every Gospel account agrees on a single point: *The witness and testimony of Mary Magdalene provided the sole reason for why the story of Jesus did not end with his crucifixion!*

...if Mary Magdalene and the other women had not returned to Galilee to inform the men of Jesus' crucifixion and resurrection, Christianity would never have been born.

There is, however, something terribly wrong with this story as far as historical reporting is concerned. There is nothing in Mark's Gospel to suggest that Mary Magdalene and the other women returned to Galilee right away, or that they returned to Galilee at all. In fact, the original ending to *The Gospel of Mark* tells us that the women fled in fear from the scene of the resurrection and told no one about their experiences. Mark implies no physical connection between the women in Jerusalem and the men in Galilee.

It is well known in New Testament scholarship that Mark's Gospel originally ended at 16:8:

> And they (the women) went out quickly and fled from the tomb; for trembling and amazement possessed them, and they said nothing to anyone because they were afraid.

At some later time, verses 9 through 20 were added to the end of Mark's Gospel, no doubt to bring it into line with the other Gospels.

There is no argument on this issue in academia because the earliest extant fragments of Mark's Gospel do not include verses 9-20. Internal evidence leads to the same conclusion: verses 9-20 do not fit with the verses that precede them, and this long ending (which I refer to throughout as Pseudo-Mark) "makes extensive use of words not employed by Mark elsewhere."[8] Because the ending of *Mark* is abrupt, it is possible that the original ending was lost, or may even have been excised.[9]

At least as far as the earliest narrative Gospel was concerned, the initial response to the Easter event was flight and silence. We almost take it for granted that the women eventually calmed down, made sense of their experience and returned to Galilee to inform the male disciples about what they had witnessed. Yet there is no necessary reason to believe that this was the case. Indeed, the earliest evidence suggests that this was *not* the case.

This is not to say that the later experience of the male disciples was not dependent on the earlier experience of the women. It simply suggests that there is no way of knowing *how much time elapsed* between the original experience of Mary Magdalene and the later experiences of the male disciples. *Mark*'s abrupt ending also suggests the possibility that there was *never* any direct contact between Mary Magdalene and the male disciples!

All of this is speculation, of course, and yet the other three canonical Gospels seem to avoid dealing with the subject of just how much time elapsed between the Easter experience of Mary Magdalene and the point when the male disciples learned of her experience.

It seems unlikely that the women would have returned to Galilee promptly. If the women were afraid and confused at first, they would have needed time to make sense out of their experiences and get their stories straight. The men, after all, would be incredulous with their report in any event. If the women were still hysterical upon their return to Galilee, the men would likely have dismissed their testimony altogether.

Then there is a matter of distance. The region of Galilee lies approximately 80 miles to the north of Jerusalem—and that's as the crow flies. The women would have had to travel by foot, which means the journey could have taken them close to a week. Furthermore, they would have needed time to secure a new male escort to protect them against bandits along the way. All of these factors argue against the likelihood that the women returned to Galilee immediately following their spiritual epiphany. It might have been weeks or months before they returned—or they may never have returned at all.

Matthew's account (28:8) tells us the women "departed quickly from the tomb with fear and great joy, and *ran* to tell his disciples," although Jesus slows them down by meeting them on the road (28:9). Obviously the women did not *run* back to Galilee, so Matthew's reference is an attempt to suggest that very little time elapsed between the Easter event and the actual testimony of the women. It is possible that the author of Matthew added this impossible detail because just the opposite was the case.

At first it seems that Luke's account of this story won't help much with the time problem because he simply states, "... and returning from the tomb they told all this to the eleven and to all the rest."[10]

John's Gospel claims that the male disciples were in Jerusalem on Easter morning, so its author contradicts the synoptic Gospel accounts entirely. Although we can feel fairly certain that the male disciples would not have been in Jerusalem immediately following Jesus' arrest and crucifixion, John's story may be pointing to a time when the male disciples returned to Jerusalem and founded the first community of "Jesus people."

But why is any of this important? What difference does it make how much time passed between Mary's experiences and the point when the male disciples heard about them? It is an important detail because the attempt to obscure time sequences suggests that there may have been two separate resurrection traditions—one matriarchal, the other patriarchal.

If "the twelve" never existed as such, and if the narratives having to do with Jesus' travels were primarily mythological, then there is no reason to suppose that the same disciples fol-

...The attempt to obscure time sequences suggests that there may have been two separate resurrection traditions—one matriarchal, the other patriarchal—right from the beginning.

lowed Jesus everywhere. In fact, the Gospels tell us that different people came out to hear Jesus when he was in their neighborhood. We know that some of Jesus' disciples (Mary, Martha, and Lazarus of Bethany, for instance) were householders and did not travel with Jesus at all.

Given these factors, there is no necessary reason to suppose that Mary Magdalene ever belonged to the same (Galilean) group of Jesus people that included Simon Peter! Perhaps Mary Magdalene and Simon Peter represented two entirely different groups of disciples from the very beginning. Certainly that particular scenario, if true, would go a long way in explaining why the traditions of Mary and Peter were often in conflict.

In addition to these factors, we also need to remember that the crucifixion/resurrection tradition of Mary Magdalene was an *independent* tradition which the evangelists grabbed hold of and placed into their narratives—just as they did with the epiphany stories having to do with the male disciples. Had all of the epiphany stories come from the same source and tradition (and we already know that this was not the case), they would have been woven together seamlessly, rather than being dropped into place, one after the other. Since the Mary legend was independent from all other legends, Mary herself may have been independent of all other disciples!

If rumors about Mary Magdalene's experiences eventually reached the male disciples in Galilee, they probably would have discounted them at first. But if those rumors persisted, the men may have left Galilee at some point and returned to Jerusalem to check them out. Here they may have come into contact with Mary Magdalene for the first time, or at least with her community.

Had this been the case, historically, then the male disciples may have had their epiphanies in Jerusalem, not in Galilee. The men's visions of a risen Jesus may have been induced as a result of coming into contact with a strong matriarchal resurrection tradition based around Mary Magdalene. In that event, *The Gospel of John*'s report that the male disciples had their resurrection experiences in Jerusalem, rather than in Galilee, would be historical after all.

Certainly we know that at least some of the Galilean men did, in fact, return to the "scene of the crime" because Paul tells us that Peter, John, and Jesus' brother James, were among the "pillars" of the Jerusalem community, and it was there that Paul visited them some three years after his conversion.[11] But these men would not have returned to Jerusalem right away because they feared that they would be arrested if they did.

Given the danger involved, even some years later, we have to wonder why these Galileans would have returned to Jerusalem at all. There must have been some compelling reason for them doing so, and for them to remain there.

Luke's account of the resurrection events informs us that when the male disciples first heard the testimony of women, they did not believe it: "But these words seemed to them an idle tale, and they did not believe them."[12] While Luke took every opportunity to diminish the importance of women, I rather suspect that on this occasion he was reporting something historical. After all, it would have been only natural for the men not to have believed the women.

Another interesting footnote to Luke's story has to do with the ascension of Jesus. This last scene in Luke's Gospel unfolds sometime after the various epiphanies, and just before Jesus ascends into heaven. Jesus tells the men: "You are witnesses of these things. And behold, I send the promise of my Father upon you; but stay in the city, until you are clothed with power from on high."[13]

This clothing with power came in the form of the Holy Spirit at Pentecost, an event Luke (who also wrote *Acts*) describes in the second chapter of *Acts of the Apostles*. Luke's narrative, in other words, is carried over from his Gospel into *Acts*. When we read the continuation of Luke's story in *Acts*, it seems—at first—that Luke is claiming that all post-resurrection events happened quickly, one after another: 1)Mary's discovery of the empty tomb; 2) her report to the disciples; 3) the disciples' subsequent visions; 4) the ascension of Jesus; and 5) the Pentecost event. A closer examination of Luke's report in *Acts*, however, suggests otherwise.

In *Acts* 1:3 Luke writes that the resurrected Jesus waited forty days before he ascended into heaven. During this time, Luke tells us, Jesus appeared to many people and spent his time giving instructions to his disciples.

Modern Biblical literalists miss the point of stories such as this by assuming that "forty days" really means forty calendar days. In the flood story in the book of Genesis, it rained forty days and forty nights. Moses and the children of Israel wandered in the wilderness for forty years. Jesus was tempted by Satan for forty days. Yet none of these time references were meant to be taken literally, since ancient mythologists regularly used the number 40 to symbolize a "long and indefinite time."[14]

> *...an appreciable amount of time passed between the Easter experience of Mary Magdalene and the time the male disciples actually started preaching the resurrection.*

By using the number 40 in *Acts*, Luke is really telling his audience that the disciples received appearances of the risen Jesus for a long time after his crucifixion, and that a long period of time passed between the crucifixion and the Pentecost event. Luke further tells us that the disciples—now apostles—did not go public until after Pentecost. We can then conclude, from Luke's report at least, that an appreciable amount of time passed between the Easter experience of Mary Magdalene and the time the male disciples actually started preaching the resurrection.

There is, then, a solid canonical foundation for suggesting the possibility that a matriarchal resurrection faith predated the faith of Jesus' male disciples. *But no matter how the Easter experience of Mary Magdalene was originally passed on from women to men, the earliest Christian belief about the resurrection of Jesus was based first on the experience of women, second on the women's testimony and third, on the fact that men eventually accepted that testimony as valid.*

One further piece of evidence on this subject should be examined before moving on. The second-century Epicurean philosopher, Celsus, made an indirect reference to the testimony of Mary Magdalene in his work, *True Doctrine*. A pagan, Celsus despised Christianity and called it a religion for stupid people, weaklings, women, slaves, and little children,[15] so it should not be surprising that he wrote, "that belief in the risen Jesus was based on the testimony of a 'hysterical female".[16]

This is a particularly interesting statement considering that it comes from a non-Christian source, and was written during the second century. Celsus did not seem to know about any resurrection traditions that were founded on the experiences of men. Instead, his sources informed him that Christian resurrection belief was based on the testimony of a woman. Certainly Celsus may have ignored other traditions in order to make a point, but even if that was the case his reference shows that a strong—and apparently popular—matriarchal resurrection tradition still existed during the second century.

WAS THERE A COMMUNITY OF MARY?

Many early Gospels that carry the name of a particular disciple (such as the *Gospel of John* and the *Gospel of Thomas*) were the products, not of a single person, but of a community of people who often produced other works such as epistles, apocalypses and apocryphons in the name of this disciple as well.[17] So it would not be surprising that at least some parts of the *Gospel of Mary* originated in a community founded, either by Mary Magdalene, or in her name.

The best arguments for the existence of a Marian community are the traditions and theology associated with Mary, particularly those which were commonly in conflict with the tradition of Simon Peter. These traditions were passed on in both oral and written form. It is doubtful that they would have been kept alive were it not for the fervor of those who defended this tradition. In the end, however, we do not have sufficient evidence to make a strong case for the existence of such a community.

IN SUMMARY:

♦ The narratives of the canonical Gospels provide us with evidence that many early Christians believed that Mary Magdalene had been a fully commissioned apostle, and an apostle *to* the apostles.

♦ Evidence in the canonical Gospels suggests that the resurrection faith of the male disciples of Jesus was dependent upon the prior faith of women.

♦ Mary Magdalene may not have been part of the same group of disciples that included Simon Peter and John.

♦ The time period between Mary's Easter experience and the subsequent resurrection faith of the male disciples may have been extensive.

IV. The Reinvention of Mary

W e now realize that the Mary Magdalene of history and the Mary Magdalene of historical tradition bears no resemblance to the Mary Magdalene of popular imagination.

But what was the process by which Mary, the holy woman, was transformed into Mary the whore? And why did the patriarchs of the early orthodox Church feel it necessary to deflower Mary?

To some extent, we have already answered this second question. Mary's tradition became associated with a form of Christian theology which the early Church fathers found unacceptable, but also because Mary had been considered a female apostle, teacher and leader, her resurrection tradition was in conflict with Peter's tradition, and because she was first witness to the Easter event.

While all of these aspects of Mary's tradition had theological implications for the early patriarchs of the Church, these men were most concerned about their political implications. If a patriarchal hierarchy in the Church was to be established, then all matriarchal Christian traditions had to be suppressed by any means necessary.

Ann Brock in her book, *Mary Magdalene, the First Apostle*, notes that in politics, the most effective way of undermining opponents is to attack them on moral grounds by suggesting sexual improprieties.[1] Theological opponents are just as vulnerable to such attacks, and the gender politics of the early Church encouraged various orthodox polemicists to use this method to discredit the historical tradition of Mary Magdalene.

Rosemary Ruether suggests that "The tradition of Mary Magdalene as a sinner was developed in orthodox Christianity to displace the apostolic authority claimed for women through her name."[2] Mary Magdalene, in other words, became collateral damage in the early Church's war over who had authority to speak for Jesus.

While the formal effort to obscure the importance of Mary Magdalene did not begin until much later, rejection of Mary's tradition was already implicit in Paul's early silence on Mary as a witness to the risen Jesus, as well as in his attack on the women prophets of Corinth—a subject we will take up again in the next chapter. Following Paul, the author of *The Gospel of Luke* also contributed to the future crucifixion of Mary Magdalene by attempting to obfuscate her traditional role as the first apostle of Christendom.

From there, the torch used to enflame rhetoric against women as leaders in the Church was passed to bishops, polemicists and heresiologists of western Christianity: Tertullian in the second century, Ambrose in the fourth, Jerome and Augustine in the fifth, and Pope Gregory in the sixth.[3] Biblical literalists made every effort to found their attacks on the authority of holy scripture and, in so doing, implicated God as a co-conspirator. In order to acquire divine support for their war against women, these men turned to the opening chapters of God's holy word: the Hebrew *Bible*.

THE SIN OF EVE

We were earlier introduced to the subject of the "sin of Eve," and here we need to address it in more detail. Tertullian, the second century Church father who was himself married, attacked the moral turpitude of all women on the basis of Eve's so-called disobedience against God in the *Genesis* creation myth. In a sermon to women, the Church father shamelessly pontificated:

> Do you know that each of you is Eve? The sentence of God on this sex of yours lives in this age. The guilt must of necessity live too. You are the devil's gateway. You are the unsealer of that forbidden tree. You are the deserter of divine law. You are she who persuaded (he) whom the devil was not valiant enough to attack (Adam). You destroyed so easily God's image.[4]

Tertullian used the *Genesis* creation story to support his belief that women were naturally sinful and wholly inferior to men. But Tertullian was hardly the only orthodox patriarch to stress that God *Himself* had condemned women. As such, these men read the creation myth of *Genesis* 2:4—3:24 as God's indictment against women for all time.

The orthodox patriarchs understood this creation myth as saying that God had created day and night, mountains and valleys, rivers and seas, land animals and fish—and Adam—with divine intention. In the case of the first woman, however, God had created Eve merely as an afterthought. God saw that Adam was lonely, so He created a playmate and helper for him. Apparently God made this decision in haste, as he soon came to regret it.

Tertullian used the Genesis creation story to support his belief that women were naturally sinful and wholly inferior to men.

God created Adam (like all the other animals) out of the substance of creation itself (dust). But in Eve's case, God chose to create her—not out of primordial matter—but out of *Adam* (one of his ribs)! Woman (womb-man) was not of heaven, and not even of earth. Woman was created from Man, and the orthodox patriarchs took this to mean that women would always be dependent on, and inferior to, men.

The *Genesis* story does not tell us how thoroughly Eve was instructed (by either Adam or God) on the subject of her subservient status. It did not make much of an impression on Eve in any case. Right from the beginning, Woman had her own ideas about things.

God told Adam and Eve they were living in Paradise, and they could eat anything they wanted in the Garden except for the fruit from "the tree of the knowledge of good and evil." God warned the couple that if they did eat of this tree, they would die. Adam and Eve didn't ask, and God didn't explain, why this was so. It was simply a rule, and that was that.

One day while wandering alone in the Garden of Eden, Eve came into the company of one very smooth talking, forked-tongued, serpent who encouraged her to eat from the very tree that God had forbidden. Eve was a woman, the serpent was persuasive, and forbidden fruit sounded delicious. What harm would there be, Eve reasoned, in taking one little bite?

Had the story ended here, perhaps only women would have been forever damned. But Eve, being a woman, wanted to share everything with Adam. For his part, Adam was an innocent and simple creature, so he did whatever anyone told him to do. He took a bite of the fruit (it was not an apple, by the way), and sealed the fate of humanity forever.

When God showed up, He was not the least bit happy with this turn of events. Adam explained that Eve made him do it, and Eve said the devil made her do it, but God was not buying any of it. He took Adam and Eve's behavior as an act of defiance and disrespect for His authority, and damned Adam to a life of toil, Eve to the pain of childbirth, and both to a future that ended in death.

The Church fathers took this story in *Genesis* very seriously, and its message seemed very clear to them: women were easily tempted by evil, had a natural inclination toward sin, were weak-minded, and spent their entire lives plotting ways to deceive men. If men were to protect themselves from sin, therefore, they first had to protect themselves from the influence of women. Women had to be kept at arm's length, and in their place. Since women were created as inferior creatures to begin with, they could not be trusted with anything important, so their proper role in life was to serve men and bear children.

Tertullian had such contempt for women that he even considered their souls to be inferior to those of men.[5] His attitude toward women and their place in the spiritual scheme of things came to represent the majority opinion within Christian orthodoxy, even if that opinion did not take root in every corner of Christendom.

Many early Christians challenged such sexist and literalistic interpretations of Hebrew scripture. Some Gnostic Christians, for example, chose to tell the creation story from an entirely different point of view. In many of these interpretations, the serpent was not an evil tempter, but the embodiment of Sophia, or Divine Wisdom. By encouraging Eve to eat of the tree of the knowledge of good and evil, Wisdom had offered Adam and Eve gnosis: the ability to perceive one's true divine nature. As for the Creator, He was not the true God, but an evil, jealous and bad-tempered demigod who wanted to deprive Adam and Eve of their divine heritage.[6]

For Gnostic Christians, scripture was not intended to be read as literal truth, or historical fact. Scripture was spiritual allegory. Quite often, a single scriptural passage held multiple layers of meaning, and its deepest meaning was revealed only to those who had attained spiritual maturity.[7]

THE PURITY OF EVE AND THE *OTHER* CREATION MYTH

Perhaps these same Christians also noted—where Tertullian and other patriarchs did not—that the story of Adam and Eve and their so-called defiance of the Creator is neither the first nor the most illumined creation myth in the book of *Genesis*. The first creation myth in *Genesis* begins at 1:1 and ends at 2:3.

In this creation myth (which actually trumps the Adam and Eve story because of its prominence), God does not prohibit Man and Woman from seeking wisdom. Except for strongly encouraging a vegetarian diet (1:29), God places no restrictions at all on the first couple. In this more libertarian Paradise, there is no tempter and no temptation. Consequently, Man and Woman do not sin, and God has no reason to condemn humanity. Instead, God blesses the first couple and wishes them well. More important to our subject, Woman is not created *from* Man, but *with* Man. Woman is born as a full equal, and in the very image of God.

It is easy to see why orthodox Christians ignored (and still ignore) the first *Genesis* creation myth in favor of the second one. It contains no basis for the doctrine of original sin, and without that doctrine orthodox Christianity cannot promote Jesus the Christ as a Savior from sin.

Furthermore, the God of *Genesis* 1:1 is not jealous or vengeful. Neither is this God so insecure as to demand obedience and worship. This is a loving God who looks upon all of creation and is pleased. Having no regrets, this God sees creation (including the pair of naked vegetarians) as perfect just the way it is. It should be no surprise, then, that the God of Genesis 1:1 is not masculine!

POLYTHEISM AND THE GODDESS

Most scholars would argue that the first creation myth in *Genesis* comes from a strata of Hebrew tradition that is later than the one that carries the second creation story. While this may be true, I believe that the myth itself carries within it the Hebraic memory of prehistory when the ancestors of the Hebrews were still polytheistic—much like the story of Abraham's near sacrifice of his son Isaac in Genesis 22:1-14, which suggests a historical memory of a time when the Hebrew ancestors still practiced human sacrifice.

The word for God used in Genesis 1:1 is not Yahweh, but Elohim (literally: "gods"). God, in this myth is not an individual, but a collective. God says, "let *us* make man in *our* image, after *our* likeness."[8] Elohim, then represents a Godhead, not an individual diety.

The singular of Elohim is "El," and El was the God of the Canaanites prior to the Hebrew's conquest of their homeland. The Canaanites were polytheistic, and their religion was absorbed (and then altered) by the

Hebrews. As a term for God, "Elohim" appears far more times in the Bible (2,500 times to be exact) than the term "Yahweh."

Although Elohim is a plural form, it is usually singular in construction. Most uses of the word in the *Bible*, in other words, are meant to represent a single deity. In those rare passages where Elohim seems to refer to a polytheistic Godhead, Judeo-Christian linguistic scholars maintain that Elohim, or "gods," refers to the "magnitude and majesty" of God.[9] I think, however, that these scholars argue from a monotheistic bias.

Certainly the use of Elohim in the first creation story refers to a Godhead, and not a single deity. The use of the sentence, "Let *us* create man in *our* image" makes this a certainty, and this same construction is repeated again in *Genesis* 3:22 and in 11:7. Here, scholars suggest that "us" refers to God's "court," i.e. the "heavenly host."

But does God's "heavenly host" (angels, etc.) have the inherent power to create heaven and earth as suggested in the first creation story? In a sense, it doesn't matter how that question is answered because any theological system that includes "divine beings"—with or without creative powers—is, by definition, polytheistic.

> *...the use of Elohim in the first creation story refers to a Godhead, and not a single deity.*

In actuality, the first creation myth in the book of *Genesis* probably originated with the Canaanites, whose nation the Israelites conquered, and whose religion the Israelites absorbed—just as they adopted and appropriated the Canaanite God, El, who they thought of in polytheistic terms.[10]

Whether modern Jews and Christians wish to accept the implications of this story or not, the Elohim of *Genesis* 1:1 created humanity (one reality) as male and female (two parts of the same reality) *in Its own image*. This precise rendering of the story strongly suggests that the author of the first Genesis myth understood God as being composed of both masculine and feminine attributes! Elohim created Man and Woman simultaneously—as equals—out of the same divine substance as His/Herself.

But El was not the only divinity the Israelites appropriated from the Canaanites. Thanks to Canaanite fertility cults that were presided over by women, the Israelites originally absorbed a host of female divinities, the greatest of which was the Goddess, Asherah, "Queen of Heaven."[11] Gradually, Asherah became Yahweh's consort.[12]

In order to combat the worship of pagan idols, however, the Hebrew prophets banished the Goddess as well. Perhaps the prophets' intent was not to create or promote a patriarchal deity in place of the Goddess, but this was what happened as the result of adopting monotheism in a patriarchal culture.[13]

As with all religious traditions that evolve theologically, earlier beliefs—no matter how ancient or obscure—are never completely eradicated. Often, well-entrenched beliefs which have become politically incorrect simply go underground, only to be revived at a later period of history.

Before patriarchal monotheism reasserted itself via the Church of Rome, the Goddess tradition passed into Christianity by way of Hebraic "wisdom theology."[14] The Goddess—in the form of Wisdom—became the divine Sophia (Wisdom) who, in turn, represented sister, wife, mother, beloved, and teacher.[15] But patriarchal monotheism sought to "eradicate the role of the Christian Goddess as it had once eradicated that of the Hebrew Goddess."[16]

Wisdom theology lies at the very heart of Jesus' teachings,[17] and the concept of the divine Sophia permeated Gnostic Christianity to the core. Schüssler Fiorenza states that "The earliest Palestinian theological remembrances and interpretations of Jesus' life and death understand him as Sophia's messenger and later as Sophia herself. The earliest Christian theology is sophialogy. It was possible to understand Jesus' ministry and death in terms of God-Sophia, because Jesus probably understood himself as the prophet and child of Sophia."[18]

While Judaism undid the myth of the "divine couple," it also needs to be understood that the purpose of such a repudiation was to eliminate gender classifications from the divine Image. The rejection of the Goddess was, in effect, the repudiation of "masculinity and feminity as

76

ultimate, absolute principles. But in doing so, it (Judaism) did not quite escape the patriarchal understanding of God, insofar as it transferred the image of the divine marriage to the relationship of Yahweh and Israel who is seen as his wife and bride."[19]

But just as metaphorical Goddess language was often used to represent a single, genderless, God in both Judaism and in the teachings of Jesus, orthodox Christianity rejected the language itself, as if it were a literal representation of God. Consequently, the early heresiologists of the Church rejected Gnostic Christian language that spoke of God as Father—Mother. It mattered not that these heterodox Christians used gender terminology metaphorically.

One group of early Christians who would have no doubt preferred the first creation story of *Genesis*, and its "polytheistic" metaphor of God as Elohim, were the "heretical" Naassenes, who worshiped God as both Father and Mother, and who claimed to have received their secret teachings from Jesus' brother, James, through Mary Magdalene![20]

MARY'S ALLIES AND ADVERSARIES

Tertullian, and most of those orthodox patriarchs who followed him, rejected the first creation story of Genesis because it was both heretical and subversive. But not every early Church father accepted Tertullian's point of view. One theologian who challenged the implications of the second *Genesis* creation myth was Marcion, a son of an orthodox bishop who was born near the end of the first century, and lived until 160 C.E.[21]

Like Gnostic Christians, Marcion did not much care for the arrogant, vindictive and angry Yahweh who had condemned humanity to death because of Adam and Eve's "sin." As a consequence, Marcion demoted the Hebrew tribal god to the office of demi-urge, and proposed that the true God—the God of love, the God of Jesus—existed far above and beyond Yahweh's creation.

Marcion's view of God, of course, was not well received by the orthodox patriarchs of the Church. For them, there could be only one

God, and Marcion's proposal was clearly polytheistic. Just as problematic, Marcion's rejection of Yahweh was also a rejection of the Old Testament and the Church's Judaic foundations. As a consequence, the Church fathers anathematized Marcion—not just as a heretic, but as an arch-heretic.[22]

In such a repressive environment, Mary Magdalene—who many Christians saw as a leader, teacher and an apostle of Christ—was an embarrassment to a Church father like Tertullian who felt he had a divine duty to uphold Paul's mandates on women in the Church:

> It is not permitted for a woman to speak in the church, nor is it permitted for her to teach, nor to baptize, nor to offer [the Eucharist], nor to claim for herself a share in any masculine function—least of all, in the priestly office.[23]

For all of his vitriolic criticism, the issue over women's roles in the Church—as well as the status of Mary Magdalene as an apostle—was far from settled during Tertullian's own day. Even though he, too, tied women to Eve's "sin," Hippolytus (c. 170 – 236), bishop and martyr, entertained a more enlightened attitude toward women in the Christian ministry:

> Lest the female apostles doubt the angels, Christ himself came to them so that the women would be apostles of Christ and by their obedience rectify the sin of the ancient Eve ...Christ showed himself to the (male) apostles and said to them: "It is I who appeared to these women and I who wanted to send them to you as apostles."[24]

Indeed, it is in the writings of Hippolytus where we find the first reference to Mary Magdalene as the apostola apostolorum. It is unlikely, however, that Hippolytus was the first to refer to Mary in this manner, and the reference probably points back to a historical tradition that affirmed Mary Magdalene as the first person to experience the risen Jesus.[25]

THE BIG LIE: MARY MAGDALENE AND POPE GREGORY'S SINFUL WOMAN

While Christian women of all stripes had many male champions, Jesus' religion of equality could not hold out against the rising tide of Christian patriarchalism as it continued to suppress Mary Magdalene's authority as an apostle by denigrating her moral turpitude. Augustine, the Church's great fifth century theologian (who led a licentious life prior to his conversion) was one Christian who would bless modernity's lusty concept of Mary:

> For how could it be otherwise than carnally that she (Mary) still believed on Him whom she was weeping over as a man?[26]

Perhaps Pope Gregory had read Augustine in his preparation for his sermon delivered at the basilica of St. Clemente in Rome on September 14, 591 C.E., [27] for he surely failed at his exegetical study of *The Gospel of Luke:*

> She whom Luke calls the sinful woman, whom John calls Mary, we believe to be the Mary from whom seven devils were ejected according to Mark. And what did these seven devils signify, if not all the vices? It is clear, brothers, that the woman previously used the unguent to perfume her flesh in forbidden acts. What she therefore displayed more scandalously, she was now offering to God in a more praiseworthy manner. She had coveted with earthly eyes, but now through penitence these are consumed with tears. She displayed her hair to set off her face, but now her hair dries her tears. She had spoken proud things with her mouth, but in kissing the Lord's feet, she now planted her mouth on the Redeemer's feet. For every delight, therefore, she hath had in herself, she now immolated herself.

She turned the mass of her crimes to virtues, in order to serve God entirely in penance, for as much as she had wrongly held God in contempt.[28]

Although Gregory did not use the term, the attentive brothers in the basilica certainly understood Gregory to mean that Mary Magdalene had been a whore, and this slanderous image of Mary has been passed down for some fourteen centuries. Gregory's disinformation about Mary has inspired numerous modern novelists and movie producers to create even more disinformation about Mary—all of which has the profound effect of impressing upon the minds of a gullible public an image of Mary Magdalene that could not be more false.

> *Gregory's disinformation about Mary has inspired numerous modern novelists and movie producers to create even more disinformation about Mary...*

Gregory's first fabrication—that Mary had been a prostitute—necessitated a second one: Mary had seen the error of her ways when she met Jesus, and repented of her sins. Now that she had repented, it was possible for Jesus to forgive her (the third part of Gregory's formula). A woman was saved, and her savior was a man. Everything was in its proper order.

This three-fold myth concerning the Magdalene allowed the Church to use the example of Mary as a teaching tool that proclaimed the very heart of the orthodox Christian message that was based on the triple doctrines of original sin, repentance and salvation. Had the Roman Catholic Church not needed to support such doctrines—as Gnostic Christianity did not—perhaps the patriarchs would have left Mary alone. As it was, the Church needed a new and penitent Eve and picked Mary to play the role.

If the canonical record clearly show's Gregory's portrait of Mary Magdalene to be false, how did the Pope come to think of Mary as a sinner in the first place? Was Gregory entirely dishonest, or just a bad exegete?

Gregory's first falsehood was in stating that Luke's Gospel portrayed

Mary Magdalene as a sinner. Gregory did not find any such reference to Mary in *The Gospel of Luke*, so he invented the idea—but not necessarily from whole cloth. Others—such as Augustine—came to this conclusion before him and, as we will see in a moment, Luke may have intentionally led these men in this direction.

In order to give birth to a sinful Mary, Gregory had to combine Luke's story of the anonymous sinful woman (7:37-50) with his first introduction of Mary Magdalene (8:2). These are two entirely different stories about two entirely different women, but Gregory justified his conflation of the two by reasoning that if Luke mentioned Mary Magdalene *after* he mentioned the sinful woman, Mary must have *been* that sinful woman!

Some scholars see in Luke's arrangement of these two stories an *intent* to falsify by *inference*. In other words, Luke may have wanted gender-biased men like Augustine and Gregory to come to the very conclusion that they did. Certainly Gregory was not the first to conflate the two women, since the idea can be traced to the fourth century, where it can be found in the writings of Ephraim the Syrian.[29]

Gregory's sermon continued with the words, "whom John calls Mary…" Again, Gregory is wrong, but creative. This time he conflated Mary of Magdala with Mary of Bethany, the sister of Martha and Lazarus (*John* 12:1-8). Gregory apparently did not care that these two Marys came from different towns. For the Pope, if both women had the same first names, they must have been the same person! Gregory also ignored the description of Mary of Bethany as a householder who lived with her two siblings, whereas Mary Magdalene was an itinerant who traveled with Jesus.

Gregory had no time for such small details, and besides, there was the *hair* connection. Luke's sinful woman bathed Jesus' feet with tears, then ointment, and dried them with her hair. Mary of Bethany bathed Jesus' feet with ointment, and dried them with her hair. It was the same act, so it must have been the same hair!

We are now able to understand Gregory's infamous and infallible equation: Jesus' feet + ointment + hair + Mary of Magdalene + Mary of Bethany + sinful woman = Mary the whore.

MARY'S DEMONS

Gregory continued to help scripture along by filling in missing pieces. Because Luke, in his story of "a woman of the city who was a sinner," failed to specify what this woman's sins were, Gregory—some five centuries later—concluded that the woman was surely a prostitute. Gregory probably also felt that he had found a smoking gun in referencing *Mark* regarding Mary's seven demons. Gregory apparently did not know that this slander was of Lukan origin, and was merely repeated in *Pseudo*-Mark.

"And what do these devils signify if not vices?" *And what vices,* Gregory did not say, *if not prostitution?* Luke's text, however, does not use the word "devils," but the Greek word, *daimon.* Daimon (pl. daimonia) originally meant "divine spirits" but gradually—mostly due to its usage in the New Testament—came to mean *evil* spirits (demons).

In first century Palestine, however, "daimons," were considered to be uncontrollable spirits which possessed an unfortunate person, through no fault of his own. One who was so afflicted was not blamed for his or her affliction, nor was he or she considered a sinner. There are numerous instances in the Gospels of Jesus performing exorcisms on people who were believed to be possessed by spirits of one kind or another, and these stories never imply that such possession had anything to do with sin or improper morals.

Yet this does not mean that Luke did not intend to stigmatize Mary by suggesting that she had been possessed by "unclean" or evil spirits. Luke was following orthodox tradition in implying that anyone who did not agree with Paul's definition of Christianity was under the power of Satan:

> For such men are false apostles, deceitful workmen, disguising themselves as apostles of Christ. And no wonder, for even Satan disguises himself as an angel of light.[30]

Sin and Satan were almost synonymous in the minds of the Church fathers—particularly when it came to determining who was a true believer and who was a heretic. Gregory was only following the tradition of men like Irenaeus (c. 180) who wrote that all those who called themselves Christians, but who rejected the Catholic faith, were inspired by evil demons, and were agents of Satan himself. Irenaeus suggested that those who rejected the moral teachings of Catholic bishops were possessed of madness and blasphemy. They were driven by the poison of the serpent to commit dark acts of passion, and lusts of the flesh.[31]

In good tradition or not, all the rest of Gregory's slanders against Mary—the perfumed flesh, forbidden acts, and scandalous displays of the body—were the product of Gregory's (sexually repressed?) overactive imagination. Covetousness, pride, holding God in contempt—the "mass of crimes" Gregory accuses Mary Magdalene of—make for a sad commentary—not on Mary, but on the pontiff himself.

> *Irenaeus suggested that those who rejected the moral teachings of Catholic bishops were possessed of madness and blasphemy.*

In spite of Pope Gregory, and in spite of the Vatican's policy on women—now as well as then—women have always had some Catholic men as allies. The debate over who should and who should not be allowed to speak for Jesus did not end in the fourth century, nor was it entirely shut out even during the sixth. Gregory's views were offset by those of his namesake and contemporary, Gregory of Antioch (d. 593). This Gregory attributed these words to Jesus in addressing Mary and other women: "Be first teachers to the teachers. So that Peter who denied me will learn that I can also choose women as apostles."[32]

IN SUMMARY:

♦ Early Church fathers used the orthodox concept of original sin —based on the so-called "sin of Eve"—to subordinate women in the Church.

♦ These patriarchs ignored the first creation myth in the book of Genesis which claims that men and women were created as equal reflections of the Divine Image.

♦ Early Hebraic faith was polytheistic and included the worship of the Goddess. This faith was eradicated by the patriarchal prophets of monotheism.

♦ The "arch-heretic" Marcion rejected this point of view, and demoted the Hebrew tribal god, Yahweh, to the lower status of demi-urge.

♦ The fiction that Mary Magdalene had been a reformed prostitute resulted from a sermon given by Pope Gregory during the sixth century, in which he conflated the figures of Mary Magdalene, Mary of Bethany, and Luke's "sinful woman."

♦ Luke's slander that Mary had been possessed by "daimonia" was used by Gregory as certain evidence that Mary had committed immoral acts.

V. Paul, Mary, and the Corinthian Women Prophets

I n this chapter I will propose that the earliest historical assault against the apostolic tradition of Mary Magdalene may not have been a war of words at all, but a siege of silence. In his first letter to the church he founded in Corinth, Paul lists those to whom the risen Jesus had appeared:

> ... he appeared to Cephas (Peter), then to the twelve. Then he appeared to more than five-hundred brethren at one time, most of whom are still alive, though some have fallen asleep. Then he appeared to James (Jesus' brother), then to all the apostles. Last of all, as to one untimely born, he appeared also to me.[1]

There are a number of inherent problems with Paul's list, not the least of which is the absence of Mary Magdalene's name. First of all, Paul did not include Peter as one of "the twelve." His mention of Jesus' appearance to "five-hundred brethren" was probably the basis for Luke's Pentecost story in *Acts*, but there is no way to be certain of that. Then Paul subordinates Jesus' appearance to James (the formal leader of the

85

Jerusalem church) to his appearance to Peter by naming Peter at the beginning of the list, and James near the end. Finally, Paul includes himself on this list, thereby making his experience of the risen Jesus equal to all the previous experiences. He does go on to say "I am unfit to be called an apostle, because I persecuted the church of God."[2]

For all of this, Mary Magdalene's name is conspicuously absent from Paul's list that honors men exclusively. The absence of Mary's name presents a serious discrepancy for New Testament scholars, and one they have puzzled over for a long time. The central problem here is chronology. No narrative Gospel was written before 70 C.E., whereas Paul's letter to the Corinthians was written during the fifties.[3] If Paul did not mention Mary Magdalene, the argument goes, it was probably because the empty tomb story, and Mary's association with it, had not yet been invented. In other words, Paul may have been silent about Mary because he didn't know anything about her.

> *The absence of Mary's name presents a serious discrepancy for New Testament scholars, and one they have puzzled over for a long time.*

I will argue here, however, that Paul did, in fact, know about the resurrection tradition associated with Mary Magdalene. I believe that he left her name off his list in order to obscure the original matriarchal resurrection tradition in the minds of his readers. The mention of Mary Magdalene would not have helped his case against the Corinthian women who are addressed in this letter.

What were Paul's problems with these women? We have discussed some of the issues earlier; here we will treat them individually. Paul's attitudes toward women in this letter are familiar to many: It is best that a man not touch a woman.[4] The head of the woman is the man.[5] Women should cover their hair with veils in church.[6] Man was not created for woman, but woman for man.[7] Women should be silent in church.[8] If women wanted to know anything about what was happening during church services, they should ask their husbands at home.[9]

No doubt, Paul's rules for women's behavior were the same in all of his churches, but given his extensive anti-feminist rhetoric in *I Corinthians*, it appears that the Corinthian women were unique among Paul's churches in their refusal to abide by his rules. And while the apostle had numerous issues with the Corinthian congregation as a whole, the women seem to have been his most important concern since they were apparently involved in the church's sudden rejection of Paul's resurrection theology. Moreover, the women were challenging Paul's status as an apostle by setting themselves up as an independent authority in the church.

Without personal credibility and apostolic authority, Paul had little control over the Corinthians, and had to remind this congregation that—in spite of the fact that he had once been an ardent persecutor of the "churches of God"—he was an apostle of Christ (which gave him authority over the congregation) by virtue of having received an appearance of the risen Jesus in a vision.[10] But the Corinthians were beginning to question these credentials.

Paul was facing a similar problem in his churches in Galatia. Both the Corinthians and Galatians were questioning Paul's right to be called an apostle based on *his own* criteria. Paul, after all, had never known Jesus, and lacked all interest in him as a flesh-and-blood man. Nor was Paul interested in Jesus' teachings, for only twice in all of his letters does Paul quote Jesus in part.[11] Paul's gospel had nothing to do with the historical Jesus, and everything to do with the Christ of faith. Paul had no pious memory of Jesus but was obsessed with "Christ crucified."[12] Geza Vermes states: "... in order to emphasize the paramount importance of the Jesus revealed in visions, Paul deliberately turned his back on the historical figure, the Jesus according to the flesh."[13]

The Jerusalem church led by Jesus' brother, James (and included Peter and John), never really accepted Paul as an apostle, partly because Paul was not interested in the historical Jesus, partly because Paul taught a gospel they did not agree with, and partly because Paul refused to submit to their authority. For his part, Paul railed against this group of disciples and insulted them in writing.[14] In the end, Paul rejected the leaders of the Jerusalem church, and they rejected him. The Jesus movement went one direction, and Paul's Christianity went another.[15]

FALSE APOSTLES

Paul respected no one as an apostle unless he preached the same gospel as he did, and he blamed "false apostles" teaching "false gospels" for turning the Corinthians against him. Yet the Corinthians were hardly alone in giving ear to Paul's opposition. In his letter to the Galatians, Paul was so angry with these other apostles that he felt compelled to put a curse on them.[16] In his letter to the church at Philippi, Paul called his competitors "evil workers" and "dogs," [17] and suggested that some of those who preached a different gospel did it just to make him miserable.[18]

Paul had a serious problem on his hands. His letters to various churches indicate that more than half of those churches were more than willing to give an audience to other—competing—Christian apostles every time Paul's back was turned.[19] Since Paul had not been commissioned an apostle by the disciples of Jesus, he constantly had to defend his right to be called an apostle.

> "Am I not an apostle? Have I not seen Jesus our Lord? Are you not my workmanship in the Lord? If to others I am not an apostle, at least I am to you; for you are the seal of my apostleship in the Lord."[20]

Paul's first letter to the Corinthians was not successful in achieving his ends. By the time he wrote his second letter to that church, the situation had deteriorated to such a degree that Paul had to defend himself against specific accusations of the congregation: "I was crafty, you say, and got the better of you by guile."[21] Since he had gotten nowhere by accusing his competitors, Paul took a somewhat different tack in his second letter to the church in Corinth:

I wish you would bear with me in a little foolishness. Do bear with me! I feel divine jealousy for you, for I betrothed you to Christ to present you as a pure bride to her one husband. But I am afraid that as the serpent deceived Eve by his cunning, your thoughts will be led astray from a sincere and pure devotion to Christ. For if someone comes and preaches another Jesus than the one we preached, or if you received a different spirit from the one you accepted, you submit to it readily enough. I think that I am not in the least inferior to these superlative apostles.[22]

Paul, like the orthodox patriarchs who followed him, called upon the image of an unfaithful Eve to make his case against the Corinthian women. Lüdemann states: "Adam was not deceived, but Eve became a transgressor. This passage explicitly restricts the image of Adam to men and Eve to women in order to stress the priority and fidelity of men over against women."[23] "Superlative" apostles were leading Paul's flock astray but, superlative or not, they were false:

And what I do I will continue to do, in order to undermine the claim of those who would like to claim that in their boasted mission they work on the same terms as we do. For such men are false apostles, deceitful workmen, disguising themselves as apostles of Christ.[24]

It was bad enough that these apostolic wolves in sheep's clothing were sneaking into Paul's flocks, but what made Paul really angry was the fact that his congregations were listening to these "deceitful workmen." Paul used sarcasm to get this point across to the Corinthians: "… you gladly bear with fools, being wise yourselves!"[25] With the Galatians, Paul had to call upon supernatural forces to aid him in his righteous battle against falsehood:

I am astonished that you are so quickly deserting him who called you in the grace of Christ and turning to a different gospel ... But even if we, or an angel from heaven, should preach to you a gospel contrary to that which we preached to you, let him be accursed. As we have said before, so now I say again, if any one is preaching to you a gospel contrary to that which you received, let him be accursed.[26]

Paul does not tell us who these false apostles were, nor what gospel they preached. We do know, however, that Paul's gospel was not taught to him by the followers of Jesus, and the apostle was proud of this fact. His gospel, Paul tells his readers, came directly from God in visions:

> For I would have you know, brethren, that the gospel which was preached by me is not man's gospel. For I did not receive it from man, nor was I taught it, but it came through a revelation of Jesus Christ.[27]

Paul makes it clear that after his conversion experience, he did not go to Jerusalem to be instructed by the disciples of Jesus, but instead went into the deserts of Arabia in order to work out his own personal theology. "I did not," Paul boasts, "confer with flesh and blood, nor did I go up to Jerusalem to those who were apostles before me."[28]

When Paul finally did meet with Peter, James and John in Jerusalem, he was totally unimpressed with their teaching and refused to submit to their authority:

> ... to them we did not yield submission even for a moment ... And from those who were reputed to be something (what they were makes no difference to me; God shows no partiality)—those I say, who were of repute added nothing to me ...[29]

Given Paul's contentious relationship with the Jesus movement—and the fact that the only followers of Jesus Paul ever mentions by name in his letters are James, Peter and John—it should not be all that surprising that Paul never mentions Mary Magdalene. Paul was not simply trying to save ink either. He spent a good deal of it writing effusively about his own friends, colleagues and companions. Paul was being quite deliberate in his silence about those who had followed Jesus.[30]

While Paul was effectively cast out of the Jewish Jesus tradition, he took his personal gospel of Jesus the Christ to the Gentile world. But even there Paul was sometimes considered an imposter.[31]

Paul was vindicated by history, however. Gerd Lüdemann writes, "It took only a century for the Jewish Christians in Jerusalem who followed James' line to be condemned along with other heresies as Ebionites by the church that canonized the letters of Paul ..."[32]

> *Paul was being quite deliberate in his silence about those who had followed Jesus.*

THE RAPE OF WOMEN'S DIVINE GIFTS

With this brief look into the mind of Paul, let us now turn our attention to his specific battle with the women in his Corinthian church. Paul's sarcastic statement, "For you gladly bear with fools, being wise yourselves" was probably targeted at these women since they were claiming to have a special wisdom that he did not.[33]

Paul wanted to silence the Corinthian women precisely because of this claim. "What," Paul says, "did the word of God originate with you, or are you the only ones it has reached?"[34] More to the point, Paul wanted to silence the women because they were claiming *direct* access to this wisdom. Paul saw himself to be the intermediary between God and his congregation, and the women were telling Paul, in effect, that they did not need an intermediary.

For Paul, spiritual wisdom came only by revelation (his own) through God's spirit in Christ.[35] Paul's "Christ" was the sole personification of God's wisdom, while it appears that the women of Corinth viewed wisdom as the divine Sophia. Such feminine personification of God's Wisdom, Antoinette Wire suggests, "could have been seen by Paul as not securely bound to the humiliation of the cross, not adequately identifying the male Christ and the female wisdom of God, or particularly prone to inspire women as her voice."[36] Paul's attempt to silence the women in his church, then, was possibly aimed at a feminist wisdom tradition that found its voice in oral expression.

Since women as a group were the only faction within the Corinthian church that Paul specifically addressed in his letter, we can safely assume that the women's influence upon the larger congregation was fairly significant. While it is impossible to know just how many Corinthian women were involved, it could not have been just a few, since the apostle did not single out any individuals.[37]

Paul intended his letter to the Corinthians to be read to the entire congregation. No doubt it was aimed at humiliating the women in public, while at the same time forcing them to take his criticisms personally. In order to *force* the women into submission, Paul was insisting that they wear the veil, remain silent, and remember that man was the glory of God, while woman were the glory of man. Paul also made it clear that none of these demands were negotiable: "If anyone is disposed to be contentious, we recognize no other practice."[38]

It still seems odd to me that Paul would not have been prepared for a certain amount of resistance to his rules for women in this church. Corinth was a sophisticated and worldly Greek city which entertained all manner of religious influences. Wearing the veil, after all, was mainly a Semitic practice and Paul was attempting to force it on Greek women. Perhaps Paul needed to force this issue because he knew that women associated with the Greek mystery religions had a specific tradition of *discarding* their veils.[39] Paul would also have been aware that his Gnostic competitors approved of the unveiling of women as an outward symbol of women's spiritual liberation and equality, and that those symbols promoted the Gnostic image of God as androgynous.[40]

As to silencing the women, Paul's purpose—as we have already noted—exceeded that of simply trying to establish proper church decorum.

The issue was not so much that women were speaking in church, it was what their speaking implied: these women were exhibiting their spiritual powers, and vocalizing them in the form of prophesy.

Paul did not discourage prophecy during worship service, except in the case of women prophets. Paul's demand that women remain silent during church services immediately follows his instructions on the subject of prophecy, so it is very clear that it was the *women's* prophecy that Paul wanted to curtail.

Once again, Paul's demands are non-negotiable: "If anyone thinks that he is a prophet, or spiritual, he should acknowledge that what I am writing to you is the command of the Lord. If anyone does not recognize this, he is not recognized."[41] If the women continue with their behavior, Paul implies, he will have no choice but to excommunicate them.

Spiritually, if not politically, the women prophets of Corinth had effectively set themselves up as an alternative theological authority to Paul. They did not require his visions, they were having their own. They did not need his wisdom, theirs came from Sophia. They did not need Paul to interpret God's truth to them, they were receiving it directly from the Source.

For Paul, this simply could not be. As a patriarch, Paul believed that God's message was passed down directly to those (male) apostles whom He enlightened and inspired through visions. These (true) apostles— now knowing God's truth and His will for humanity—would graciously interpret both for the benefit of average men, and most especially for the benefit of women. For Paul, it was simply not possible for others (especially women) to access God's truth directly.

Antoinette Wire sees in Paul's refusal to recognize the Corinthian women prophets as an "attempted rape of women's divine gifts."[42] If not rape, certainly Paul was using ecclesiastical blackmail.

THE RESURRECTION AND PAUL'S SILENCE ON MARY

Immediately following his demand that the Corinthian women be silent, Paul launches into a lengthy defense of his doctrine on the resurrection of Jesus and his belief in the general resurrection of the dead at the end of time.[43] Since there is no segue between these two topics, the back-to-back arrangement of subject matter strongly suggests that the Corinthian women were the main force behind the challenging of Paul's doctrine on the resurrection.[44]

...the back-to-back arrangement of subject matter strongly suggests that the Corinthian women were the main force behind the challenging of Paul's doctrine.

If we read Paul's words carefully, it appears as if the Corinthian women were not denying that Jesus had risen (in some sense of the term) from the dead. What they were challenging was Paul's belief that there would be a general resurrection of dead believers when the world ended. For Paul, these two beliefs (the resurrection of Jesus, and the general resurrection) were inextricably linked together, and the women of Corinth had broken that link.

For Paul, it was not enough that the Corinthians still believed in a risen Christ. After all, Paul argued, if Jesus had risen, then the dead would also arise in Christ. If, on the other hand, there was no such thing as the resurrection of the dead, then Jesus had not risen either. If this were the case, Paul argued, the Corinthians' faith—and his own preaching—had been in vain. On this last point, at least, the Corinthians were in full agreement with Paul. They rejected much of his preaching as vanity, and may have rejected him as an authentic resurrection witness as well.

The doctrine of bodily resurrection would have been a tough sell to the Greeks in Corinth in any case. This belief arose out of Semitic religious philosophy, and was popular among the Pharisaic party of Judaism during Paul's time. By the same token, it was rejected by the Sadducees (who believed that no part of a human being survived death) and the Essenes (who believed in the immortality of the soul). Greek philosophy also promoted the idea of the immortality of the soul, so Paul's Pharisaic notions of the after-life must have seemed quite strange to the Corinthians—even though Paul believed that spiritual, not physical, bodies would rise on the last day.[45]

Paul believed that God had revealed himself (in Christ) in secret and mystical ways. But he also believed that Jesus the Christ was only revealed to certain men, and never to women. Moreover, Paul believed that he was the last man on earth who would ever receive an appearance of Jesus prior to the "parousia"—the return of Jesus from heaven (an event that Paul considered imminent).

In Paul's mind, it was the unique reality of Christ's appearance to *him* that set him apart as an apostle. Since the Corinthians could never have such experiences themselves, Paul offered himself as a gift from God to them. Since God spoke directly to him, Paul's duty was to interpret God's message for the benefit of all.

The Corinthian women prophets, however, were challenging Paul's sense of self-worth by eliminating him as an intermediary. They were claiming their own visions of the risen Christ. These women angered Paul further by rejecting his theology of the general resurrection of the dead by claiming a resurrected life in Christ in the here and now.[46]

If Paul's doctrine of the resurrection contradicted their own experience, these women reasoned, then Paul was not the final resurrection witness because "... they themselves know the living Christ in spirit." Moreover, the women believed that the resurrected life in Christ did not end with physical death.[47]

Such claims, of course, were heresy to Paul. Women could not receive appearances of Jesus, they could not already be living the resurrected life, and the soul could not be immortal because it could not exist independent of the body.

We now have a basis for understanding why Paul might want to leave the name of Mary Magdalene off his list of resurrection witnesses. To have included her name would have sabotaged his case against the Corinthian women prophets.

Wire suggests three possible motives for Paul's silence on Mary: 1) Paul may have wanted to make Peter primary in the resurrection tradition; 2) he did not consider women's testimony to be credible; or 3) he did not want to provide support for the Corinthian women's movement.[48]

The first two possibilities are tenable but, as Wire points out, only the third motive is thoroughly consistent with Paul's previous arguments against the Corinthian women. He mandates women's silence, then immediately moves to a topic (the resurrection) in which women are entirely missing.[49]

Not only would Paul's exception of Mary Magdalene as a witness to the resurrection effectively deny her the status of an apostle, but such a denial would also strengthen his case against the women of Corinth. If Mary Magdalene were known to the Corinthian women as a resurrection witness (and an apostle because of that experience), then Paul's case against the women of Corinth would have collapsed. Wire therefore suggests that Paul's omission of Mary's name as a resurrection witness was intentional.[50]

For the Corinthian women, "resurrection" had nothing to do with rotting corpses coming back to life. Nor did it have to do with the raising of "spiritual bodies" as Paul believed.[51] "Resurrection" was a metaphor for a new state of being—a new life in Christ—and for the Corinthians, that new life had been achieved at baptism.[52]

For the women of Corinth, the state of resurrected life in Christ did not begin with an apocalypse, or end with physical death. The resurrection was a permanent state, discovered in the here and now, and continued—without interruption—after death. The women were already living with Christ in the kingdom of God.[53] In this, the women agreed with the authors of *The Gospel of Philip* and *The Treatise on the Resurrection*:

> Those who say they will die first and then rise are in error. If they do not receive the resurrection while they live, when they die they will receive nothing.[54]
>
> But the resurrection ... is the truth that stands firm. It is the revelation of what is, and the transformation of things, and a transition into newness. For imperishability [descends] upon the perishable; the light flows down upon the darkness...

> Therefore, do not think in part ... nor live in conformity with
> this flesh for the sake of unanimity, but flee from the divisions
> and the fetters, and already you have the resurrection.[55]

In claiming direct access to the resurrected life, the Corinthian wom-
en seized what Paul had given to the Galatians, but had denied them: a
state of being where "There is neither Jew nor Greek, slave nor free, male
nor female."[56] The women had simply assumed this state of being, and
did so without Paul's blessing. We can feel all of Paul's jealousy, anger,
and personal hurt over this issue in the words he chose to respond to
these ungrateful new Christians:

> Already you are filled! Already you have become rich!
> Without us you have become kings! And would that you did
> reign, so that we could share the rule with you![57]

Wire sums up with what she considers a tentative reconstruction
of the philosophic assumptions and spiritual beliefs of the Corinthian
women prophets:

> Christ is alive in the prayer, prophecy and authority of
> those he set free. The spiritual life is not subject to an external
> tradition or past witnesses. It is a 'present communal experience
> of coming to a life in Christ.' The Corinthian community incor-
> porated a memory of men and women who experienced Christ's
> presence from the beginning.
>
> Salvation is not dependent upon a future cosmic event
> where evil is subdued. 'Death's weakness and pain are over-
> powered now with health and life.
>
> Christ's resurrection was not the 'first fruits' of some cosmic
> plan that required some sequence of events to take place. It is the
> immediate disruption of all that causes spiritual death in life.
>
> Resurrection is not a reward or punishment for past sin,
> but is the initiation of liberation from all human structures

that bind people in this life. Resurrection is not the preserve of the dead, but of the living.[58]

While no direct link can be shown between the tradition of Mary Magdalene and the women prophets of Corinth, there are enough intriguing parallels between these two matriarchal traditions to make one wonder if the women of Corinth might not have been directly or indirectly influenced by Mary's tradition. Certainly the theological tradition that Mary Magdalene came to be associated with has parallels in the feminist tradition of the Corinthian women prophets. Certainly these two early Christian traditions demonstrate that more than a few early Christian women naturally and unapologetically accepted their natural state as one of equality with men.

JAMES, MARY, AND PAUL THE ENEMY

While most Christians have always thought of Simon Peter as the leader of the earliest Jesus movement, this was not the case historically. Certainly Simon, aka Petros, aka Cephas, was *a* leader in this movement, but the earliest Jesus community that we know of—the one which was based in Jerusalem—elected as its leader, not Peter, but James, Jesus' brother and a Nazirite priest.[59]

As leader of the Jerusalem community, James was also considered to be the main leader of the Jesus movement throughout Judea and Palestine. The existence of James, and his role as leader is widely attested to in early writings. References to James' leadership can be found in *Acts of the Apostles*, Paul's letters, *The Gospel of Thomas*, the writings of the Jewish historian, Josephus, and Clement of Alexandria—to name just a few. The third-century Church historian, Eusebius, goes so far as to refer to James as Christianity's first bishop.[60]

When James was murdered in the Temple in 62 C.E., hostilities between the Jews and their Roman overlords were beginning to break out in all directions. Four years later the first Jewish/Roman war began, and by the time it ended in 70 C.E., the Temple—and Jerusalem itself—lay in ruins. The holiness of James was such that some ancient traditions attributed the downfall of Jerusalem itself to the death of James.[61]

With so little left of their homeland, and with the symbolic center of faith now nothing more than rubble, those Jews who hadn't already fled during the war became refugees after it was over. It is at this point that we lose touch with the original Jesus movement, but there is substantial evidence that Jewish Christianity—finally considered heretical by the Church—continued to exist in various forms down through the fourth century—in Palestine, in the Transjordan, and in Syria.[62]

Many of these Jewish forms of Christianity can be traced back to James and include Thomas Christians, the Ebionites (the poor ones), the Nazarenes and the Naassenes—who claimed the authority of both James and Mary Magdalene. None of these groups believed that Jesus was a divine being, and ultimately ran afoul of those Gentile Christians who—like Paul—taught that Jesus was a Savior-God.[63]

It is likely that Mary Magdalene was in some way associated with those early Jesus people who identified James as their leader. And it is certainly possible that she was caught up in the battles between Paul and the leaders of the Jesus movement. In his letter to the Galatians, Paul writes of his bitter enmity with James and Peter, and of his attack on Peter in Antioch (the center of the Hellenistic Christ cult).[64]

It was here that Paul condemned Peter (and by extension, James) for his adherence to the purity codes of the Jewish Torah, or Law, and this led to a final schism between the Jerusalem community and Hellenized Christians. There is no evidence that this schism was ever mended, so scholars have often suggested that Paul—in his letter to the Galatians—gave a false report about what took place in Antioch.[65]

Paul did make one last trip to Jerusalem, ostensibly to mend fences. *Acts* paints a rosy picture of this meeting, but most scholars believe that the meeting went badly. Instead of winning over the "pillars," Paul forced his issues to such a degree that the Jesus people—led by James—finally denounced *him* as a heretic.[66]

One ancient collection of documents known as the Pseudo-Clementines[67] tells the story of what took place after this final, fatal, meeting between James, the leader of the Jesus movement and Paul, the Christian. In this work, Paul is clearly represented as the enemy of the Jerusalem community and of Jewish Christianity in general.[68]

The vigorous polemic against Paul in the Pseudo-Clementines repudiates the legitimacy of his apostolate. Peter explains to Paul that he cannot be an apostle because he had never walked and talked with Jesus. Furthermore, Peter goes on, Paul could not have had a vision of Jesus at all. Paul's visions must have been the product of an evil demon or a lying spirit. Proof of this was the fact that Paul's teachings contradicted Jesus' teachings.[69]

According to the Pseudo-Clementines, Paul's hatred of James and the Jerusalem church culminated in an event in which Paul entered the Temple where James was speaking, shouted him down, physically attacked him, and "threw him headlong from the top of the steps."[70] *Acts* reports that Paul—with his entourage of Hellenized Christians—was, in fact, accused of desecrating the Temple and starting a riot on two separate occasions.[71]

Regardless of the historicity of such reports, there is significant evidence suggesting that—at the very least—Paul made a big mistake in claiming that his apostolate was on the same level as those who led the Jerusalem community. Paul's further claim of having the authorization of the Jerusalem community to preach Jesus (without the Law) to the Gentiles was also probably false and led to significant friction.[72] In the end, while Paul disallowed women their claim to legitimacy as visionaries and preachers of the risen Christ, the Jesus people stripped Paul of the very same legitimacy.

In the Clementine *Homilies*, Peter makes a formal case against Paul:

> If Jesus really appeared to you in a vision and made himself known to you, then he has become angry with you as an adversary; that is why he spoke through visions or dreams or even through revelations which are from outside. Can anyone be made skilful in teaching on the basis of an appearance?

And if you say, 'It is possible,' why then did the teacher remain and spend a whole year with those who were awake? But how can we believe you, even if you say that he has appeared to you? How can he also have appeared to you if what you think is contradictory to his teaching? But if you have been visited by him for an hour and instructed and thereupon become an apostle, then proclaim his words, expound his teaching, love his apostles. Do not fight with me, his disciple, for you are hostile to me, firm rock that I am, the foundation stone of the church. If you were not an adversary, you would not shame me by calumniating my preaching, so that people do not believe me when I say what I heard personally from the Lord, as if I had been condemned without dispute and you had a good reputation. But if you say that I am 'condemned,' you are accusing God, who revealed Christ to me, and disparaging the one who called me blessed on the basis of revelation. Now if you truly want to further the truth, then learn first from us what we learned from him, and if you are a disciple of truth, then come and work with us.[73]

Many early Christians (and probably some modern ones as well) vilified Paul for all the reasons listed in this speech. The speech itself has the ring of historical authenticity. But since "the historical Peter was relatively close to Paul," Gerd Lüdemann suggests that this speech does not go back to Peter, but to "circles around James, or to James himself."[74] Whatever the historical value of this speech, it does point up the early opposition to Paul that was eventually silenced by Christian orthodoxy.

The rejection of Paul by the Jesus movement, however, was not enough to overcome Paul's rejection—which led to the Church's rejection—of the historical Jesus and his Jewish followers. In the end, Paul had his way. Jesus the Jewish reformer became Jesus the Gentile Christ. Hellenistic Christianity replaced the religion of Jesus and his followers—including Mary Magdalene.

IN SUMMARY:

♦ The patriarchal Christianity of Paul became the chief reactionary movement against women in the Church.

♦ Paul was an early patriarch who used the "sin of Eve" myth as a means of denigrating all women and suppressing their influence.

♦ Paul attacked Mary's tradition through silence, excluding her name from his list of those who had experienced the risen Jesus.

♦ Paul's attack on the Corinthian women prophets was a means of suppressing an early feminist Christian movement.

♦ The Corinthian women believed that they were already living a resurrected life in Christ, and Paul sought to disavow such a theology.

♦ Paul's enemies included the leaders of the Jerusalem church.

♦ Paul rejected the historical Jesus in favor of the mythological Christ.

♦ The religion of Jesus' followers was eventually supplanted by the religion founded by Paul.

VI. Sex, Myth and Metaphor

REVISIONIST MYTHOLOGY AND MARY

Mythologizing and romanticizing the historical figures of early Christianity is an ancient art. The canonical Gospels themselves represent the earliest attempts to give life to oral tradition and community memory through the use of myth and metaphor.

Romances based on the lives, travels and adventures of the disciples and apostles continued to be written for centuries. Much of this pious fiction was fanciful and fantastic to the extreme—none more so than the so-called infancy gospels which claimed to fill in information about Jesus' childhood:

> But the son of Annas the scribe was standing there with Joseph; and he took a branch of a willow and dispersed the waters which Jesus had gathered together. And when Jesus saw what was done, he was angry and said to him: 'O evil, ungodly and foolish one, what harm did the pools and the waters do to you? Behold, now you too will be withered like a tree, and

will bear no leaves, nor root, nor fruit.' And immediately the boy wholly withered away ...

After that he again went through the village, and a child ran and bumped against his shoulder. And Jesus was provoked and said to him: 'You will not go all the way (on your journey)'. And immediately he (the boy) fell down and died.[1]

Like Damian in *The Omen*, Jesus' petulant and sociopathic behavior did not win the hearts and minds of the local townspeople. The parents of the children whom Jesus had caused to die came to Joseph and told him to pack up the family and get out of town. When Joseph confronted Jesus with all of this, Jesus caused his father to go blind.

Miracles abounded in late apocryphal literature, and no theme seemed too fantastic. The *Book of the Cock*, for instance, tells a story in which Jesus is served a cut-up chicken for dinner. Instead of eating the chicken, Jesus caused the neck bone to be connected to the wing bone and the wing bone connected to the breast bone—and so on —until all of the chicken's parts were reassembled. Back together again, complete with feathers, the chicken follows orders from Jesus to leave the house for the purpose of spying on Judas Iscariot.[2]

Neither was Mary Magdalene spared such abuses from the media. Epiphanius (367 – 404 C.E.), as mentioned earlier, claimed that the lost *Questions of Mary* contained obscene practices, and provided his readers with a paraphrase from this work:

... Jesus gave Mary a revelation, taking her aside to the mountain and praying, and he brought forth from his side a woman and began to unite with her, and so, forsooth, taking his effluent, he showed that 'we must do, that we may live'; and how when Mary fell to the ground abashed, he raised her up again and said to her: 'Why did thou doubt, O thou of little faith?'[3]

Since the actual text of the *Questions of Mary* did not survive, we cannot evaluate the authenticity of Epiphanius' quotation. But Epiphanius had a reputation for stretching the truth.[4] Like many other orthodox fathers who were battling heresies, Epiphanius was not above manufacturing or altering the content and meaning of texts to suit his theological needs.

Epiphanius, for instance, associated the *Questions of Mary* with Nicolaus, the founder of the heretical Nicolaitans (Nicolaus was one of the seven deacons of the Jerusalem church mentioned in *Acts of the Apostles* 6:5). Epiphanius claimed that Nicolaus and the Nicolaitans were well known for their licentious practices.[5]

> *Like many other orthodox fathers who were battling heresies, Epiphanius was not above manufacturing or altering the content and meaning of texts to suit his theological needs.*

We have good reason to doubt the accuracy of Epiphanius' testimony, however. While evidence about the practices of the Nicolaitans themselves is scant, Nicolaus himself was vindicated of such charges by Clement of Alexandria (c. 150-215).

Clement had heard rumors about Nicolaus, but had reliable information that the deacon had actually lived a chaste and holy life, and that his own children had remained celibate all of their lives.[6]

While an "Acts of Mary" has never been discovered, the author of the Greek version of the *Acts of Philip* included Mary in a fantastic adventure story and even gave her superhuman powers. In this text Mary Magdalene battles a dragon and subdues it through an act of exorcism. Along with Bartholomew, Mary holds a chalice in the air and sprinkles water over the beast while making the sign of the cross.[7]

The *Acts of Philip* also represented the Mary of earlier tradition: a woman who was a comforter, leader, teacher and disciple; one whom the Savior calls "good," "courageous," and "blessed among women."[8] The *Acts of Philip* attests to the fact that as late as the fourth century, Mary Magdalene was still perceived as a holy woman of highest repute in some orthodox circles.

Within Gnostic Christian circles, the reputation of Mary as a holy woman is nicely embellished in a third-century Manichean psalm book which expanded on the "apostle to the apostles" theme in the canonical *Gospel of John* (20:15-17):

> Miriam, Miriam, know me: do not touch me. Stem the tears of thy eyes and know me that I am thy master. Only touch me not, for I have not yet seen the face of my Father.
> ... thy God did not die, rather he mastered death. I am not the gardener ... I appeared [not] to thee until I saw thy tears and thy grief.
> Cast this sadness away from thee and do this service: be a messenger for me to these wandering orphans. Make haste rejoicing, and go to the Eleven.
> Say to them: 'Arise, let us go, it is your brother that calls you.' If they scorn my brotherhood, say to them: 'It is your Master.' If they disregard my mastership, say to them: 'It is your Lord.' Use all skill and advice until thou hast brought the sheep to the shepherd.[9]

As in *The Gospel of John*, the *Psalter* places Mary at the resurrection scene where Jesus commissions her to go to the male disciples as a skillful advisor and teacher, and as one who proclaims a distinct theology of the resurrection. But the *Psalter* also goes beyond John's account of the resurrection in explaining why Jesus specifically chose Mary for this interdiction. The risen Lord indicates that, while he loves the male disciples, *he cannot appear to them directly because they do not yet have sufficient faith to recognize him.*

The Jesus who speaks to Mary is an avatar who, in another psalm states:

> I am in everything, I bear the skies, I am the foundation, I support the earths, I am the Light that shines forth, that gives joy to the souls. I am the life of the world: I am the milk that

is in all trees: I am the sweet water that is beneath the sons of matter ... [10]

Since Jesus was an avatar (who had previously appeared in India as the Buddha, and in Persia as Zoroaster)[11] only Mary—with her elevated powers of perception—could see him. Only Mary—with her powers of persuasion—could convince the male disciples that Jesus did not really die on the cross. Only Mary—with her great compassion—could generate faith in weak and fearful men.

While the avatar Jesus had been manifested by the Father, so also did He create the feminine principal in the form of the Maiden, the Soul, and sent her forth to subdue the powers of darkness.

> He held her fast, he spread her over them like purified clouds of water, she thrust herself within them like piercing lightning. She crept in their inward parts, she bound them all, they not knowing it.[12]

The arch-heretic Mani (b. 216 C.E., the founder of Manichaeism), was strongly influenced by Buddhism, and that influence is especially apparent in Manichean ethics. This Gnostic Christian system promoted vegetarianism, poverty, abstention from marriage and bearing of children. It further instructed its adherents to avoid, as much as possible, harming the divine Light which exists in all sentient lifeforms.[13]

In one of several fragments of (orthodox) Coptic literature associated with the disciple Bartholomew, Mary is represented as a holy woman who goes with other holy women to Jesus' tomb where she falls into conversation with the gardener, who is given the name of Philogenes. The gardener relates the events of the resurrection, after which Jesus himself appears and talks with Mary—blessing her, promising her that she will be with him in his Kingdom and, once again, charging her with informing his other disciples.[14]

Reverence for Mary in orthodox apocryphal works was, of course, not

> *The Epistula Apostolorum can be seen as one of orthodox Christianity's earliest attempts to obscure the resurrection tradition of Mary Magdalene, and withhold her apostolic credentials in the process.*

universal. In the resurrection story in the *Epistula Apostolorum*—a mid-second-century work—Mary's importance to Christianity's myth of origin is almost nil. In this version of events, the risen Jesus doesn't seem to care who goes to tell the male disciples of his resurrection. The women just happen to be present, so Jesus tells them, "But let one of you go to your brothers and say ..." [15] By not having Jesus assign this apostolic role specifically to Mary Magdalene, the author's intention was to diminish her importance as an apostle.

In the Ethiopic version of this text it is Mary Magdalene who first goes to inform the male disciples of Jesus' resurrection, but they do not believe what she tells them. Mary returns as a failure, at which point Jesus sends "Sarah," a figure who does not even appear in the canonical Gospel accounts of the resurrection.

In the Coptic version of this text, Mary's importance is diminished even further. It is Martha (also not in the canonical accounts) who goes to inform the male disciples, while Mary is merely her back-up. From the patriarchal point of view of the author of this work, none of the women had any credibility, so they all fail in their mission. In a great turn of revisionist mythology, the risen Jesus is forced to appear to the male disciples without the benefit of a feminine introduction.

The *Epistula Apostolorum* can be seen as one of orthodox Christianity's earliest attempts to obscure the resurrection tradition of Mary Magdalene, and withhold her apostolic credentials in the process. But this was just the beginning. In another work known as the *Acts of Pilate*, the resurrection account excludes Mary Magdalene altogether and refers only to anonymous "women."[16]

In other orthodox texts that will be discussed in the conclusion of this work, Mary Magdalene's importance is not just diminished. Mary is erased altogether and replaced by Peter, or by Jesus' mother, Mary.[17] With Mary Magdalene out of the way, the Church was able to more easily elevate Simon Peter to a position of absolute primacy among the apostles. Even though Mary had walked with Jesus, held a position of great importance in the early Jesus movement, and had been a witness to the resurrection, she was denied her apostolic status by having her tradition either "altered, weakened, or eradicated."[18] Ann Graham Brock states:

> The fluidity with which early Christian figures such as Mary Magdalene, Mary, the mother, and Peter appear in—and disappear from—different textual traditions suggests that the presence or absence of these figures may well have had political or theological significance. The displacement of a figure, either in texts or translations is unlikely to be an arbitrary, confused or unmotivated act, but is in all probability intentional and deliberate.[19]

THE METAPHOR OF THE DIVINE CONSORT

Modern media sensationalists who have a vested interest in reinforcing the false image of Mary Magdalene as a highly charged sexual being, often use as one of their pieces of "evidence" a reference in *The Gospel of Philip* in which Mary is called the "companion" of Jesus. However, in the Valentinian system of Gnostic Christianity which produced *The Gospel of Philip*, the words "companion" and "consort" are metaphors referring to the divine feminine principle, or aspect, of the Godhead. Such words *never* refer to literal, historical personalities or physical acts.[20]

In *The Gospel of Philip* Mary is also equated with the divine Sophia, or Wisdom, who is called "the barren" (one who does not produce progeny) and "the mother of the angels, and the companion of the Savior."

In the *Pistis Sophia*, Sophia is the spiritual consort of the "son of man," and here Sophia is also sometimes identified as the "mother of all." At other points in the text, Sophia is an emanation of divine Will, which manifests itself in the Savior himself.[21] Wherever Mary is associated with the consort, Sophia, Mary's relationship to the Savior is one of cosmic union.

Mary Magdalene is Jesus' "companion," in the sense that she represents that part of divine nature that is inherently "feminine" or "receptive." The Valentinian system ordered creation into *syzygies*, or "couples"—much in the same way that Taoism teaches that the Tao comprises all pairs of opposites. Mary, in other words, was understood as yin to Jesus' yang.

Elizabeth Schüssler Fiorenza points out that the Valentinians believed in three Christs (or a three-fold Christ) so, … "it is possible that Mary Magdalene was thought of as a consort of the earthly Jesus, just as the Holy Spirit was the consort of the aeon Christ in the Pleroma, and Sophia was the consort of the Savior."[22] But Fiorenza goes on to say that *"Gnosticism … employed the categories of 'male' and 'female', not to designate real women and men, but to name cosmic-religious principles or archetypes."*[23]

Ultimately, gender designations in this type of literature were metaphors for the divisions in the human psyche—divisions which were meant to be transcended in spiritual practice. For the human being to approximate the divine Image, as Karen King has pointed out, all gender distinctions had to be transcended by the seeker of gnosis. The ideal psychic state, then, is one of androgyny.

There are other instances in Gnostic Christian literature which seem to suggest that the ideal spiritual state is distinctively masculine. In logion 114 of *The Gospel of Thomas*, for instance, Peter says to Jesus, "Let Mary (Magdalene) leave us, because women are not worthy of life." Jesus replies, "Observe, I will lead her so that I can make her male in order that she also may become a living spirit resembling you males. For every woman who makes herself male will enter the kingdom of heaven."

On the face of it, this logion certainly seems sexist. But some background is needed to understand its intended meaning. Peter, for instance, metaphorically represents the orthodox Church's position on women. Peter's vitriolic discourse is also intended to be a set-up for Jesus' teaching about spiritual androgyny, although this does not seem apparent at first.

Here the term, "male," is used in a way that is not necessarily gender specific. "Male"—defined in antiquity as the highest possible spiritual state of the soul—is both gender specific and non-gender specific at the same time, and the early Church fathers would not have overlooked this double meaning.

To a large extent the orthodox Church fathers moved toward a similar understanding of the human soul as androgynous based on Paul's statement, "There is neither male nor female" in Christ.[24] But the problem for the Church fathers was this: How could a Christian woman—who was created as an inferior being—achieve the kind of equality that belonged to her as a disciple of Christ?

The Church fathers answered this question by declaring that a Christian woman was no longer a *woman*. While a female nonbeliever was defined by her physical sex, the believing woman 'progresses' to the 'perfect man', to the measure of maturity in Christ."[25] Fiorenza states:

> The nonsexual monism of the divine pertains to the soul redeemed from the duality of bodily sexuality. The soul is equal and of the same essence in man and woman. Male and female are equal in divine likeness because on the level of the soul there is neither male nor female, but on the historical-creational level woman has to be subordinated to man. The anthropological corporeal duality of the sexes is subsequent to the fall and does not pertain to the original spiritual creation in the image of God. Therefore, the virgin or 'single one' represents the original 'spiritual, angelic' human being created in the image of God. Having progressed to 'the perfect man,' she ceases to be woman and can be called 'man.'[26]

Even if Christian women achieved near equality in the spiritual realm, their status in the real world remained unchanged. "Since it was restricted to the soul, the discipleship of equals could neither transform patriarchal marriage nor prevent the formation of a patriarchal church and the elimination of women from its leadership."[27]

MARY, SOPHIA, AND THE GODDESS

It is doubtful that Gnostic Christian women considered themselves to be emancipated, but they were certainly better armed in the struggle for equality. The debate over the status of women in everyday life *had* to be self-critical in those theological systems which spoke of God as a *dyad*. To those modern women who consider Gnostic Christianity to be their ally in reviving the ancient pagan "goddess," it should be pointed out that those Gnostic systems which spoke of the "Divine Mother" did not revere Her as an independent deity, but as part of a divine couple.[28] Elaine Pagels states:

> One might expect that these texts (the Gnostic Gospels) would show the influence or archaic pagan traditions of the Mother Goddess, but for the most part, their language is specifically Christian, unmistakably related to a Jewish heritage. Yet instead of describing a monistic and masculine God, many of these texts speak of God as a dyad who embraces both masculine and feminine elements.[29]

Recognizing the dyadic nature of the All, however, did not limit such Christians from using the metaphor of the Mother of All in a practical sense. "Followers of Valentinus," for instance, "prayed to her for protection as the Mother, and as 'the mystical, eternal Silence.'"[30] And those Christians who traced their secret tradition back to James, through Mary Magdalene, prayed: "From Thee Father, and through Thee, Mother, the two immortal names, Parents of the divine being ..."[31]

In Sophia mythology, Sophia was sometimes identified as the *facilitator* of the Savior's enlightenment or "resurrection." The aspect of the consort as a figure who is often responsible for a god's rebirth is a common theme found in the ancient Greek and Roman mystery religions. Here the consort is a goddess figure as well.[32] Attis was accompanied by

Cybele, Dionysus by Mother Rhea, Osiris by Isis, Adonis by Aphrodite, Baal by Anath, Tammuz by Ishtar.[33]

Some scholars believe that an early Christ cult once existed that saw the goddess figure in just this way: as the facilitator of Jesus' resurrection. The evidence, some suggest, is contained within the New Testament itself. Robert Price is one scholar who has made an interesting case for the very early existence of goddess worship in Christianity. And he casually notes that Mary Magdalene would have been the logical choice to play the role of Christ's "divine consort."

Price believes that trace evidence of a parallel Christian goddess tradition can be found in a rather strange story recorded in *Acts* 17:18. In this narrative, the apostle Paul is in Athens trying, as always, to convert everyone within earshot. His audience is made up of Epicurean and Stoic philosophers in this instance. Listening to Paul, some of the philosophers think he is just babbling, while others in the audience comment, "He seems to be a preacher of foreign gods, because he preaches Jesus and the resurrection."

A modern Christian would probably find nothing unusual about this sentence: Paul seems to be preaching his usual message about the resurrected Christ. But Price points out that, beginning with the early Church father, Chrysostom, textual critics have recognized that not one, but two, *proper names* are intended here: "Jesus and the Resurrection" or (in Greek) Jesus and Anastasis.[34]

According to Price and others, Anastasis was seen as the divine consort who—as in other mystery religions which feature a dying and rising god—*assisted* in the resurrection of Jesus. The philosophers, in other words, believed that Paul was preaching a mystery religion whose "foreign divinities"—a God and a Goddess—were Jesus and Anastasis. If there was such a cult, then it is possible that Mary Magdalene was related to it by virtue of the fact that she was the one woman always associated with the resurrection of Jesus.

Price suggests that the author of *Acts* in telling this story was attempting to both criticize and obscure evidence of an early Christ cult that included Goddess worship. If Price is right in his speculation, then the existence of a Christian Goddess cult may have been partly responsible for some of Mary Magdalene's early popularity. On the other hand, the opposite scenario is just as compelling: Mary Magdalene's popularity may have *spawned* a Goddess cult.

Did the story of the empty tomb, and Mary Magdalene's involvement in the resurrection of Jesus, begin as a more or less typical god/goddess mystery myth? The evidence is far too scant to allow us to make such a leap, but such a scenario is certainly not inconsistent with my hypothesis that Christianity's resurrection story—its myth of origin—began as a matriarchal tradition.

This much is certain: If such a goddess cult existed in early Christianity, it was firmly suppressed by orthodox clergy who reasserted patriarchal monotheism. Just as the Goddess was excised from Hebrew faith by the original sponsors of a single, male divinity, orthodox Christians may have "sanitized" the resurrection mystery story and eradicated the role of the Christian Goddess altogether.[35]

THE REAL RELATIONSHIP BETWEEN JESUS AND MARY, OR WHEN A KISS IS NOT A KISS

An interesting story in the *Pistis Sophia* that compliments the theme of the divine feminine consort assisting in the enlightenment of her masculine counterpart is also rich in sexual metaphor. In this narrative, "Spirit" comes to earth seeking to unite with his "brother," Jesus. As it happens, Jesus is not in the house when Spirit arrives, so Mary Magdalene is compelled to tie him to the bedposts so that he won't escape before she has a chance to find Jesus.

Mary locates Jesus working in the vineyards with his father, Joseph, and tells him about Spirit's arrival. Jesus rushes back to the house and releases the divine visitor. Jesus then enters a state of rapture, and Mary later has to tell him what took place while he was in this altered state:

> ... we looked upon you, and found you to be like him. And the Spirit bound to the bed was set free, and he embraced you, and kissed you, and you also kissed him—and you became one.[36]

Clearly the metaphor of the "kiss" is not meant to be taken literally. Elaine Pagels points out that in Gnostic Christian literature, the "kiss" is a means of transferring spiritual energy—of signifying mystical communion. As a metaphor, the "kiss" was hardly unique to Gnostic Christianity. The same imagery has been in common use in mystical traditions throughout history.[37]

Jesus' love for Mary Magdalene is a theme that appears frequently in the Gnostic Gospels, but every text is clear that his love for her is purely *spiritual*, and predicated upon her unique spiritual gifts. In the *Pistis Sophia*, for instance, Jesus is unequivocal about why he loves Mary and compares her to the beloved disciple in *The Gospel of John*:

> But Mary Magdalene and John, the virgin, will surpass all my disciples and all those who will receive mysteries in the Ineffable, they will be on my right hand and on my left, and I am they and they are I ...[38]

As with most of the Gnostic Gospels, the *Pistis Sophia* argues against marriage and virtually every other kind of sexual intimacy. Instead, it supports the practice of celibacy as a necessary part of overcoming worldly desires in order to attain enlightenment, or gnosis. In this text, Jesus tells his followers to "Renounce the whole world ... and all of its relationships."[39]

The relationship between Jesus and Mary in virtually every Christian text ever written is unquestionably one of master and disciple.

The relationship between Jesus and Mary in virtually every Christian text ever written is unquestionably one of master and disciple.

115

But in Mary's case, the relationship with Jesus is intensified due to her unique ability to perceive the true meaning of his teachings. A perfect example of this relationship can be found in *The Gospel of Mary*, where Mary is the Savior's star pupil; the next master–in–waiting. As his intern, Mary is being groomed by Jesus to take his place and, indeed, she does just that.

Mary's unique spiritual status is confirmed by her titles and descriptions: "The Blessed One,"[40] The "companion of Wisdom,"[41] the "Pure Spiritual One,"[42] the "woman who understood completely."[43] Rather than lusting after Mary, the enlightened Jesus fully recognizes and respects the enlightened Mary:

> Mary, thou blessed one, whom I will perfect in all of the mysteries of the height, speak openly, you whose heart is raised to the kingdom of heaven more than any of your brothers.[44]
>
> For you are blessed before all women on the earth, because you will be the fullness of all fullness, and perfection of all perfections.[45]
>
> Excellent, Mariam, the blessed one, who will inherit the whole kingdom of Light.[46]

Understanding how the word "kiss" is used in mystical literature, let us turn to the sentence about Jesus and Mary Magdalene in *The Gospel of Philip* that Dan Brown made so much of in his novel, *The Da Vinci Code*. For Brown, and those who read his fiction as fact, this sentence "proves" that Jesus and Mary Magdalene had a physical relationship:

> Jesus loved her (Mary Magdalene) more than all the disciples and used to kiss her often on the mouth.[47]

Dan Brown's version of this sentence, however, does not exist. The actual sentence from *The Gospel of Philip* reads like this:

> ... her more than ... the disciples ... kiss her... on her ...

The words above are all that remain of this part of *Philip's* text. As it happens, the papyrus manuscript of *Philip* (Codex II, tractate 3 of the *Nag Hammadi Library*) is badly damaged. Based on the *context* of the surrounding text, however, scholars have reconstructed this sentence and feel confident that the reconstruction accurately represents the intention of the author. The *reconstructed* sentence that appears in *The Nag Hammadi Library in English* reads:

> [… loved] her more than [all] the disciples [and used to] kiss her [often] on her […].[48]

The brackets around the words above indicate "lacunas" or blank spots in the text. Given the context we can feel confident that the sentence has to do with Jesus and Mary. As for the word "kiss," just when we are about to discover what part of Mary's anatomy Jesus used to plant his lips on … there is a *hole* in the papyrus![49] Some translators supply the word "mouth" here to fill the lacuna because they understand the context within which this sentence fits. And that *context* makes all the difference. Although it was ignored by Brown, the author of *The Gospel of Philip* is very clear about how he is using the word "kiss":

> It is from being promised to the heavenly place that man [receives] nourishment. […] him from the mouth. [And had] the word gone out from that place it would be nourished from the mouth and it would become perfect. For it is by a kiss that the perfect conceive and give birth. For this reason we also kiss one another. We receive conception from the grace which is in one another.[50]

Now that we know the author's intent, let's put the kiss sentence back into its original context:

> As for Wisdom (Sophia) who is called 'barren' (without

117

progeny) she is the mother of [of the] angels. And the companion of the [...] Mary Magdalene. [... loved] her more than [all] the disciples [and used to] kiss her [often] on her [...]. They said to him, 'Why do you love her more than all of us?' The Savior answered and said to them, 'Why do I not love you like her? When a blind man and one who sees are both together in the darkness, they are no different from one another. When the light comes, then he who sees will see the light, and he who is blind will remain in darkness.'[51]

Jesus' love for Mary obviously has nothing to do with erotic love, and he answers the disciples' pointed question by reversing it. What single quality, Jesus asks, does Mary have that justifies his special love for her? It is the very quality that they lack. Like Mary, the other disciples are in the presence of the Light (Jesus), but they are blind to it. Only Mary is capable of seeing Jesus for who he really is.

Jesus is saying that all of the disciples except for Mary still remain in ignorance and in the darkness of their own jealous minds. Since Mary is the only disciple with the ability to perceive the Light, she is the only disciple worthy of receiving the mystical kiss which provides spiritual nourishment—the symbolic act that transfers illumination from master to disciple.

The Gospel of Mary also uses the metaphor of the kiss, but in a unique and very feminine way:

[... Mary stood up and greeted] them; she tenderly kissed [them all and said, brothers and sisters, do not weep, do not be dis]tressed nor be in doubt ...[52]

As the one who took over Jesus' role after he departed, Mary's kiss, too, is full of spiritual nourishment, but being feminine it also carries with it non-judgment, great compassion, purity and innocence.

THE ISSUE OF CELIBACY

The Gospel of Philip, like the *Pistis Sophia* and every other Gnostic Gospel, promotes the celibate life-style, going so far as to consider acts of the flesh a defilement of one's essentially spiritual nature:

> The bridal chamber (the crucible in which enlightenment takes place) is not for the animals, nor is it for the slaves, nor for defiled women; but it is for free men and virgins.[53]

The "bridal chamber" (which appears in the Gospels of *Matthew*, *Mark* and *Luke* as well) was a sacrament in the Valentinian system of Gnostic Christianity, of which *The Gospel of Philip* was a part. Elisabeth Fiorenza states that it was used "as a spiritual-symbolic means for individual perfection and psychological unification."[54] Physical marriage, Philip tells us, is nothing compared to one's marriage to God:

> Indeed marriage in the world is a mystery for those who have taken a wife. If there is a hidden quality to the marriage of defilement, how much more is the undefiled marriage a true mystery! It is not fleshly but pure. It belongs not to desire but to the will.[55]

For Philip, as well as for the authors of other Gnostic Gospels in which Mary Magdalene appears, sexual abstinence is a necessary part of the spiritual path. Jean Doresse states that the Naassenes—those Gnostics who claimed to have received their teachings from Jesus' brother James, through Mary Magdalene—"were against carnal intercourse, which they looked upon as a defilement for the race of the elect ... "[56]

SISTER-WIVES

Those today who wish to make a case for the union of Jesus and Mary by demonstrating that the early apostles were married, often point to a passage from Paul's first letter to the Corinthians. Paul writes: "Do we not have the right to be accompanied by a wife, as the other apostles and the brothers of the Lord and Cephas?"[57]

Paul himself, however, was celibate, so his question was entirely rhetorical. He had no intention of claiming this "right" for himself, but merely wanted to point out that he should be afforded the same rights as any other apostle. But what can we make of Paul's mention that other apostles and the "brothers of the Lord" brought along wives on their missionary journeys?

Nearly all English translations of this verse are misleading. Translators—perhaps intentionally—generally leave out the Greek word, *adelphene* or "sister" that precedes the word *gunaika*, or "wife," in this passage. Correctly translated, Paul's question actually reads: "Do we not have the right to be accompanied by a sister-wife ... ?"

> *"Sister-wives" were married women who accompanied their apostolic husbands on their travels and who, like their husbands, had taken vows of celibacy.*

In using the term adelphene-gunaika, Paul was not trying to confuse the issue. "Sister-wives" were married women who accompanied their apostolic husbands on their travels and who, like their husbands, had taken vows of celibacy. The second-century Church father, Clement of Alexandria, was well aware of this tradition:

> Peter and Philip fathered children, and Philip gave his daughters in marriage. Furthermore, Paul did not hesitate to mention his 'companion' in one of his epistles ... He says in his epistle, 'Do I not have the right to take along a sister-wife, as do other apostles?' However, the other apostles, in harmony with their particular ministry, devoted themselves to preaching without distraction. Their spouses were with them, not as wives, but as sisters, in order to minister to housewives.[58]

Clement is saying that all of the apostles save for Peter and Philip had been celibate even though some were married. The sister-wives had withdrawn from sexual relations along with the men. They traveled with the men in order to assist and support the housewives of those churches which they visited. John Dominic Crossan also adds that sister-wives were often missionaries themselves, and were accompanied by men for their own protection.[59]

Paul wished that everyone could be celibate like himself, and he had practical reasons for encouraging celibacy.[60]

> I wish you to be without care. The unmarried care for the things of the Lord, how he shall please the Lord; but he that is married cares for the things of the world, how he shall please the wife. The wife and the virgin are divided. The unmarried cares for the things of the Lord, that she may be holy both in body and spirit; but she who is married cares for the things of the world, how she shall please the husband.[61]

Clement of Alexandria was saying essentially what Paul had said, and Paul was saying essentially what Jesus had said: that one cannot successfully serve two masters at once. There is no judgment in this pronouncement. Unlike many Gnostic Christians, Jesus, Paul and Clement did not believe that the flesh was evil, sex was sinful or that marriage was wrong. They simply pointed out that if one wanted to devote their lives entirely to God, and heighten their spiritual powers, then they needed to look beyond all worldly concerns, especially the desires of the flesh.

Paul, however, was also a realist. He believed that it was better to marry than to burn with lust. Since Paul believed that human history was about to end, and even though he believed in celibacy as the highest ideal, he counseled the Corinthians to remain in the state in which they found themselves. If they were married, they should remain married. If they were single, they should remain single.[62]

Nothing was ever that simple for our rebellious Corinthians, however, and Paul found himself with another serious problem on his hands. The Corinthian women prophets had apparently decided to become celibate. For those who were married, this meant denying their husbands' conjugal rights![63]

A HEADACHE IS NO EXCUSE

Even though Paul made his own celibate life-style well known, he did not encourage anyone who was already married to renounce his or her marital obligations—not even for the sake of their spiritual lives. His opinion applied to the Corinthian women prophets even more than it did to other members of the congregation. These women, in addition to all the other problems they were causing Paul, were no longer honoring their marital vows.

The women had not become frigid, they were simply honoring their spiritual yearnings, and these had to do with what scholars call "realized eschatology." For the women of Corinth, the "end" of the world had already come, and the "second coming" of Christ had already taken place. The women saw themselves as already leading a resurrected life in Christ. Caught up in ecstasy, their new dimension of spirituality encouraged them to become celibate in order to enhance their spiritual powers.[64]

Understandably, those husbands who had not made a similar commitment were not happy about this new development. Someone from their group had apparently asked for Paul's intercession, so the apostle was forced to do some serious marriage counseling.

In consecrating their bodies (together with their minds and souls) to God, the Corinthian women were living no differently than Paul himself. But Paul still found this new turn of events another occasion where he had to take issue with these women, and in this case, the issues were more practical than theological or personal. Paul knew that if he supported the women in their new undertaking, their frustrated husbands would further destabilize an already shaky congregation.

Once again Paul had to overrule the women, and wrote to them: "The wife does not have authority over her own body, but the husband does." But

Paul was not being sexist. He went on to write, "Likewise the husband does not have authority over his own body, but the wife does. Do not defraud one another ("I have a headache") unless by consent for a season that you might be at leisure for fasting and for prayer, and again come together in one place so that Satan will not tempt you because of your incontinence."[65]

Temporary celibacy for the sake of spiritual exercise was OK if both partners agreed. Prolonged celibacy, however, could lead men into temptation. Although Paul does not say what form temptation might take, prostitution is certainly implied. This was a real concern for Paul because in Corinthian society many men were forced to frequent prostitutes due to that society's practice of female infanticide. There simply were not enough women to go around.[66]

Paul recognized that his church was headed for a moral meltdown if the spiritually oriented wives continued to deny their husbands. He tried to deal with the situation by being a good pastor and offering sage advice, but in doing so he was also begging the question as to what was best for the women's spiritual lives. They had made a decision to abstain from sex in order to enhance their spiritual powers, but Paul considered those needs secondary to church order.

Had the circumstances been different, perhaps Paul would have addressed this situation in some other manner. But Paul believed—and wanted his parishioners to believe—that life as they knew it was about to end abruptly. In Paul's view, once this evil world and its relationships passed away, God in Christ would create a new spiritual kingdom in which marriage and even sexual differentiation would no longer exist. In the meantime, the Corinthian women's responsibility was to keep their husbands' libidos in check by fulfilling their marital obligations. After all, they could look forward to celibacy for all eternity.

EUNUCHS FOR THE KINGDOM: MARY, JESUS AND CELIBACY

The situation involving sexual continence in Corinth was only a foretaste of a practice that would become pandemic in early Christianity.

Christian men and women, both married and single, Gnostic and or-thodox, took up the celibate life in great numbers during the first several centuries of the Christian era. They did not invent the reasons for doing do, they were simply following Jesus' teachings on the subject:

> The sons of this age marry and are given in marriage; but those who are accounted worthy to attain to that age and to the resurrection from the dead neither marry nor are given in marriage.[67]
>
> Not all men can receive this precept, but those to whom it is given. For there are eunuchs who have been so from birth, and there are eunuchs who have been made eunuchs by men, and there are eunuchs who have made themselves eunuchs for the sake of the kingdom of heaven. He who is able to re-ceive this, let him receive it.[68]
>
> The disciples of John (the Baptist) marry and are given in marriage; but my disciples neither marry nor are given in mar-riage, but are as the angels of God in heaven.[69]

Some of those who attempt to make a case for the physical union of Jesus and Mary Magdalene point out that absolute celibacy was not part of the Jewish way of life for men in first century Palestine. After all, didn't God tell Adam and Eve to "be fruitful and multiply"?

Apparently ignoring the celibacy of John the Baptist before Jesus, and Paul after him, these critics further inform us that by the age of thirty, most men—apart from the celibate Essenes—were married. According to rabbinic rules, a Jewish man was expected to marry by the age of 18, or by the age of 20 in the case of those who belonged to the married branch of the Qumran community.[70] This logic is simple: If most Jewish men in first-century Palestine were married, then Jesus must have been married.

Giles Vermes, however, probably speaks for most scholars in chal-lenging such logic: "… there is one aspect of life in which Jesus seems to have been completely different from the men of God of his age. The Hasidim were all married, with children and grandchildren; with Jesus ... everything points toward a celibate existence."[71]

In fact, Jesus was nothing like other Jewish holy men of his day. Jesus rejected, and spoke out against, the social customs and religious wisdom of his day. He took up the itinerant life and called men and women alike to leave their livelihoods, their wealth, their homes, and even (and especially) their families (with all of their implied responsibilities) in order to devote their lives entirely to their search for the kingdom of God within.

> *The Hasidim were all married, with children and grandchildren; with Jesus ... everything points toward a celibate existence."*

Such behavior—in most cultures, in most times—is generally viewed as irresponsible, especially in the case of men who are expected to be husbands, fathers, family providers and responsible members of the community. For Jesus, however, the kingdom of heaven trumped societal expectations.

> The various call stories in the gospels show that Jesus called young men to leave their father's fishing boats or work in the fields, their household and family groups. That is, they left their places of responsibility, the tasks that they were supposed to fulfil (sic) as men, sons and/or husbands and fathers in the household. These tasks were not only economic roles. They were social, religious and cultural expectations. If they left all this to walk around with Jesus, they had left a 'man's place' ...[72]

Jesus seemed to have had little regard for the value of blood relationships, and rejected the concept of the nuclear family in favor of the family of God. It should not be surprising, then, that Jesus—like every spiritual giant and great saint in recorded history—encouraged others to reject cultural expectations, transcend desires of the flesh, and renounce the attractions of the material world in favor of building up treasures in heaven: "For where the treasure is, there will be the heart also."

Jesus, like the Buddha, was a renunciate but not a strict ascetic. Both spiritual giants chose the "middle way" that allowed them to live *in* the world without being *of* it. Jesus ate what was put before him, attended wedding parties and raised a cup of cheer now and again. And even though he had chosen the path of celibacy, Jesus reaffirmed the sanctity of marriage as an institution of God. For all of his heroic domination of the flesh, Jesus fully recognized that in every age only a few are so passionate for God that they will enter through the narrow gate to take up the difficult journey that leads to enlightenment.

With these things in mind, what can we make of Jesus' statement about becoming eunuchs for the sake of the kingdom? Even among those New Testament scholars who have reduced the authentic sayings of Jesus to a mere handful, there is general agreement that the "eunuchs" saying comes from the *historical* Jesus.[73] But did Jesus expect his audience to understand these words literally?

The author of Matthew's Gospel places this saying in the context of Jesus' teachings about marriage, adultery and divorce. In this context, it is a direct response to his disciples' rhetorical statement that—given the pitfalls of marriage—perhaps it was better to remain single. Many scholars, however, feel that *Matthew* 19:12—which has to do with the controversy over divorce and remarriage—was a separate saying of Jesus, and the two teachings did not originate together.[74]

While the Greek word, *eunoukos*, most often referred to males who had been castrated, it was also applied to men with impotency from birth, and to those who abstained from sexual practice and marriage by choice.[75] The circumstances mattered little to most people; however, being a eunuch was most often regarded as a shameful condition. Jesus' favorable comments about eunuchs, then, were meant to challenge this common prejudice.

Many scholars maintain, therefore, that Jesus' saying about eunuchs was a response to accusations that he and his group of followers were "like eunuchs" because they had rejected the social conventions of masculinity in Jewish society. They had left "a man's place," so they were not "real men."[76]

In relating *eunoukos* to the kingdom of heaven, Jesus used a controversial example of chastity and asceticism to reject Jewish prejudice that—because eunuchs were unfruitful—they were to be despised. Jesus turned this around: "No longer are eunuchs despised: rather they have merited grace and are invited to enter into the kingdom of heaven."[77]

Jesus may have also used the term, eunoukos, in the same sense as early Christian and Roman writers: to indicate asceticism as a laudable and masculine enterprise which, in a figurative sense, spiritualized the eunuch into a male ideal by virtue of cutting out the passions of the soul without touching the body.[78]

As was always the case, Jesus' wisdom was out of step with traditional social and religious customs and prejudices. Elaine Pagels notes that such a social theology must have horrified Jewish traditionalists:

> ... for barren women, whom Jesus blessed, had traditionally been seen as accursed, and eunuchs, who Jesus praised, were despised by rabbinic teachers for their sexual incapacity. Unmarried himself, Jesus praised the very persons most pitied and shunned in Jewish communities for their sexual incompleteness—those who were single and childless ... [79]

Thus Jesus dismisses the family obligations considered most sacred in Jewish life, including those to one's parents, siblings, spouse, and children. By subordinating the obligation to procreate, rejecting divorce, and implicitly sanctioning monogamous relationships, Jesus reverses traditional priorities, declaring, in effect, that other obligations, including marital ones, are now more important than procreation. Even more startling, Jesus endorses—and exemplifies—a new possibility and one he says is even better: rejecting both marriage and procreation in favor of voluntary celibacy, for the sake of following him into the new age.[80]

In early Christianity, the celibacy preached and practiced by Jesus spread like wildfire. "In sharp contrast to contemporary Christianity, the early churches were not strong defenders of 'family values', although there was strong debate on the subject."[81] The marital state was certainly not condemned, but authors of Christian literature often encouraged readers to follow Jesus and Paul's practice of celibacy, as did the early Church fathers:

> Blessed are the solitary and elect, for you will find the Kingdom. For you are from it, and to it you will return.
> *The Gospel of Thomas*

> For when you come forth from the sufferings and passions of the body you will receive rest.
> *The Book of Thomas the Contender*

> He who has married should not repudiate his wife, and he who has not married, should not marry.
> *The Gospel of the Egyptians*

> They are the ones who were not defiled with women, for they are virgins. These are the ones who follow the Lamb wherever he goes ...
> *The Book of Revelations*

> Blessed are they that keep the flesh chaste, for they shall become the temple of God. Blessed are they that abstain, for unto them shall God speak. Blessed are they that have renounced this world, for they shall be well-pleasing to God.
> *The Acts of Paul*

> Wherefore, ye servants of God, arm yourselves every one in your inner man with peace, patience, gentleness, faith, charity,

knowledge, wisdom, love of the brethren, hospitality, mercy, abstinence, chastity, kindness and justice.

The Acts of Peter

It is not possible for you to obtain that woman, seeing that for a long time she has even separated herself from her husband for godliness' sake.

The Acts of John

Our ideal is not to experience desire at all... . We should do nothing from desire. Our will is to be directed only toward what is necessary. For we are children not of desire but of will.

Clement of Alexandria

If anyone is able in power to continue in purity, to honor the flesh of our Lord, let him continue to do so without boasting.

Ignatius

Many who have been Christ's disciples from Childhood—both men and women—remain pure at the age of sixty or seventy years.

Justin Martyr

You would find many among us, both men and women, growing old unmarried, in hope of living in closer communion with God.

Athenagorus

There are many who do so and seal themselves up to being eunuchs for the sake of the kingdom of God, spontaneously relinquishing a pleasure so honorable and permitted.

Tertullian

The Savior teaches us that absolute chastity is a gift given
by God … Therefore, God will give the good gift—perfect purity in celibacy and chastity—to those who ask Him with the
whole soul, with faith, and in prayers without ceasing.

Origen

As all sides agree, no one will ever be able to *prove* that the relationship between Jesus and Mary Magdalene was only one of master
/disciple. As with any subject having to do with the murky past, we
always have to admit that anything is possible. But we will conclude
with Robert Price's observation in his article, "The Da Vinci Fraud,"
that possibility is not probability:

The notorious tendency of conservative apologists and
New Age paperback writers alike is to leap from mere possibility to the right to believe. 'If there might be space aliens, we
can assume there are.' 'If the idea of Atlantis is not impossible,
we can take it for granted.' 'If the traditional view of gospel
authorship cannot be definitively debunked, we can go right
on assuming its truth.' No you can't. And though Jesus might
have had sex with one or many women and men, the mere
possibility is no help. He might have been a space alien, too.
Some think he was. But historians do not.[82]

IN SUMMARY:

◆ Pious romances about Jesus, Mary, and the apostles continued to be written long after the New Testament period.

◆ References to Mary Magdalene as Jesus' "companion" or the "consort" of the Christ in the Gnostic Gospels were meant to be understood spiritually and metaphorically. As such, they did not refer to the historical Jesus or the historical Mary Magdalene.

◆ Sexual metaphors are common to the literature of the world's mystical traditions.

◆ Some evidence exists that suggest that there may have been an early Christian goddess cult, and Mary Magdalene may have been associated with it.

◆ The metaphor of the "kiss" in Gnostic Christian literature refers to the transfer of spiritual energy.

◆ All the evidence suggests that the relationship between Jesus and Mary Magdalene was strictly one of master and disciple.

◆ Jesus was celibate and taught celibacy. Many early Christians followed his example.

VII. Peter - the Tarnished Saint

PETER AS MYTHOLOGICAL FIGURE

Looking for the historical Peter turns out to be, in many respects, even more difficult than looking for the historical Mary Magdalene. If one were to consult the subject indexes of most scholarly works on New Testament subjects, one will rarely find Peter's name. While Peter may be mentioned many times in these books, it would appear that— as a subject—he doesn't seem to merit a subject listing.

Perhaps this is the case because Peter is nearly always mentioned only in the context of his relationship to someone else: to Jesus, to Mary Magdalene, to James, to Paul. Paul is a good case for comparison, for while literally thousands of books have been written about Paul—who never even met Jesus—few scholarly tomes have been devoted to the man who was supposedly Jesus' chief disciple.

Cephas, Petros, Simon, Peter, the Rock! Along with Paul and Mary Magdalene, Peter's place as a major force in early Christianity is still assured by the shear volume of references to him in the *New Testament*, orthodox apocryphal literature and in the Gnostic Gospels. We know that Peter lived, and we know that he was associated with Jesus and with Paul. We know that he played an important role in the origins of Christianity, but we do not know precisely what that part was, and we certainly have very little biographical information about him. Peter, it would seem, was so mythologized by early Christians that scholars have rarely attempted to discover who he really was.

Most Christians, for instance, think of Peter as the leader of "the twelve," and yet there are no early traditions to support such a belief. Peter was not considered the preeminent leader of "the twelve" until Matthew's Gospel made him out as such—some fifty years after the death of Jesus.[1] By the time Luke wrote his Gospel—some ten to thirty years later —the lore about Peter had already become legend. Burton Mack states:

> Peter became a prime figure for mythmaking because, if you could recast the Peter of Paul's Galatians (letter) and imagine the Peter of the synoptic Gospels to represent and validate the Christ myth, centrist interests would gain an exceptionally solid foundation. Just think what it would mean if the leading figure of the Jerusalem congregation had taken the gospel to Rome. So that is what happened.[2]

The Roman Catholic Church has always considered Peter its first honorary pope, based on an ancient tradition that claims that Peter, like Paul, traveled to Rome, had something to do with the founding of the church there, and died in Rome as a martyr. There is, however, no real evidence to support such claims.[3]

Much of the history about Peter is based only on later Church tradition itself, such as the writings of Eusebius and Justin Martyr.[4] But while Eusebius was the first "historian" of the early Church, his work was often revisionist in nature. When the Gospel accounts suggest otherwise, how can we believe Eusebius when he referred to Peter as "great and mighty," "the leader of all the other apostles," "a noble captain of God, clad in divine armour."[5] The evidence suggests that all of these claims are at least partly false.

We know, for example, that Peter was *not* the primary leader of all the other apostles. If anyone has a legitimate claim to that title, it was James, Jesus' brother. As to Peter's illustrious character, reviews are mixed.

Luke, in *Acts of the Apostles*, says nothing at all about Peter traveling to Rome, or anything about his later life. In the twelfth chapter of *Acts*, the author claimed that Peter had been arrested by Herod and thrown into prison. But then, like Houdini, Peter made good his escape in spite of the fact that he was in a cell, in chains, and physically guarded night and day.

> *Many scholars in the past have considered the possibility that Peter was expelled from the Jerusalem community for some reason.*

Luke, as one might expect, attributed Peter's escape to the assistance of an angel from heaven. Once free, Peter appeared at the home of Mary, the mother of John Mark, and told the gathered assembly there to report to James and his "brethren" that he had made good his escape. Others were asked to make this report because Peter "departed and went to a different place."[6]

This is the last we hear of Peter in the New Testament. The rest of *Acts*—more than half of the entire work—is devoted solely to adventures and travels of Paul. Thus, if Luke—writing no earlier than 90 C.E.—had information about Peter having traveled to Rome—where he became a martyr—he surely would have reported such historical facts. The fact that he didn't suggests that Luke had no idea whatsoever what became of Peter.

How and why did Peter fall off Luke's radar? In *Acts* 21:18, the author reports that when Paul made his third and final journey to Jerusalem, he paid his respects to James alone. We know, then, that at some point Peter was no longer part of the Jerusalem community.

Many scholars in the past have considered the possibility that Peter was *expelled* from the Jerusalem community for some reason. Of course, Peter may have left of his own free will. But reasons for Peter's departure seem to have been so embarrassing to the early Christian community that the author of *Acts* refused to reveal them. We have only one clue as to what happened: Peter's vanishing act may have had something to do with his relationship with the apostle, Paul.

PETER AND PAUL, FRIENDS AND ENEMIES

Historically, it appears that early in their relationship Peter and Paul were friends, or at least friendly acquaintances. Paul tells us in his letter to the Galatians (c. 55 C.E.) that he went to Jerusalem to "visit" Peter some three years after his own conversion. Paul claims to have stayed with Peter for fifteen days. While he was there, Paul met with Jesus' brother, James, but he claims to have seen no other apostles during this visit.[7]

We know from Paul's testimony in this same letter that at some point after this visit, an adversarial relationship developed between Paul and the "pillars" of the Jerusalem community: James, Peter and John. The tension between the Jesus movement (based in Jerusalem) and Paul's Hellenist Christ cult (based in Antioch) seems to have been well known to all concerned by the time Paul made a second trip to Jerusalem some fourteen years later. "Paul did not say what the gospel according to the pillars was, but he made it very clear, both in *Galatians* and elsewhere in his correspondence, that his gospel and their gospel did not match."[8]

Paul's stated purpose for making this second trip was to mend fences and receive support for his Gentile mission. But Paul seems to have come armed and ready for a fight, bringing his co-workers, Barnabas and Titus, with him as allies. These three men then met with James, Peter and John, as well as with the community as a whole.

According to Paul's testimony, the meeting turned into a disaster, with accusations flying in all directions. Paul blamed the problems on "false brethren" and "spies" who were "secretly" brought in to challenge his doctrine of freedom from the Law. We don't know what the other side of the argument was, but Paul proudly stated that his group of Christians "did not yield submission (to James, Peter and John) even for a moment."[9]

Given the intense acrimony, many scholars believe that Paul was probably not telling the whole truth in later claiming in *Galatians* that Peter,

James and John extended to him "the right hand of fellowship." It is further evident that the wounds had not healed between these two movements by the time Peter journeyed to Antioch and met with Paul and the other Hellenists there. Rather than mending fences, Paul states that he "opposed him (Peter) to his face, because he stood condemned."[10]

Paul supposedly wanted to win over the "pillars" to his cause, but that was not to be. The meeting at Antioch—like the Jerusalem meeting before it—turned into another fiasco. Paul's expressed hope for unity and support turned out to be entirely unrealistic since neither he nor the Jesus people were willing to compromise. Instead of unity, the meeting at Antioch resulted in a final schism between the Jesus movement and the Christ cult.

Paul accused Peter of being a hypocrite because Peter—in Paul's opinion—vacillated between living as a Gentile, free of the Law, then siding with the "Judaizers" whenever he was in their company.[11] To this extent, Paul's picture of Peter's personality agrees with later portraits painted by the evangelists who wrote the Gospels. Hardly the solid rock of Christian tradition, the historical Peter seems to have been someone who never took a solid position on anything. He seems to have been continuously susceptible to outside influences and the winds of change. The Gospels did not altogether succeed in redeeming Peter's character, only illuminating his hypocrisy in numerous and devastating ways.

PETER - THE TARNISHED SAINT

Peter, according to the Gospels, was a man of extremes. One moment he had great faith and insight, the next he was consumed with doubt and negativity. As one of the mythical "twelve,"[12] Peter often took a negative position on issues. More often than not, Peter failed to understand what Jesus was teaching, and was not above arguing with him for his own point of view. On one occasion, Jesus became so frustrated with Peter that he compared him to Satan—a man who was "not on the side of God, but of men."[13]

The historical Jesus made no Messianic claims about himself, nor did he predict his future.

Peter's reputation for intransigence seems to have been so well known in early Christian circles that the authors of the canonical Gospels did not attempt to hide it. It was a simple matter, then, for the author of *The Gospel of Mary* to use this canonical caricature of Peter as a metaphor for the orthodox Church: Peter was stubborn—the Church was stubborn. Peter did not understand Jesus' teachings—the Church did not understand Jesus' teachings. Peter was combative and narrow-minded, and so was the Church.

But since Peter was mythologized into an important figure in early Christian orthodoxy, the authors of the Gospels were compelled to at least try to rehabilitate his reputation, and they did this by turning him into a Christian. Peter, the Gospels tell us, was a dullard while Jesus was alive, but became a rock of faith after Jesus was crucified and then rose from the dead.

After the resurrection of Jesus, Peter suddenly becomes enlightened. He now sees that Jesus was the Messiah, just as Jesus had implied while he was alive. Jesus suffered, died, and rose again, just as he said he would. Peter understood now that Jesus had been telling the truth in all things. Except that, historically, Jesus never said any of those things.

Peter's "illumination" is pious Christian retrospective from a later era. Neither Jesus nor his earliest followers were interested in Messianic expectations, and Jesus' followers had little interest in giving meaning to Jesus' death and resurrection. The historical Jesus made no Messianic claims about himself, nor did he predict his future. Christian evangelists put such words into his mouth, and then into Peter's. So, if Jesus' earliest followers did not believe—even after adopting some kind of resurrection faith—that he was the Messiah (as evidenced in *The Gospels of "Q" and Thomas*) —then neither did Peter, at least not at first.

It seems probable that Peter did become a "Christian" at some point, since numerous early Christian traditions saw him in that light. But his conversion from Jesus person to Christian may have been due—at least partly—to Paul's influence during those early days when Peter and Paul had been friends. Paul may have criticized Peter for being a hypocrite, and a Judaizer, but he certainly believed that he was a *Christian* hypocrite and Judaizer.

Those that followed in the tradition of the Jerusalem community were *not* Christians in the usual sense of the term. Burton Mack points out: "Judging from later evidence for Jewish Christianity in general, Jesus was esteemed as 'the anointed' teacher of a Jewish ethic of very high standards. He was not revered, held to be divine, or worshipped on the model of the Hellenistic congregations."[14]

Since Jesus' earliest followers were not Christians, and since those who followed the Jerusalem community were not Christians either, we must assume that the "pillars" of the Jerusalem church were not Christians in the way that Paul was. If Peter eventually became a Christian because of Paul's influence, it is possible that Peter was expelled from the Jerusalem community precisely for that reason. Certainly we must account for the disappearance of Peter from the Jerusalem community in some way, and we must also account for Peter's reputation as a disciple who had "denied" Jesus.

I KNOW HIM NOT

Mark's story (14:66-72) of Peter's three-fold denial of Jesus after his arrest is well known by Christians. It is, however, a poorly crafted attempt at obfuscating the truth about Peter's denial of Jesus. One group of scholars puts it simply: "The fellows of the Jesus Seminar are convinced that the tale of Peter's denial is a Markan invention. Peter did not deny Jesus because he was not there (in the courtyard of the high priest); he had fled with the rest of the disciples. Moreover, the narrative has Mark's literary fingerprints all over it."[15]

Is it possible that Peter's reputation for having denied Jesus resulted from events that took place *after* Jesus was crucified? Did Peter become an apostate of the Jesus movement? Was he ultimately converted by Paul at Antioch, and therefore expelled from the Jerusalem community by James? Why else would Peter and Paul—together—be considered the co-founders of orthodox Christianity?

In *Acts of the Apostles*, Peter does, in fact, disappear from the Jerusalem community. The fact that the author of *Acts* offers no explanation for this disappearance suggests that he was embarrassed by the truth. If there had been a schism between Peter and the Jerusalem church due to Peter's defection to Paul's Christ cult, and if Mary Magdalene had been aligned with the Jerusalem Jesus people, then such a schism might help explain, as well, the early tension and rivalry between the disciples of Peter and the disciples of Mary Magdalene.

THE SLEEPY SENTRY

The author of Mark's Gospel fictionalized, in Peter's favor, the scene in which Jesus was arrested, and he may have done this to obscure a tradition which accused Peter of being complicit in the arrest of Jesus. Using Mark's master story as a basis, all four canonical Gospels tell us that on the night he was arrested, Jesus went with his disciples to the Garden of Gethsemane on the Mount of Olives, not far outside the walls of Jerusalem. Jesus' supposed purpose for going there was to pray.

Jesus takes all of his disciples to the Mount of Olives, but leaves most of them at the foot of the hill. He then continues further up the mount with Peter, James (the son of Zebedee), and John. Then Jesus stops at a certain place, and tells Peter, James and John to remain at this location while he goes further up the hill. Jesus also tells the men to *gregoreite*— which, in Greek, means "to watch," "to remain awake," to "keep one's eyes open," to "**be on the alert**"!

Leaving these three behind, Jesus disappears into the trees. After awhile, he returns to find all three disciples fast asleep. Jesus specifically reprimands Peter: "Could you not watch one hour?" After again instructing Peter and the other two disciples to remain awake, Jesus again goes off alone. Still later, Jesus returns a second time, and again finds the

140

disciples asleep. Again he chastises the men, and again he charges them to remain awake, and again he goes off to pray alone.

When Jesus returns the third time and finds the men asleep, he does not bother to chastise them because now it is too late. His betrayer is at hand, and all is lost. Judas Iscariot—a disciple gone bad—and an arresting party made up of Roman soldiers and Temple police arrive on the scene and immediately take Jesus into custody.

No doubt most Christians who have read this story in Mark's Gospel (which is repeated in *Matthew, Luke* and *John*) have wondered why it was so important to Jesus for the disciples to remain awake. When we add up all the details in all of the accounts of this story we find the answer.

Luke (22:36) fills in one important piece of information that Mark left out. He narrates a scene which took place shortly after Jesus' "demonstration" in the Temple. For an innocent lamb of God, Jesus does something shocking: he tells his disciples to go out and buy swords! Why such a request? The reason is simple: the disturbance in the Temple had brought Jesus and his disciples to the attention of the authorities, and those authorities were seeking to arrest Jesus.

Any charismatic Jew who had the potential for inciting crowds was viewed as a revolutionary by the Roman occupiers of Palestine. The Romans crucified first and asked questions later, so Jesus could not have been unaware of the potential consequences of his actions in the Temple. He knew that he could be arrested at any time, and it is even possible that he had narrowly escaped capture at the time of the incident itself.

It seems likely that Jesus was in hiding at this point in time, hoping to return to Galilee just as soon as the authorities tired of looking for him. But Jesus had a need to come out of hiding and go to the Garden of Gethsemane on Mount of Olives, outside of the walls of Jerusalem. It seems rather irrational that he would leave his safe house and go walking about with a group of armed men.

Certainly Jesus did not go to the Mount of Olives just to pray. He could talk to God anywhere. For some reason, Jesus was willing to risk capture by appearing in a public park with an armed guard. In Chapter

VIII we will discover what Jesus was really doing on the Mount of Olives, but we will not tell that story just yet.

All of the canonical Gospels agree that the disciples were armed with swords at the time Jesus was arrested. Thus armed, Jesus instructed Peter, James and John to remain awake because he needed them to warn him of any impending trouble. In other words, Peter, James, and John had been posted in the Garden of Gethsemane *as sentries*.

By falling asleep, the three men utterly failed their master, and that failure resulted in Jesus' arrest and crucifixion. No wonder the Christian evangelists didn't want to tell the true story of Jesus' arrest. Instead, they gave the story a Christian "spin," and used it to their advantage. Jesus *had* to be arrested, because he *had* to be crucified, because he *had* to die, so that he *could* rise from the dead, so that through his *sacrifice*, God could initiate His plan of *salvation*. Jesus, in other words, went to his death willingly and with complete foreknowledge that he was God's own son, and must suffer and die.

> *By falling asleep, the three men utterly failed their master, and that failure resulted in Jesus' arrest and crucifixion.*

This is Christian theology, however, not history. The fact that Jesus' disciples were armed suggests that Jesus had no intention of being captured, much less crucified. The Gospel narratives also tell us that when the arrest went down, the disciples actually *used* their swords. The sword play apparently did not last long, but at least one disciple sliced off the ear of the "slave of the high priest." In *Mark, Matthew* and *Luke*, that disciple is anonymous. In *John*, however, the swordsman is identified as the hot-headed Simon Peter![16]

Although the historical arrest scene may have been quite different from the one recorded in the Gospels, Christian community memory of this event may have held Peter partly responsible for Jesus' arrest and crucifixion. The evangelists spun the story as best they could, and did their level best to clean up Peter's reputation at the same time. History confirms that they were successful.

PETER THE ENFORCER

Two stories in *Acts of the Apostles* which feature the dark side of Peter's personality are probably not based on historical events, but they are important stories because they tell us more about the nature of the Church—an institution with which Peter became permanently identified.

The first story (*Acts* 5:1-11) has to do with a married couple: Ananias and Sapphira. This couple, who belonged to the Jerusalem community of Jesus people, sold their personal property and gave the money to the community (which held all things in common).

Unfortunately for them, the couple held back part of the profits from the sale. Worse still, when the husband, Ananias, brought the partial proceeds from the sale to the apostles, he failed to mention that he had kept some money out for a rainy day which was, surely, an act of bad faith.

Peter—who after Jesus' resurrection has developed psychic powers—knows of Ananias' deception, and confronts him. Peter accuses Ananias of being filled with Satan, and charges him with lying to the Holy Spirit. Upon hearing Peter's words, Ananias immediately falls down dead.

The body is cleared away by young men, and the scene is reset for Sapphira's eventual entrance. When she appears, Peter confronts her. Sapphira lies to Peter about the amount she and her husband had collected from the sale of the property, and this lie seals her fate. When Peter tells her that he knows that she is lying, and that her husband is dead because of his deceit, Sapphira immediately falls down dead at Peter's feet. Luke ends the story by stating: "And great fear came upon the church and upon all who heard of these things."

Peter in this story actually represents the *authority* of the Church, and the Church claimed that its authority came directly from Jesus. In *Luke* 22:30, Jesus tells the disciples that they will sit on thrones, and judge all of Israel. It is Peter's (the Church's) right, therefore, to both judge and dispense punishment just as Israel had judged Achan in the Biblical book of *Joshua*. Achan was put to death for the very same crime as Ananias and Sapphira: holding out on the holy community.[17]

Peter's judgment and sentencing is therefore an act of God's will. Luke then tells his readers that great fear came upon everyone in the "Church" (a term used for the first time in *Acts*) upon hearing this story. Luke's intention seems to have been one of intimidation, and the implication is that the Church had the power to judge its members, and even impose the death penalty if necessary.

The early Church had, and used, this power. The reader will recall that Clement, Bishop of Rome, threatened the troublesome Corinthians with death for heresy and rebellion, and Clement no doubt justified his stance based on Paul's prior judgment of the Corinthians.

In one particular case discussed in *I Corinthians*, Paul accused a male member of the congregation of sleeping with "his father's wife" (mother or stepmother?), which was, for Paul, the worst sort of abomination. Paul judged the man in absentia, and ordered the church to "deliver this man to Satan for the destruction of the flesh."[18] If Paul did not expect the congregation itself to put this man to death, he did expect Satan to take care of the execution.[19] Paul makes a point that because the members of his church are Christians, they have the right to both judge and condemn: "Do you not know that the saints (Christians) will judge the world? And if the world is to be judged by you, are you incompetent to try trivial cases? Do you not know that we are to judge the angels?"[20]

SIMON PETER VS. SIMON MAGUS

The second story in *Acts* (8:9-24) having to do with Peter's lack of charity tells of a showdown between Simon Peter and a Samaritan known as Simon Magus (the Magician). Luke tells us that Simon had an inflated sense of himself, and that he had previously practiced the craft of magic.

The disciple, Philip, was preaching Jesus Christ in a Samaritan city one day, and Simon happened to be in the audience. Simon was impressed with what he heard and immediately became a believer, asking Philip to baptize him.

Philip did baptize Simon, along with many other Samaritans, and when the other apostles back in Jerusalem learned how successful Philip had been in winning new converts to Christ, they dispatched Peter and John

> *Peter accused Simon of wickedness, and wished him to perish along with his silver.*

to Samaria to continue the crusade. One day after they arrived, Peter and John were baptizing as well as practicing the ritual of the laying on of hands, which invoked the power of the Holy Spirit.

Simon watched Peter and John perform this ritual and was very impressed. Simon was so impressed, in fact, that he offered Peter money to teach him how to call down the Holy Spirit. Rather than graciously accepting the money as a donation to the community of the poor in Jerusalem, Peter accused Simon of wickedness, and wished him to perish along with his silver.

To a non-Christian it might seem that it was Simon Magus, not Simon Peter, who acted like a gentleman. He offered to pay for his education, and did not demand the teaching as a gratuitous favor—which would have been his right as a baptized Christian. To the unbiased reader, it is Simon Magus who excels as a gentleman in this story, bearing Peter's reprimands with patience and humility.

While *Acts* says no more about Simon of Samaria, the Church father, Justin Martyr, reported that Peter had such animosity toward Simon Magus, that he followed him all the way to Rome in order to denounce him even further.[21] For all of this, it is highly unlikely that there is anything historical about this account.

Simon Magus was considered by the early Church (and by many modern scholars) as the founder of Gnosticism, so Luke in *Acts* used "Peter" to stand for "the Church" in its opposition to "Simonists" who were rivals of orthodox Christians in Rome where Simon was worshipped as a God.[22]

What is particularly revealing about Luke's account of Simon, however, is that he states that Simon was a *former* practitioner of magic and

145

a *current* Christian in good standing. While Luke intended to criticize "Simony" in the telling of this story, it is rather amazing that he considered Simon (and by implication, his followers) to be Christians.

PETER—DISCIPLE OF JOHN THE BAPTIST

The author of Mark's Gospel claims that Simon Peter and his brother, Andrew, were fishermen plying the Sea of Galilee at the time that Jesus came along and called them to be his disciples.[23] Shortly thereafter, Jesus, Peter and Andrew made a courtesy call on Peter's mother-in-law who was sick with a fever. With these notations, Mark wanted his audience to believe that Peter had been a married man, a fisherman, and a householder who—along with his brother—gave up their settled lives to follow Jesus around Galilee.

The Gospel of John, however, tells us something entirely different about Peter. Rather than being fishermen from Galilee, John claims that when Jesus met Peter and Andrew, the brothers were disciples of John the Baptist.[24]

In the synoptic Gospel accounts of Jesus and John, Jesus came to John the Baptist to be baptized by him, but there is also a general implication that Jesus was originally a disciple of John's. After John was beheaded by King Herod, Jesus began his own ministry, and some of John's disciples began to follow him. In *The Gospel of John*, however, Jesus does not even come to John to be baptized, much less become his disciple. In John's Gospel, the implication is that Jesus and John's ministries were concurrent, and they are essentially leaders of different communities.

Most scholars prefer—as being closer to historical fact—the synoptic accounts about Jesus' and John's relationship. That is, Jesus was a disciple of John's at one point, and may not have started his own ministry until after John was dead. At the same time they also believe that Jesus' earliest disciples were Baptists from John's community.[25]

Luke, in *Acts*, adds that Jesus' earliest disciples were with him even while he was still with John the Baptist.[26] Inasmuch as Peter and Andrew were the first disciples "called" by Jesus, it therefore seems all the more likely that Peter and Andrew were originally Baptists.

Of the four canonical Gospels, only John's Gospel suggests that Jesus and John the Baptist may have been rival teachers (which they probably were). Certainly the author of *John* did not want his audience to believe that Jesus' teachings were the same as the Baptist's. Since John the Baptist believed that God was about to break into history and judge Israel, he preached repentance and practiced water baptism. Jesus believed that the kingdom of God was already present, so he did neither. Consequently the Jesus of John's Gospel baptizes no one—although he permits *his disciples* to do so.[27]

John's Jesus in some ways is closer to the historical Jesus as he is portrayed in the earliest layer of the *Gospel of Q*, or Q^1. The Jesus of Q^1 is not an eschatological preacher—believing, instead, that the kingdom of God was already present.[28] Only after the *Gospel of Q* was redacted at a later date (Q^2 and Q^3) by a different group of Jesus people, does Jesus himself become an apocalyptic preacher (in Matthew and Luke's Gospels) like the Baptist.[29] Helmut Koester states:

> The most obvious signs of a secondary redaction of Q can be found in the apocalyptic announcement of judgment and the coming Son of man which conflicts with the emphasis upon the presence of the kingdom in wisdom sayings ...
>
> The announcement of judgment characterizes this opening section (the introduction of John the Baptist in *Matthew* and *Luke*) of Q in which John the Baptist calls for repentance and announces the coming of God... for judgment with fire and spirit.[30]

Such teachings, then, were not original to Jesus. Nor were they original to the earliest followers of Jesus. These beliefs eventually entered the Jesus movement (and Christianity) through the direct influence of disciples of John the Baptist who joined the Jesus movement and infected it with John's theology. If Peter brought the Baptist's ideas into the Jesus movement, then it stands to reason that Peter was not a member of the earliest Q1 community.

Because John's disciples became followers of Jesus, all of the canonical Gospels had to accommodate the tradition of John the Baptist to one degree or another. The later the Gospel composition, the greater the accommodation. John's Gospel, however, was an exception to this rule, as was the Jewish–Christian *Gospel of the Nazaraeans*, in which we read:

> Behold, the mother of the Lord and his brethren said to him: 'John the Baptist baptizes unto the remission of sins, let us go and be baptized by him.' But he said to them: 'Wherein have I sinned, that I should go and be baptized by him? Unless what I have said is ignorance.'[31]

To all of the Gospel authors, the suggestion that Jesus had been baptized by John was a scandalous proposition, and each author dealt with the scandal in a different way. Early in the second century, Ignatius of Antioch suggested that Jesus was not immersed in water so that it would purify him, but so that he would purify the water.[32]

None of the evangelists would have had to deal with the relationship between John and Jesus, however, were it not for the fifth column of Baptists in the early Jesus movement. John was only important to the Jesus story-line because Baptists made him important.

In the end the Baptists had their way. Although Baptist ideas were not part of the earliest Jesus tradition, those ideas were assimilated into early Christianity. W. Barnes Tatum states:

> This kind of assimilation—if not rivalry—apparently did occur around the middle of the first century when the Q community expanded its emerging collection of Jesus' sayings to include sayings by and about John the Baptist. As-

similation of John the Baptist's followers into the emerging Church may also be presupposed by Luke's infancy traditions about John.[33]

None of this would be important to us in dealing with the subject of Mary Magdalene were it not for *The Gospel of John's* notation that Peter and Andrew had been disciples of John the Baptist before they were disciples of Jesus. If John's report is historically credible, then we can, hypothetically, trace a trajectory directly from John the Baptist to Peter to Paul to *orthodox* Christianity. This trajectory is parallel to, but entirely separate from, the tradition that begins with Jesus and was handed down through Jesus' brother, James, Mary Magdalene, *The Gospel of Mary*, the Jewish-Christian Gospels, and Jewish-Christian Gnosticism.

Mary's tradition, for instance, entirely rejects all Baptist theology. Sin, repentance, baptism, and the end of days, are all ideas antithetical to early Jesus movements such as the community of Q^1, Thomas Christians, and those who wrote *The Gospel of Mary*. If such ideas entered Christianity, in part, through Simon Peter, then we have yet one more possible explanation for the historical rivalry between Peter and Mary and/or between Peter and Mary's followers.

Admittedly, the evidence for Peter being the source of Baptist influence on the early Jesus movement is circumstantial. If the connection could be demonstrated conclusively, however, it would go a long way toward solving a number of mysteries about the evolution of early Christianity. It might, for instance, provide a basis for Peter's early friendship and association with Paul, who carried the Baptist's beliefs into Gentile Christianity. It might also explain why Peter virtually vanished from *Acts of the Apostles*.

PETER VS. MARY IN GOSPEL TRADITIONS

In the Gnostic Gospels in which Mary and Peter both appear, there are often common elements. In *The Gospel of Thomas*, for instance, Peter is portrayed as less enlightened than Mary Magdalene.[34] Peter demonstrates how little he has learned from Jesus by asking him to throw Mary out of their group because "Women are not worthy of life."

In the *Pistis Sophia*, Peter wants Jesus to make Mary shut up because she is entirely dominating the question/answer session. Peter complains, "Who can endure this woman?"[35] For her part, Mary expresses to Jesus that "I am afraid of Peter because he threatened me, and hates our sex."[36]

In *The Gospel of Mary*, Peter is on his worst behavior. He accuses Mary of lying, and of faking a special relationship with the Savior. Wherever Peter and Mary appear together in these texts, Peter consistently challenges Mary's authority or diminishes her status.[37]

Ann Brock contends that those works in which battles between Peter and Mary play out, the works themselves show no literary dependence upon one another. That is, no author used any other author as a source for his own work. This suggests to Brock that the tension between Mary and Peter played out in many independent traditions, and in widespread locations!

The tension between Peter and Mary played out in the canonical traditions as well—in the only place they could: in the stories about Jesus' resurrection. Brock notes that Peter and Mary never both receive individual resurrection appearances in the same text. It is always Mary *or* Peter, never Mary *and* Peter.[38]

So, even in the orthodox Christian tradition, Mary and Peter were used as pawns of opposing colors on a chessboard of Christian politics. The political issue was the same as it was in the Gnostic texts: whether or not women had the right to speak and teach in Jesus' name.

The most explicit anti-Marian / pro-Petrine Gospel is, of course, that of Luke's. Luke consistently treats women as subordinates,[39] heightens Peter's importance in general,[40] and excludes altogether Jesus' rebuke of Peter (otherwise found in *Mark* 3:32b and *Matthew* 16:22).

In Luke, the risen Jesus appears only to Peter, so the evangelist has an excuse for not including a story commissioning Mary as an apostle to the apostles. And whereas Mark and Matthew state that Mary and other female disciples ministered to Jesus, Luke has Mary and the other women minister to "them," that is, the male disciples.[41]

Luke does not even allow Mary (by name) to stand with the other women at the crucifixion of Jesus, thus diminishing her importance even further.[42] And only Luke reports that the male disciples did not believe Mary and the other women's report that Jesus had risen from the dead.

In *Matthew*, by contrast, Mary receives not one, but two commissionings as apostola apostolorum: one by an angel, and one by Jesus himself. One story parallels Mark's "go and tell the disciples," and the other parallels John's "go tell my brothers." Brock suggests that the two commissioning stories represent two different traditions about Mary.[43]

In *The Gospel of John*, Mary receives an appearance of the risen Jesus at the empty tomb, but Peter—even though he goes to the empty tomb—does not see Jesus.[44] In fact, Brock believes that John's entire story about Peter and "the disciple whom Jesus loved" rushing to the tomb, only to find it empty, is a later interpolation created for the purpose of inserting a masculine resurrection tradition, and two male witnesses.[45]

John's Gospel further diminishes Peter by not including a story in which Jesus actually calls Peter to follow him, and withholds from Peter the privilege of confessing Jesus as the Messiah. John, instead, grants that honor to a woman! It is Martha who says, "I believe that you are the Messiah and the son of God."[46]

It cannot be stressed enough that the mythological tensions that play out between Peter and Mary Magdalene in the various Gospels reflected political tensions within the Church itself. To claim to have "seen the risen Lord" had political consequences,[47] since only those who could make this claim could be considered apostles.

In the end, however, it still did not matter that Mary Magdalene had been commissioned as an apostle in three of the four canonical Gospels. The Church could not allow apostolic succession to pass on to women in the Church through Mary Magdalene. Even though Mary's tradition as an apostle is certain, the Church still restricted "the circle of leadership to a small band of persons (men) whose members stand in a position of incontestable authority."[48]

IN SUMMARY:

♦ In the canonical Gospels, Peter was often portrayed as a man of extremes who was represented as someone who was often faithless, uncomprehending and argumentative.

♦ There is no hard evidence to support the Church's claim that Peter was the founder of the church of Rome, or that he ever traveled to or was martyred there.

♦ Peter was originally a friend of Paul's, but was later attacked by Paul for being a hypocrite and a "Judaizer." A complete schism eventually developed between the two men.

♦ The tradition that Peter "denied" Jesus may have been based on a schism that developed between Peter and the Jerusalem community of Jesus people. Or it may have been based on rumors that Peter's negligence led to Jesus' arrest and crucifixion.

♦ Peter, in *Acts of the Apostles*, plays the role as the Church's "enforcer."

♦ Originally, Peter may have been a disciple of John the Baptist, and brought the Baptist's theology of sin, repentance, baptism, Messianism and eschatological expectation into a Jesus movement that was originally free of such ideas.

VIII. And Mary Wept:
Mary in the *Gospel of Mary*

AND MARY WEPT

I n contrast to the reputations of Peter and Paul, virtually all ancient
accounts of Mary Magdalene portray her as an innocent. She never
argues or debates, never makes accusations, and never calls anyone a liar. And even though Mary is almost entirely silent in the
canonical Gospel accounts of her, she is still consistently portrayed as
supportive, completely faithful, entirely honest, and wholly unassuming.
It should not be surprising, then, that this is the role that Mary plays in
the Gospel attributed to her.

In *The Gospel of John's* account of the resurrection of Jesus, we find
Mary weeping outside an empty tomb.[1] When asked by an angel why
she was weeping, Mary answered that it was because she did not know
what had happened to Jesus' body. But we can easily imagine that Mary
had been weeping at the cross of Jesus as well.

In the Coptic version of *The Gospel According to Mary*, Peter
asks Mary to speak of the things the Savior had discussed with her
when they were not present. Mary agrees to tell the disciples what

she remembers of the Savior's teachings and states: "I will teach you what is *hidden* from you"—indicating that she is going to reveal esoteric knowledge.

Shortly after Mary begins to speak, the text breaks off, and pages 11-14 are missing. When the text picks up again, we find ourselves in the middle of a treatise on the ascent of the liberated soul at the time of death.

When Mary finishes speaking, Peter's brother, Andrew, challenges her by saying that he doesn't believe that the Savior had ever taught such strange ideas. Peter agrees with Andrew, and accuses Mary of lying. Because Peter's accusation is false and unjust, Mary begins to weep.

There are other instances in other texts in which Mary weeps as well, and we might be tempted to view such reports as insensitive male stereotyping. But I believe that the image of a weeping Mary is meant to convey something important about Mary.

The very ability to weep defines one as fully human. Weeping can be understood as a metaphor for one's ability to be open and vulnerable to all that life has in store for us. The ability to weep demonstrates that we are fully engaged in life. Tears demonstrate that we are willing to respond to life's tragedies and joys from the very center of our being—from our "heart."

In the *Pistis Sophia*, Mary weeps in front of Jesus because she is worried that the celestial powers of judgment at the time of death might keep them from being in His presence eternally. And, at the end of this, the fifth book of *Pistis Sophia*, all of the disciples weep after Jesus gives them the secret words to use in overcoming these same powers.[2]

In Mark's Gospel, Peter wept after he realized that he had denied Jesus.[3] In John's Gospel, Jesus himself wept upon learning that his friend Lazarus had died. In Luke's Gospel, Jesus wept for Jerusalem, knowing its unhappy destiny, and knowing that he had no power to change the course of history or the effect of national karma.

> Would that even today you knew the things that make for
> peace! But now they are hid from your eyes. For the days shall

come upon you, when your enemies will cast up a bank about you and surround you, and hem you in on every side, and dash you to the ground, you and your children within you, and they will not leave one stone upon another in you.[4]

In *Luke*, Jesus was weeping because his people, the Jews, were unable to do the right thing; that is, to wage peace instead of war, to open minds instead of close them, to soften hearts instead of harden them. Jesus wept because he understood the human condition and the *inevitability* of human tragedy. Mary wept for the very same reason.

Great sorrow, however, can also lead to great compassion. Weeping for the injustices of the world is not wasted energy. Neither does it necessarily indicate attachment to the way we would *like* things to be. The Buddha, already liberated from all attachments to the material world, was known as "the compassionate one." Bodhisattvas in the Buddhist tradition renounce their final liberation until every sentient being is also liberated. It is this same gnosis, or deep understanding of how the universe works, that enables the current Dali Lama to have such profound compassion that he can refer to the Chinese Communists who occupy his homeland as "my friends, the enemy."

Tears are inevitable for anyone who has unbearable compassion for all life, and they are the natural and necessary bi-product of the spiritual seeker. Rather than desensitizing us, the inevitability of pain in life is intended to make us *feel* all the more. An ever-expanding consciousness cannot help but invigorate our emotional sensibilities, even with an understanding of the secret purpose of tragedy.

The Buddha did not teach people how to transcend the pain of feeling for life. Instead he taught how not to suffer in the midst of such pain. Modern Buddhists put it simply, "Pain is inevitable, but suffering is optional." Jesus taught much the same thing:

Blessed are they who have been persecuted within themselves. It is they who have truly come to know the Father.[5] If you knew how to suffer you would not be able to suffer. Learn how to suffer and you shall be able not to suffer.[6]

So will you not cease loving the flesh and being afraid of sufferings? Do you dare to spare the flesh, you for whom the Spirit is an encircling wall? If you consider how long the world existed before you, and how long it will exist after you, you will find that your life is one single day and your suffering but a single hour.[7]

Hearken to the Word; understand knowledge (gnosis); love life, and no one will persecute you, nor will anyone oppress you, other than you yourselves.[8]

For when you come forth from the sufferings and the passions of the body, you will receive rest.[9]

Jesus taught that by going *through* suffering (rather than avoiding it) one could learn how to transcend it. Mary's "weeping," therefore, is a useful metaphor in this context. The Mary who weeps is a woman filled with compassion, and out of compassion Mary comforts and instructs the other disciples. But Mary's support for others is not limited to words alone. Mary teaches by example. Her compassion manifests in behavior and in action.

Mary represents a person who has gained spiritual maturity in spite of life being a veil of tears. The Mary who weeps is the same Mary who tenderly kisses each of the disciples. The Mary who weeps is the same Mary who comforts the disciples by reminding them of the encircling wall of Spirit that protects them. As a model of spiritual strength, Mary is able to turn the disciples' hearts toward the good.[10]

By contrast, Peter is represented in this Gospel as a spiritually underdeveloped person who is angry, fearful, arrogant, jealous and ignorant.[11] The underlying message of *The Gospel of Mary* is that such radical differences in personality and behavior are the result of one's theological world view. Mary represents the authentic Christian, while Peter manifests the perversion of Christianity in the form of Christian "orthodoxy."

THE CONCEPT OF SIN IN THE *GOSPEL OF MARY*

Earlier we discussed the origin of orthodox Christianity's belief in original sin, and how such a concept defined the human condition of sinfulness and alienation from God. The wages of sin, the Church maintained, was death, and the only way humanity's fate could be changed in this respect was through the intervention of God.

The ancient belief that God demands sacrifice from humanity survived in Pauline theology and orthodox Christianity, but the historical Jesus preached against both the concept and the practice of sacrifice.

Humankind could do nothing to save itself, so it was necessary for God to become man. As man, God sacrificed Himself to appease Himself, and thereby offered humanity the opportunity for salvation from His own condemnation.

Such a theology could scarcely have arisen out of Judaism a century later. When the Temple in Jerusalem was destroyed by the Romans in 70 C.E., the cult of priests, and the ancient practice of sacrifice, ceased to exist. Jews never again believed that their God had to be appeased by sacrificial offerings.

The ancient belief that God demands sacrifice from humanity survived in Pauline theology and orthodox Christianity, but the historical Jesus preached against both the concept and the practice of sacrifice.[12] Jesus' demonstration against the Temple cult resulted in his crucifixion.[13]

Jesus' brother, James, continued to challenge the cult of priests and their sacrificial practices. Ultimately, however, James paid the same price as Jesus for his protest. It is interesting to note that, according to one ancient text, the person accused of instigating and participating in the murder of James was himself heavily invested in the theology of sacrifice. According to the Pseudo-Clementines, the "Enemy" (of both Jesus and James) was none other than Paul.[14]

Gnostic Christianity believed neither in the concept of original sin, nor the need to appease a wrathful God by offering sacrifices. Consequently, Jesus was not the Savior of humanity because he died on the cross. Jesus was the Savior of humanity because he brought the Light of knowledge to the world.

Jesus in *The Gospel of Mary* proposes a model for Christian living in which the concept of sin is entirely absent. In this Gospel, Peter—who represents the orthodox Church—asks Jesus: "What is the sin of the world?" Jesus' answer, however, takes Peter by surprise:

> There is no such thing as sin; rather you yourselves are what produces sin when you act in accordance with the nature of adultery, which is called 'sin'. For this reason, the Good came among you, pursuing (the good) which belongs to every nature... This is why you get si[c]k and die: because [you love] what de[c]ei[ve]s [you]. [Anyone who] thinks should consider (these matters)!
>
> [Ma]tter gav[e bi]rth to a passion which has no Image because it derives from what is contrary to nature. A disturbing confusion then occurred in the whole body. That is why I told you, 'Become content at heart, while also remaining discontent and disobedient; indeed become contented and agreeable (only) in the presence of that other Image of nature'. Anyone with two ears capable of hearing should listen![15]

In Mary's Gospel, sin has nothing to do with good and evil actions. It is the result of an improper mixing of spiritual and material natures, and the domination of one's spiritual self by fleshly needs.[16] Karen King states,

> Salvation is achieved by overcoming attachment to the body and the material world, for it is attachment which keeps people enslaved to suffering and death. Ultimately it is attach-

ment to the body that produces sin. From this perspective, sin doesn't really exist, because the material world and the body associated with it are merely temporary phenomena, soon to pass away.[17]

As with Hinduism and Buddhism, *The Gospel of Mary* teaches that the body is not one's true Self. Only the soul infused with spirit (Atman or Self in the *Bhagavad Gita*), is eternal. *The Gospel of Mary* therefore teaches that one should seek that Self within rather than attend to desires of the physical (but temporary) body. If one is successful in this spiritual endeavor, if one overcomes all attachments to the world, the true Self at the time of death will return to its Source. Spirit returns to its own nature.[18]

Since sin does not really exist in this system of thought, there is no need for atonement, and no need for a savior from sin. King states, "Because sin is attachment to the world, turning from the love of the world to the love of God removes humanity from the power of sin."[19]

Modern New Testament scholars almost universally consider the idea of spirit returning to Spirit, and matter returning to Matter, as dualist philosophy, but this is a gross misunderstanding of Gnostic Christian philosophy at its most profound level. In Mary's Gospel, Jesus taught that the non-reality of "sin" was the same thing as the non-reality of material existence itself. And if the material world is ultimately an illusion—or a delusion of the human mind—then dualism is, by definition, impossible. There is only one ultimate Reality, and that is God. Duality exists only in the human mind.

In *The Gospel of Mary,* Jesus taught that:

> Every nature, every modeled form, every creature, exists in and with each other. They will dissolve again into their own proper root. For the nature of matter is dissolved into what belongs to its nature.[20]

Spirit and matter are both "real," but since matter has a beginning and an end, it does not have the nature of *ultimate* reality. All that truly exists in the Universe is One, pure, unchanging, Spirit. All else is illusion.

THE KINGDOM OF GOD IN THE *GOSPEL OF MARY*

Earlier I made the claim that Jesus' concept of the kingdom of God was at the very heart of all his teachings. Because of Paul's teachings, orthodox Christianity took Jesus' teachings on the kingdom to mean a future time when Christ would return from heaven, and God would rule on Earth.

The Jesus Seminar understands Jesus' term to mean a present rule of God on Earth. The Seminar's translation of "kingdom of God" in all of its books is usually: "God's imperial rule," or "imperial domain."

I would contest this translation in that I think it destroys Jesus' intended meaning. I understand Jesus to be saying that the "kingdom" is not a physical place. It is a state of *consciousness*—a way of perceiving one's relationship with the cosmos. The "kingdom" of God lies within oneself.

> Some Pharisees asked Jesus when the kingdom of God would come. His answer was, "The kingdom of God does not come in such a way as to be seen. No one will say, 'Look, here it is!' or, 'There it is!'; because the kingdom of God is *within* you.[21]

The Greek preposition used for "within" in *Luke* is "entos." This word can be translated as either "within" or "among," but most Christian translators choose to render it "among" because "within" has mystical implications. Still, "entos," rendered as "within," was the most popular use of this Greek word, and is the correct translation in this case. In *Matthew* 23:26, the evangelist used the word to mean the "inside" of a cup. In the Septuagint, the Greek version of the Old Testament (the Hebrew *Bible*), it always refers to the "inward parts of a person."[22]

C. H. Dodd, in *The Parables of the Kingdom* wrote:

Entos is properly a strengthened form of *en* used where it is important to exclude any of the possible meanings of that preposition other than 'inside'... When Luke means 'among' he says *en mesoi*... 'Among' does not give a logical sense. A thing which is 'among you' is localized in space, more or less. On the other hand you cannot say 'Lo here, or there!' of that which is "within,' and the Kingdom of God is said not to be localized in space, because it is *entos humon* (within the individual)... In other words, the ultimate reality, though it is revealed in history, essentially belongs to the spiritual order, where the categories of space and time are not applicable.[23]

"The kingdom within" saying in *Luke* has a number of parallels in heterodox Christian texts. It is found in *The Gospel of Thomas* 3:1-3, and 113; in *Dialogue of the Savior* 9:3; and in *The Gospel of Mary* 4:4-5:

If those who lead you say, 'Look, the kingdom is in heaven,' then the birds of the air will precede you. If they say, 'It is in the sea,' then the fish will precede you. Rather, the kingdom is within you and outside you.[24]

His disciples said to him, 'When will the kingdom come?' He said, 'It will not come by watching for it. They will not say, 'Look here!' or 'Look there!' Rather the kingdom of the Father is spread out upon the earth, and people don't see it.[25]

... And I say to [you, ...] what you seek [and] search for, lo[ok, it is wi]thin you, ...[26]

Be on guard so that no one deceives you by saying, 'Look over here!' or 'Look over there!' For the son of Man (or, child of true Humanity) exists within you.

Follow it! Those who search for it will find it.[27]

Each rendering of this saying has precisely the same sense to it: the kingdom is not something up there, down here, or over there. God's kingdom is everywhere simultaneously—most especially within oneself. The kingdom cannot be localized in time or space because "it is instantaneous and ubiquitous."[28]

In Mark, Matthew and Luke's Gospels, Jesus teaches that the kingdom is a "secret" and a "mystery,"[29] and is known only to those who have true spiritual perception—that is, eyes to see and ears to hear. To all others the parable of the "kingdom" is nothing more than a puzzle without a solution.[30]

Jesus taught that such spiritual perception was attainable only by becoming as innocent and pure as very young children, for they perceive reality directly, having not yet been conditioned by human interpretations of reality. Jesus, in *The Gospel of John*, says that everyone who seeks God within will become as if born again.[31] He or she who seeks and finds becomes an entirely new person, with a new ability to perceive *all* of reality as it truly is. *Finding* the kingdom is tantamount to becoming "enlightened" in the religions of the Far East.

With this understanding of what the kingdom or God (or the kingdom of heaven, or the child of true Humanity) really meant to Jesus, it is possible to go back and re-read all of Jesus' parables about the kingdom with a new sense of understanding—although many of the kingdom parables in the Gospels were put into Jesus' mouth by the evangelists themselves, and were eschatological in nature.[32]

The omnipresence of the kingdom was, in fact, the core of Jesus' teaching, and the essence of his gospel. Certainly, in such works as *The Gospel of Thomas, Dialogue of the Savior*, and *The Gospel of Mary*, the presence of the kingdom "within" every person was Jesus' "good news." In Mary's Gospel, Jesus (after stating where one can find the kingdom) tells his disciples to "Go then, preac[h] the good news about the kingdom."[33]

Jesus, in Mary's Gospel, warns that no external power can save anyone. Instead, the key to salvation lies in understanding the true nature of the spirit that exists within oneself. The "son of Man," or "the child of true Humanity," is not an apocalyptic figure. It is the Self, a divine spark from the Light of God.[34]

In *The Gospel of Mary*, Peter also challenges Mary's authority to teach on the basis of her gender. Mary's Gospel, however, makes it clear that men are not superior to women. Rather, "the natural state of humanity is ungendered... the divine, transcendent Image to which the soul is to conform is non-gendered; sex and gender belong only to the lower sphere of temporary bodily existence."[35] King points out that God in *The Gospel of Mary* is not called Father, but only "the Good": "In order to conform as far as possible to the divine Image, one must abandon the distinctions of the flesh, including sex and gender."[36]

After Peter's accusations against Mary, Levi (who, like Mary, had an individual vision of the risen Jesus, but was not counted among Jesus' disciples) comes to Mary's defense. He argues that the Savior considered Mary to be worthy, and that his judgment about this was completely reliable. "That is why," Levi states, "he loved her more than us."[37]

Mary's status as teacher and spokesperson for Jesus had been confirmed by Jesus himself. She could be trusted with the gospel of the kingdom, and recognized as a leader and teacher of men because she was a spiritual athlete. What is more, "Only those apostles who have attained the same level of spiritual development as Mary can be trusted to teach the true Gospel."[38]

We have found, then, more than enough justification to support the ancient tradition that claimed that Mary Magdalene was a true apostle. Her credentials stand out against those of Paul and Peter. The battle for recognition of Mary's apostolic rights in the early Church are confirmed by the contest between Mary and Peter in *The Gospel of Mary*—although that contest also metaphorically represented the war between Gnostic and orthodox Christians.

While Paul was silent about Mary, the tradition of Peter was not. The Gospel attributed to Mary is hard evidence that the battle for women's rights to become teachers and leaders in the early Church was a major issue well into the second century. Can we claim any more than this?

Can we claim Marian and Petrine theologies as having been separate Christian traditions from the very beginning? Mary Thompson writes:

> It is difficult, if not dangerous, to read these Gospels with too literal an interpretation, but the continuing presence of conflict between Peter and Mary of Magdala is pervasive and gives rise at least to the suspicion that there was such a conflict in the early churches and the disciples of Mary Magdalene may well have been in serious conflict with the disciples of Peter.[39]

IN SUMMARY:

♦ The theology of the Gospel attributed to Mary Magdalene rejected the concept of original sin, and considered the material world—including the body—to be illusory. Salvation in this system of thought was achieved by overcoming attachments which keep human beings enslaved to suffering and death.

♦ The kingdom of God for Jesus was not a future event, but already existed both within and outside the individual. Jesus' "program" was aimed at helping others achieve consciousness of the Kingdom.

IX. Mary Magdalene According to *Mark*: The Master Story

GENERAL CONSIDERATIONS

This chapter on *Mark* is considerably longer than those devoted to the three other canonical Gospels. It also contains a good deal of detail and even goes off on a (seeming) tangent to discuss the discovery and contents of the *Secret Gospel of Mark*.

There are a host of compelling reasons for giving this much attention to Mark's Gospel. First, *Mark* was the earliest narrative Gospel to be written, which means it stands closest to the historical events of Jesus' life. Second, the authors of *Matthew* and *Luke* copied the *entirety* of Mark's Gospel and embedded it within their own narratives (with various changes). And even though the author of John's Gospel went his own way, it is evident that he referenced Mark's narrative. Mark's Gospel was, in other words, the "master story."

The *Gospel According to Mark* is full of difficult problems, one of which is its ending(s). As we will discover in this chapter, the earliest extant manuscripts of Mark's Gospel abruptly end at 16:8, and they do not include any resurrection-appearance stories.[1] Jesus does not ap-

Many scholars, however, believe that the original version of Mark included a longer ending and suggest that that ending was either lost, or purposely excised!

pear to Mary Magdalene, nor does he appear to anyone else.

The earliest manuscripts of Mark's Gospel, in fact, end with Mary (and the two women with her) running away from the empty tomb in fear—telling no one at all of their experiences. A longer ending (16:9-20) which does contain appearance stories (including one in which Jesus appears to Mary Magdalene) was actually appended to Mark's Gospel by a Christian redactor sometime during the second century.

Many scholars, however, believe that the original version of *Mark* included a longer ending and suggest that the earliest ending was either lost, or purposely excised! To complicate matters even further, a fragment of a "secret" version of Mark's Gospel was discovered in 1958. Not only does this fragment raise new issues about canonical *Mark*, it suggests that Jesus was a teacher of a secret tradition! Moreover, there is evidence suggesting that this secret tradition—like parts of Mark's Gospel itself—may have been suppressed by the early Church.

Since all such details are important in better understanding the crucifixion and resurrection tradition of Mary Magdalene, I would ask for the reader's patience as we examine them. I would recommend, as well, that he or she have the actual text of Mark's Gospel on hand as a reference guide.

With the single exception of Luke's reference to Mary Magdalene (from whom seven demons had gone out) as a disciple of Jesus, the canonical Gospels refer to Mary only in connection with Jesus' crucifixion and resurrection. Formerly, I raised the possibility that the Marian crucifixion-resurrection story began as an independent tradition, and was only later made a part of other early resurrection traditions. Here we will explore that possibility further.

I have also suggested that the Christian evangelists who wrote the canonical Gospels were forced to include the Marian crucifixion-resurrection legend in their Gospels (albeit with their own redactions) because of its widespread popularity, and because it was—in my opinion—the *original* tradition. Mary's importance to early resurrection faith could not, apparently, be minimized or excluded. Now we must ask: what can the evangelists' individual representations of this core myth tell us about Mary; and, what really happened to Jesus after he was arrested?

First of all, we must note the differences between the crucifixion and resurrection legends themselves. Gerd Lüdemann has pointed out that, whereas the passion of Jesus was an observable event that took place in a few days, the experiences of the risen Jesus included "a variety of events of different kinds which extended over a long period, probably over a number of years."[2]

There is no reason to believe, then, that the resurrection tradition of Mary was closely associated with other resurrection traditions, either in time or in place. We cannot automatically assume that Jesus appeared to Mary Magdalene "three days" after his crucifixion, or that all other appearances took place shortly after her experience. Instead, we must create a broader historical stage upon which events took place.

Many scholars consider the Mary/empty tomb tradition as being somewhat late in construction. They conjecture that the "empty tomb" was invented to address Jewish accusations that the body of Jesus had been stolen by his disciples and/or to support a growing belief in the physical resurrection of Jesus. The fact that Paul did not mention a resurrection tradition having to do with Mary Magdalene further convinces scholars that the empty tomb legend involving Mary was not constructed earlier than the fifth or sixth decade of the first century.

As to the first argument, I believe the cart has been placed before the horse. The rumors about Jesus' body being stolen had to have been a *reaction* to the empty tomb legend, not the motive for its creation. The second argument can be dismissed out of hand because all the resurrection-appearance narratives (with only a couple of exceptions) were apparitions, visions and "revelations." They have nothing to do with a resuscitated corpse. As to the third argument, we have already dealt with the subject of Paul's silence on Mary Magdalene.

What is far more important to consider is the possibility that the original resurrection tradition involving Mary Magdalene had nothing to do with an empty tomb. Mark may have grafted an early resurrection legend, having to with Mary Magdalene, to an empty tomb story of his own making.

Whatever its original construction, and whenever it was constructed, the resurrection legend involving Mary Magdalene was the earliest Easter tradition. Had the evangelists known of earlier traditions involving Jesus' male disciples, they would have made those traditions primary in their narratives. Instead, each and every author subordinates the patriarchal-resurrection traditions to the tradition having to do with Mary Magdalene. This fact virtually guarantees that Mary's tradition was both the earliest and most widely known.

Some scholars, in fact, have suggested the possibility that the evangelists invented patriarchal resurrection stories for the specific purpose of minimizing the role Mary had played in the original story. It is, therefore, possible that Mary Magdalene was not just the *first*, but the only disciple to have an experience of the risen Jesus.[3]

Paul, in his first letter to the Corinthians, claimed that the risen Jesus had appeared to Peter, James, the "twelve," "the apostles," "five hundred brethren," and to himself. But Paul did not define what he meant by "appearance." In his letter to the Galatians, for instance, Paul only goes so far as to say that God "was pleased to reveal his son to me," whatever that meant. Later Christians wanted more specificity, so the evangelists may have invented patriarchal-resurrection legends based on Paul's list of "appearances" in *I Corinthians*.

It is particularly interesting to note that the second-century anti-Christian Greek philosopher Celsus argued that belief in the risen Jesus was based on nothing more than the testimony of a "hysterical female."[4] So even detractors of Christianity held the Marian mythos to be dominant.

Ann Brock believes that the long history of literary tension between Mary Magdalene and Peter was probably founded upon early disagreements about which of these two disciples had had an *authentic* resurrection experience. Brock also disagrees with those scholars who claim that such tension existed only in later Christian communities, and was projected back to New Testament times. Brock writes, "... the tension is already implicitly present in the discrepancies regarding the identity of the first resurrection witness."[5]

The earliest Gospel reports about the resurrection of Jesus were contradictory, and this indicates that early Christian communities held varying views about who participated in the resurrection event. Some of the Gospel authors tried to please everyone by inventing stories in which many different people saw the risen Jesus, but this practice only served to further confuse the issue. The Gospels lump together apparition stories, visionary experiences and psychological "revelations."

While the early appearances of Jesus were varied in nature, later Christian belief made it necessary for the authors of Luke and John's Gospel to include the idea that Jesus had *physically* risen from the dead. Lüdemann states, however, that "... . the fleshly objectification is a secondary addition and unhistorical. The original seeing of the Easter witnesses was a seeing of the spirit; they did not see a revived corpse."[6]

How important was resurrection faith to the early Jesus movement? *The Gospel of Q* and *The Gospel of Thomas* show no interest in the subject at all. In fact, these Gospels were not even interested in Jesus' crucifixion! Their faith, in other words, was not yet "Christian." These early followers of Jesus were only interested in his *teachings*. That Jesus was crucified and that some disciples "saw" him after his death only became important considerations to later Christians who needed to make sense of what had happened to Jesus.

THE CRUCIFIXION IN *MARK*

> And there were also women from afar off looking on,
> among whom was Mary the Magdalene, and Mary the mother
> of James the less and of Joses, and Salome who also when

he was in Galilee, followed him, and ministered to him, and many others who came up with him to Jerusalem.

(*Mark* 15:40)

In Mark's narrative of the crucifixion of Jesus, Mary is accompanied by two other women who are named: Mary, the mother of James and Joses, and Salome. But these three women, according to Mark, were accompanied by other women as well.

While it is historically plausible that other women besides Mary witnessed the crucifixion of Jesus, it is unlikely that Mark—a Roman, writing forty years after the death of Jesus—knew who these women were. He did know of a tradition having to do with Mary Magdalene, but everything else was probably speculation on his part.

Subsequent Gospels suggested that the women were interchangeable, which is another way of saying that the other evangelists certainly had no idea who—outside of Mary—witnessed the crucifixion of Jesus. In Matthew's Gospel, Mary Magdalene is accompanied by Mary the mother of James and Joseph, and the mother of the sons of Zebedee.[7] True to his Paulinist roots, Luke doesn't give names to any of the women at the crucifixion, thereby diminishing their importance.[8] Finally, John names Mary Magdalene, Jesus' mother, Mary, and her sister (also called Mary), as being present.[9] The author of *The Gospel According to Philip* probably referred to John's Gospel in coming up with the names of the three Marys who "always walked with the Lord."

Mark's text goes on to tell us that the women present at the crucifixion had followed Jesus while he was in Galilee. Some New Testament scholars have made much out of the next words in Mark's text: "… and (had) ministered to him" (15:41). Based mostly on Luke's identification of women followers of Jesus as those "who provided for them out of their means,"[10] some scholars have concluded that Mary and the other female disciples were financial backers of Jesus' ministry.

But this is not Mark's implication in my opinion. He merely informs his readers that the women took care of Jesus' daily needs in some fashion, not that they financed his mission. Luke is entirely alone in representing the women as financial sponsors and, as we already know, Luke invented new information wherever it suited his purposes to do so. Still, this subject must remain an open question since scholars are divided on this issue.

There are also scholars who believe that Mark invented the entire crucifixion scenario, as he certainly did in the case of Jesus' "trials." Mark names no witnesses to those events, so they are obviously Markan inventions. In the case of the crucifixion, however, Mark tells us that there were witnesses, and that those witnesses were women. This much of Mark's story is probably historical and came down to him through oral tradition.

> *Mark may have known of traditions that claimed that the male disciples of Jesus were not present at the crucifixion, and that a woman known as Mary of Magdala was.*

Mark may have known of traditions that claimed that the male disciples of Jesus were not present at the crucifixion, and that a woman known as Mary of Magdala was. Perhaps this same tradition also held that other women had accompanied Mary, but Mark at least knew that Mary Magdalene was the source for all subsequent Christian beliefs about the crucifixion.

Mark probably knew of a tradition that claimed that the male disciples had gone into hiding when Jesus was arrested. Reporting that the male disciples of Jesus had been cowards must have been very embarrassing, so it is doubtful that Mark would have told this story if it did not have some historical validity.

But Mark probably knew little else about the crucifixion of Jesus. He could not have known any details, since he admits in 15:40 that the only witnesses (Mary and the other women) watched "from afar." Two thousand years of Christian art depicting women grieving beneath the foot of Jesus' cross may invoke Christian piety, but does nothing to further the cause of historical accuracy. The Romans, after all, did not allow family and friends to interfere with crucifixions by being anywhere near the crosses.

All the details of Mark's crucifixion scene —Jesus being mocked and struck, his hands and feet being pierced, his clothing being divided after the casting of lots, and even his words on the cross: "My Lord, my Lord, why have you forsaken me" came not from historical reports remembered by witnesses at the scene, but (almost word for word) from Psalm 22 of the Hebrew *Bible*!

In the end, only two things can be confirmed as probable in Mark's passion narrative: Jesus *was* crucified, and Mary Magdalene watched the event from a distance. But was Mary present when Jesus actually took his last breath? Did she see his body being taken down from the cross? Did she follow Joseph of Arimathea and note the location of the tomb in which her teacher was laid to rest? Probably not, because it is highly unlikely that Jesus died on the first day of his crucifixion, and even more unlikely that his corpse was ever formally buried.

From the time Pompey conquered Jerusalem in 63 B.C.E., until Rome put down the final Jewish revolt of Bar-Cochba in 135 C.E., the Romans crucified literally thousands upon thousands of Jews during their long occupation of Palestine. The Jewish historian, Josephus, mentions that the governor Varus crucified "about two thousand" Jews in 4 B.C.E., that Florus crucified "about three thousand six hundred" Jews in 66 C.E., and that, in 70 C.E., Titus crucified "five hundred or sometimes more ... *daily*."[11]

But even though the Romans crucified thousands of Jews, in all of the archaeological digs ever conducted in Israel, **only one crucified skeleton has ever been found!**[12] How could that be possible? The answer is that the Romans did not allow crucified victims to be buried.

The single skeleton that was discovered was of a young man known as Yohanan, according to the rough inscription on his ossuary—a limestone burial box. The very fact that Yohanan's bones had been preserved in this manner suggests that he came from a Jewish family of means and influence, since it was not customary for Rome to hand over the corpses of crucified criminals.

The discovery of Yohanan's remains confirms two important things: We now know that it was at least *possible* for a family to retrieve a corpse for proper burial if they had sufficient influence with the authorities. But we also know that such instances were *extremely* rare.

What, then, happened to the skeletons of thousands of other crucified victims? No doubt, they decomposed above ground. The standard Roman practice was to leave corpses on their crosses to be picked apart by vultures and other birds. This practice was a warning to others: *This will happen to you if you dare challenge the power of Rome.*[13]

Not all bodies were left on their crosses, however. When necessary, the Romans took corpses down and threw them into open pits, and left them to decompose under layers of lime, or to simply be torn apart by crows and dogs.[14]

The examination of Yohanan's bones by Israeli pathologist Dr. Nicu Haas also tells us much about the Roman practice of crucifixion. It tells us what Jesus probably experienced, and what Mary Magdalene probably saw on that dark day two thousand years ago.

The cross itself was a diabolical torture device. The purpose of crucifixion, after all, was to make the victim suffer for as long as possible. To that end, the Romans affixed the arms of the victim to the crossbeam, but not by pounding nails through that person's hands. Dr. Hass found that the nails had entered through the two bones of Yohanan's forearms, just above the wrists.

Every time the crucified victim moved—which was constantly—these bones became worn and abraded through constant friction. While it was too painful to remain still, it was even more excruciatingly painful to move.

A single iron spike had been driven through both heel bones of Yohanan's feet. The spike was still in Yohanan's heel when his skeleton was discovered, and that spike had been bent over and down, ostensibly to help secure Yohanan to the cross. In order to remove Yohanan's body from the cross, his legs had been cut off at the ankles!

Attached to every cross was a wooden seat called a "sedile." This seat allowed Yohanan to flex his legs and bear his weight, easing the agonizing strain on his arms. But the sedile was itself a torture device. In the end, it only prolonged the victim's suffering.

The Romans wanted those who were crucified to suffer for as long as possible, and for most victims, the unspeakable agony lasted for days, not hours. Finally, when the crucified victim had no more strength to continue the struggle, the entire body collapsed upon itself, causing instant asphyxiation. If the Romans wanted to hurry the process for any reason, they used a device known as the "crurifragium," a blunt mallet, to break the victim's legs so that the body could no longer support its own weight.

This was the scene which Mary Magdalene and, perhaps, other female disciples of Jesus witnessed. We can only imagine the effect that watching such horror had on them.

Mark's reference to the women, however, comes at a point in the story that seems out of context. It is only after Jesus had taken his last breath that he mentions the female witnesses. And this mention is immediately followed by Mark's introduction of a heretofore unknown figure—Joseph of Arimathea. Joseph, according to Mark, was a "respected member of the council" (the Jewish Sanhedrin) who "was also looking for the kingdom of God."[15] After Jesus died, Mark claims, Joseph went to Pontius Pilate to ask for the body of Jesus so that he might bury him. We are led to believe that Joseph was successful in his quest because he was a man of means and influence.

If we were to extract the two verses between Jesus' death and Joseph's request for his body, Mark's story would read smoothly. As it stands, the mention of the women is out of place. As a good storyteller, Mark should have introduced the women at the beginning of the crucifixion, not at the end—after Jesus was already dead!

But Mark had a good reason to write the story the way he did; he needed to connect the women to the *actions* of Joseph of Arimathea. Joseph enters Mark's story for no other reason than to bury Jesus, and the women are introduced precisely at the point where Mark needed them to witness Joseph carrying the body of Jesus to the tomb. Had the women not followed Joseph and seen where Jesus was buried, they would not have known where to come on Easter morning. This entire scenario is a setup for the Easter event.

Mark's invention of the Joseph story addressed a number of negative rumors that were circulating during his own time. His story was meant to establish that Jesus had died on the cross, and that his corpse had not been taken down and revived by his disciples. Mark also wanted his readers to believe that the body of the Messiah did not suffer the final indignity of most crucified victims. Jesus' corpse was not left on the cross to be picked apart by birds, but was buried in a traditional manner. Finally, Mark's story made it clear that there were witnesses to the burial (the women), and this element of the narrative was intended to dispel Jewish rumors that the women had found an empty tomb only because they had gone to the *wrong* tomb.

Mark tells us that Jesus was crucified in the "third hour" and died in the "ninth hour," which means that he was on the cross for just six hours. When Joseph of Arimathea went to Pontius Pilate to ask for Jesus' body for burial, Pilate was amazed that Jesus was already dead, since most crucifixions lasted for days.

Mark tells us that Jesus was crucified on a Friday and, because Hebrew Law mandated that all corpses had to be buried prior to the beginning of Sabbath (sundown on Friday), Jesus had to be off the cross in record time. Mark also needed Jesus to be dead and buried for at least part of *three days* in order to have the resurrection event correspond to Jesus' statement in 14:58: "I will destroy this temple that is made with hands, and in three days I will build another, not made of hands." The three-day interment also allowed Mark to link Jesus' death and burial to ancient Hebrew prophecy in the Old Testament books of *Jonah* and *Hosea*.[16]

Who was Joseph of Arimathea? Mark implies that Joseph—although a member of the Jewish council which supposedly condemned Jesus to death—knew about Jesus and his teachings that had to do with the kingdom of God, and that he himself was seeking the kingdom.[17] But Mark's story doesn't work. Had Joseph been sympathetic to Jesus, the women could have approached him and asked to be allowed to anoint Jesus' body for burial. Instead, the women followed Joseph at a distance, not knowing that Joseph was an ally, and only witnessed where Jesus was laid to rest.

If the women were afraid to approach Joseph, it would only have been because he was *not* a friend or a disciple of Jesus. And if that had been the case, we must ask why Joseph would have taken responsibility for Jesus' burial in the first place? Along with the fact that no such place as Arimathea has ever been located,[18] there are simply too many inconsistencies in Mark's story to allow us to accept Joseph as a historical figure, or Mark's story as a historical report.[19]

> *...it is statistically more likely that Jesus' body was never removed from the cross at all. Crucifixion was, after all, designed to be death without burial!*

It is doubtful that Jesus died after only six hours on the cross. And it is statistically more likely that Jesus' body was never removed from the cross at all. Crucifixion was, after all, designed to be death *without* burial! The entire event was meant to humiliate—not just the victim—but his family and his friends as well. Left on the cross, or tossed into a pit, the crucified was carrion for wild animals and this, the Romans held, was a fitting end to the life of a criminal.[20]

Neither is it at all likely that Pontius Pilate would have released Jesus' body to *anyone*. Far from being the conflicted soul of the Gospels, the historical Pilate was a cruelly repressive dictator who did not hesitate to shed innocent blood. Neither was he a respecter of Jewish customs and law.

Pilate's violence and lack of compassion is well documented, and he was finally recalled to Rome for his excessive cruelty. The historian, Philo—writing around 41 C.E.—made the point that Pilate's administration was well known for its "briberies, insults, robberies, outrages, wanton injuries, constantly repeated executions without trial, ceaseless and supremely grievous cruelty."[21]

Little of Mark's passion story—from the "trials" of Jesus to his burial—can be considered historical. John Dominic Crossan states that Mark's story *"originated as a scribal composition years, even decades, after the death of Jesus."*[22] But no scholar doubts that Jesus was crucified, or that his crucifixion was witnessed by women:

> The only item in the Markan account of Jesus that has any claim to historical veracity is the presence of women followers at his execution. They are depicted as watching from a distance, which conforms to Roman practice: relatives and loved ones were not permitted to interfere with executions. The followers of Jesus, including the women, might well have been in danger had they attempted to become involved.[23]

THE RESURRECTION IN *MARK*

Mark tells us that early on "the first day of the week" following the crucifixion, "Mary Magdalene and Mary, the mother of James, and Salome, brought spices, so that they might go and anoint him."[24] This would have been a strange plan on the part of the women. The women supposedly saw where Jesus was buried, and they saw Joseph roll a large stone in front of the entrance of the tomb. Knowing that they could not roll away this stone, the women would have given up on any idea to anoint Jesus' corpse.

Certainly the women could mourn Jesus near the tomb, but they could not conduct burial rites. They would not have brought oils and spices with them to the tomb because there was no point in doing so. Mark's story is fiction.[25]

As Mark's narrative continues, the women arrive at the tomb of Jesus and find that the stone covering the entrance has been miraculously rolled away. When the women entered the tomb, instead of finding Jesus' corpse, they found "a young man sitting on the right side, dressed in a white robe; and they were amazed."[26] Were the women amazed that Jesus' body had disappeared, or were they amazed to find a serene young man sitting in the tomb—someone who just happened to have a message for them?

Seeing their expressions of amazement, the young man said, "Do not be amazed; you seek Jesus the Nazarene, who was crucified. He is risen. He is not here; see the place where they laid him."[27] In other words, You didn't come to the wrong tomb, but you arrived too late. The tomb is empty only because Jesus has risen from the dead. But who, according to Mark, was the young man who delivered this message?

YOUNG MEN IN WHITE AND THE *SECRET GOSPEL OF MARK*

Christians think of Mark's "young man" as an angel because Matthew, Luke and John all upgraded him to angelic status by virtue of their own narratives. Yet, if Mark—who wrote the master resurrection story—had meant "angel," he would have written "angelos." Instead, he used the Greek word, "neaniskon," which means "young man." Since "neaniskon" is *never* used in the New Testament to mean a heavenly messenger, Matthew, Luke and John made the leap from young man to angel(s) entirely on their own.

If not an angel, then, who—or what—was the young man, and what was Mark trying to tell us by making him a critical part of the resurrection story? One possible answer comes in the form of a strange entry in *Mark* at the scene of Jesus' arrest in the Garden of Gethsemane which I called the reader's attention to previously.

Returning to the arrest scene for a moment, Mark tells us that after the disciples of Jesus fled, "a young man followed him (Jesus) with nothing but a linen cloth about his body; and they (the arresting party) seized him, but he left the linen cloth and ran away naked."[28]

Christians and scholars alike have never been able to make any sense of this bizarre footnote to Mark's arrest story. Who was this young man, why was he naked under a linen cloth, why was he with Jesus in the Garden of Gethsemane, and why did Mark mention him in the first place?

Because it is so bizarre, and seemingly so out of place, we can be certain that Mark would not have included such a detail in the arrest story unless he had reason to believe that his readers would understand his meaning. Unfortunately, the key to understanding the meaning of both the naked man in the Garden, and the young man in white in the empty tomb, is missing from Mark's Gospel. It is missing because at some point in early Christianity that key was intentionally removed.

By an act of cosmic serendipity, the key to Mark's meaning was discovered by Columbia University professor, Morton Smith, in 1958.[29] During the summer of that year, Smith had been a guest at a Greek Orthodox monastery in the desert at Mar Saba, not far from Jerusalem. Smith was there to study the monastery's extensive manuscript collection, much of which was very ancient. Quite by accident, Smith came across a fragment of a letter by the second-century Church father, Clement of Alexandria. This discovery was, in itself, stunning; but it was the *content* of Clement's letter that truly excited Smith.

According to Smith, Clement had addressed his letter to a certain Theodore, who was probably a priest under Clement's authority. Theodore had previously written to Clement concerning certain words in a manuscript he believed to be a *secret* version of *The Gospel of Mark*. Theodore suspected that the manuscript in his hands had been altered from the original by a heretical group of Christians known as the Capocratians and wanted Clement to confirm his suspicions.

Apparently Clement was very familiar with what he considered to be the *authentic* secret version of *Mark* and informed Theodore that the verses in question were, in fact, falsifications. In the process of his explanation, Clement quoted from the *authentic* secret Gospel, and that quote turns out to be very revealing.

When Smith published his findings on this "lost Gospel" in 1973, he was scoffed at by most of the academic community because he was unable to produce the actual manuscript, or even photographs of the pages. The manuscript had mysteriously disappeared from the monastery library and could not be found by any of the monks. Smith, perhaps not expecting the negative reaction his book received, could do nothing to prove that the letter of Clement of Alexandria ever existed.

So, even though Morton Smith had the right credentials, scholars doubted his claim, and most considered it a fraud and a hoax. It probably did not help Smith's credibility that he used the content of the secret version of *Mark* to make a case for a secret tradition within the early Jesus movement and, even more startling, a case for an historical Jesus who was a magician, or shaman. But, fortunately, this is not the end of the story.

In the year 2000, several scholars traveled to Mar Saba in order to confirm or put to rest Smith's claim once and for all. They discovered that the manuscript had indeed disappeared temporarily, that there was no conspiracy behind its disappearance, and that the manuscript had subsequently been recovered. They were also able to document that Smith himself had read the manuscript because his initials were found on one of the pages.

Photographs of the manuscript containing Clement's letter were produced for study, and scholars eventually determined that Morton Smith had been telling the truth all along. As a result of this further research, the *Secret Gospel of Mark* is now considered to be an authentic "lost" Gospel.[30]

Many important questions remain. Is Clement's letter itself authentic? Was the secret version of *Mark* a later, expanded version of canonical *Mark*, or was canonical *Mark* an edited version of a more original *Mark* that is now lost to us?

Scholars also have to investigate whether or not the story about Jesus in *Secret Mark* goes back to the historical Jesus, or was a product of later Christian mythology. Although these are still open questions, what we do now know is that more than one version of Mark's Gospel was used in early Christian churches.

The most intriguing feature of *Secret Mark* is the actual text that Clement quoted in his letter. And Morton Smith immediately recognized the importance of this Gospel's portrayal of Jesus as a hierophant of a mystery tradition:

And they come into Bethany, and a certain woman,

whose brother had died, was there. And, coming, she prostrated herself before Jesus and says to him, 'Son of David, have mercy on me.' But the disciples rebuked her. And Jesus, being angered, went off with her into the garden where the tomb was, and straightway a great cry was heard from the tomb. And going near Jesus rolled away the stone from the door of the tomb. And straightway, going in where the youth was, he stretched forth his hand and raised him, seizing his hand. But the youth, looking upon him, loved him and began to beseech him that he might be with him. And going out of the tomb they came into the house of the youth, for he was rich. And after six days Jesus told him what to do and in the evening the youth comes to him, wearing a linen cloth over [his] naked [body]. And he remained with him that night, for Jesus taught him the mystery of the kingdom of God. And thence, arising, he returned to the other side of the Jordan.[31]

Clement indicated that these verses belonged in canonical *Mark* between 10:34 and 10:35. After more explanation, Clement also quoted a subsequent line to this story from the "secret" version of Mark:

And the sister of the youth whom Jesus loved and his mother and Salome were there, and Jesus did not receive them.[32]

These words, Clement maintained, belonged between the words "And they came to Jericho" and "and as he was leaving Jericho" in canonical *Mark* 10:46. Scholars have recognized for centuries that something was missing from *Mark* 10:46, which now reads, "And they came to Jericho; and as he was leaving Jericho ... "

This verse makes no sense as it stands. Information about what Jesus *did* in Jericho is obviously missing. Something was edited out of Mark's Gospel at this point, and Clement claimed that it was the sentence having to do with

Jesus not receiving the sister of the young man, his mother and Salome.

Clement maintained in his letter that *Secret Mark* was an expanded version of canonical *Mark*, and was written to be read only by those who were "initiated into the great mysteries." Yet, if sentences had been edited out of canonical Mark—as they seem to have been—then *original* Mark must have contained the passages. If so, then The Gospel of Mark that was passed down through history is an edited version of the original Gospel.

> *Some scholars have gone so far as to suggest that the original version of Mark was edited in order to remove all of its esoteric passages!*

Smith also noticed the similarities between *Secret Mark's* story of Jesus resurrecting a young man and the story in *The Gospel of John* (11:1—12:19) about Jesus raising Lazarus (the brother of Martha and Mary) from the dead. To explain the parallels, Helmut Koester has suggested that the authors of both Gospels accessed an earlier miracle story about Jesus and individually rewrote it to suit their own theological purposes.[33]

All of this brings us back to the resurrection story in canonical *Mark*. As mentioned earlier, Mark's Gospel abruptly ends at 16:8 without anyone having seen the risen Jesus. Then we must now ask, did the same hand that removed the "secret" portion of *Mark* also remove the original ending of this Gospel as well?

Obviously, one of two things happened: either a page of canonical *Mark* was lost at some early point, or *Mark's* original ending was deliberately excised.[34] With the discovery of *Secret Mark*, the second scenario now seems more likely. Some scholars have gone so far as to suggest that the original version of *Mark* was edited in order to remove all of its esoteric passages![35]

With this possibility in mind, we can now return to Mark's resurrection story and read it with new eyes. According to *canonical Mark*, Mary Magdalene, Mary the mother of James and Joses, and *Salome* (!) entered the tomb of Jesus and found—not the body of Jesus—but a *young man*, dressed *in a white robe*, sitting on the "right" side of the tomb.

Was this the same young man who fled the Garden of Gethsemane? Was this the same young man whom Jesus raised from the dead in *Secret Mark*? And is there any significance to the report that three women attempted—and failed—to see Jesus in both the story from *Secret Mark and* the resurrection story in canonical *Mark*? Or that one of these women, Salome, is mentioned in both stories?

Some scholars have proposed that the young man being initiated in the secret version of *Mark*—and the young man fleeing upon the arrest of Jesus in canonical *Mark*—was the same young man who was seated in the empty tomb.[36] It seems a good deal more likely, however, that the three young men were all different initiates of Jesus—since initiation was a one-time event.

In *Secret Mark*, the risen young man who immediately "loved" Jesus was required to undergo *six days* of preparation prior to being initiated into the mysteries of the kingdom of God by Jesus. The young man then presented himself to Jesus, naked beneath a white linen cloth. At this point, a nocturnal initiation ceremony began and continued throughout the night.

The young man in the Garden of Gethsemane who ran away naked was also dressed as an initiate (naked beneath a white linen cloth). Was Jesus arrested while conducting an all-night initiation ceremony? If so, we can theoretically revise Mark's edited arrest story accordingly: Jesus put himself into jeopardy by coming out of hiding—not to *pray* in the Garden of Gethsemane—but to conduct an all-night initiation ritual. In this event he would have needed sentries to warn him of impending danger because he was completely involved, perhaps even in a trance state.

"Very early" on Easter morning—at first light, or even before—Mary Magdalene and two other women came to the tomb and found, not Jesus, but a young man dressed as an initiate. Since dawn was only now breaking, the young man had been with Jesus' corpse, in the tomb, during the night.

The young man had a message for the women: "Jesus the Nazarene, who was crucified, is not here (the realm of the dead), he is risen (has taken on a new existence)."

If we understand Mark's empty tomb story as a metaphor, then it might be fair to say that the message the young man gave to Mary Magdalene and the other women was that—even though Jesus had been crucified—he did not exist in the realm of the dead. He was a living spirit, and could only be found in the land of the living.

Mark's resurrection narrative had yet another purpose for being written. By the time Mark wrote his Gospel (70 C. E.), many Christians had begun to think of Jesus as the son of God, if not yet *the* Son of God—but some sort of divinity in any case. So Mark's resurrection story probably had a good deal to do with spreading the idea of Jesus' divinity, since divine beings often rose from the dead.

Gregory Riley points out that "Resurrection from the dead did at least prove that one was a son of god in the minds of the people whom these (Gospel) writers addressed, the Romans and Greeks."[37] And, "if you rise from the dead, you had a divinity as one of your parents."[38] Mark, like the other evangelists, was not writing to Jews of Judea, but to Hellenistic Jews, Romans and Greeks elsewhere in the Roman Empire—all of whom were familiar with the resurrected gods and saviors of the Greek and Roman mystery religions.

Mark recognized that a resurrection story was a necessary prerequisite for making the claim that Jesus was something more than just a flesh-and-blood man. By introducing his "young men in white," Mark was also telling this same audience that Jesus had initiated people into the mystery of the kingdom of God,[39] and that they, too, could enter this mystery by virtue of Jesus' resurrection.

MARK'S NARRATIVE AS MAGIC AND MYSTERY

If we interpret Mark's death, burial, and resurrection narrative as the foundation story for a mystery religion, then a number of interesting parallels come to light. In *Secret Mark* we have a young man in a tomb. The stone is rolled away from the tomb entrance by Jesus himself. There is a resurrection. The resurrected young man immediately "loves" Jesus.

Later, the young man dons a white robe after six days of preparation and presents himself to Jesus. The initiation ceremony takes place all through the night, and at dawn Jesus disappears from view. Three women—the sister and mother of the resurrected young man, along with Salome (who was also with Mary Magdalene at the empty tomb)—discover where Jesus is and attempt, but fail, to see him.

In canonical *Mark*'s passion/resurrection story, Jesus himself undergoes six days of "preparation" (his kingly entry into Jerusalem, his protest against Temple sacrifice, the sacred meal, the death, and the burial) prior to his resurrection. In the tomb, it is Jesus himself who was naked beneath a white linen shroud. And where Jesus himself had rolled the stone away from the initiate's tomb in *Secret Mark*, the stone is rolled away from his own tomb by an initiate in canonical *Mark*.

It would seem, then, that Mark wanted his readers to understand that these two resurrection stories—the one in *Secret Mark*, and the one in canonical *Mark*—were somehow connected.[40] Mark even goes so far as to suggest that the three women were the same in both cases.[41]

Are all of these parallels mere coincidence? Or was Mark trying to say something about "resurrection" that only initiates of Jesus would have understood? Certainly we can not know this for sure, but it does seem clear that Mark knew of a secret Jesus tradition and left hints of it here and there throughout his Gospel.

Canonical *Mark* hints that the secret tradition had to do with gnosis, or inner knowing, for these are precisely the words Jesus uses to qualify those who have the ability to understand the *mystery* of the Kingdom of God:

> To you it is given to *know* the mystery of the kingdom of God, but to those who are without (outside the inner circle of initiates), all things are done in parables, that seeing they might not perceive; and in hearing they might not understand...[42]

Morton Smith in *The Secret Gospel of Mark* supports the idea that Jesus can only be understood in terms of a secret tradition because he was—among other things—a magician, or shaman. Orthodox Christian scholars quickly part company with Smith at this point, and we can certainly understand why. Such ideas of magic and miracles smack of supernaturalism, which is no longer part of the consciousness of liberal Christian scholars and clergy.

But if the first-century evangelists only hint at Jesus being a magician, Smith maintains, it is only because being a magician was a criminal offense.[43] But the miracle stories themselves seem to make this claim about Jesus.

> Besides the reports that Jesus ordered spirits about, the miracle stories in the Gospels show many minor traits of magical procedures... : Jesus' curing touch, manipulation, looking upward, sighing or groaning, use of Aramaic phrases in Greek, use of typically magical words, use of spittle in a salve, conspicuous use of the hands, touching the tongue, claiming to use 'the finger of God.' Anger at the demons, prohibition of their return, requirement that the patients have 'faith,' secrecy in performing the cures, performance in private and commands that the cures be kept secret, instructions to the disciples to pray and fast before exorcisms, the requirement of three-day or seven-day preparatory periods, *the use of a sheet over the naked body as a costume for initiations* ...[44]

Smith also points out that the stories told about Jesus are very similar to the stories told about many ancient magicians.

> Among these are: the power to make anyone he wanted follow him, exorcism, even exorcism at a distance, remote control of spirits and the power to order them about, giving his disciples power over demons, miraculous cures of hysterical conditions including fever, paralysis, hemorrhage, deafness, blindness, loss of speech, raising the dead, stilling storms, walking on water, miraculous provision of food, miraculous escapes ..., making himself invisible, possessing the keys of the kingdom or of the heavens, foreknowledge of his own fate, of disasters on coming cities, etc., knowledge of

other's thoughts, introduction of religious reforms and of new magical rites, claiming to be united with others, so that he is in them and they in him, claiming to be a god, or son of god, or united with a god, notably in statements beginning, 'I am,' … claiming to be the image of the invisible god.[45]

Whether or not Jesus actually did any of these things—I think Smith would agree—is beside the point. The *point* is that Jesus' followers saw him in this light. Since early apostles like Peter were represented as having acquired some of these same powers in Jesus' name makes such an argument irrefutable.

Would it be fair to interpret Mark's resurrection story in such a light as a divine magical event? Perhaps. Perhaps not. But I think there is a hidden meaning in Mark's empty tomb story and that Mary Magdalene is part of that hidden meaning. The mysterious woman, Salome, also seems to have been important in Mark's esoterica, since she does not later appear in any of the other canonical Gospels.

Mark leaves yet another clue having to do with initiation into the mysteries by having his young man sitting on the right side of the tomb when the women arrive. Why did Mark make such a notation? And why did Matthew, Luke and John ignore this detail?

Perhaps the position of the young man within the tomb held no hidden meaning for Mark. Perhaps the notation was nothing more than an honorific. Throughout the Hebrew *Bible*, and the Christian New Testament, "the right side" simply meant the place of honor. The most honored guest would be invited to sit on the right side of the host.

Then again, it is also possible that Mark intended this notation to be understood on two different levels. To the Gnostic, "right" and "left" held a good deal more meaning—just as "above" and "below" did. In Gnostic systems, "right" signified the psychic realm, while "left" referred to the realm of matter.[46] In some systems, "right" and "left" were also related to the four directions, with the right hand denoting the East, where the stars rose and ascended into the heavens.[47]

On the subject of the Gnostic doctrine of the syzgies, or pairs of opposites, the Pseudo-Clementines put the following words into Peter's mouth:

> As God, who is one person, in the beginning made first the heaven and then the earth, as it were on the right hand and on the left, he has also in the course of time established all the pairs of opposites.[48]
>
> Now that he might bring men to the true knowledge (gnosis) of all things, God, who himself is a single person, made a clear separation by way of pairs of opposites, in that he, who from the beginning was the one and only God, made heaven and earth, day and night, life and death. Among these he has gifted free-will to men alone so that they may be just or unjust. For them he has also permuted the appearing of the pairs of opposites, in that he has set before their eyes first the small and then the great, first the world and then eternity, this world being transitory, but the one to come eternal; so also ignorance precedes knowledge (gnosis).[49]

A Gnostic Christian reading Mark's empty tomb story might, then, consider that *the tomb itself was a place of initiation*, and the young man in white an initiate. As a metaphor, they might have suggested that during the darkness of the night, as long as the initiate remained in ignorance, he sat on the left side of the tomb. As dawn broke, the young man moved to the right side, signifying that the initiation was complete.

JESUS THE NAZARENE

Another oddity of Mark's story of the young man in white is that he tells the women that they seek Jesus of Nazareth—as if they didn't know who they were looking for. What would have been Mark's purpose in pointing out the obvious?

The Greek text, however, does not say Jesus "of Nazareth," but Jesus "the Nazarene." It requires a Greek transliteration in order to come up with "of Nazareth," and such an effort was not necessarily called for.

For one thing, the existence of a town called Nazareth during Jesus' time has never been confirmed. There is no mention of such a town in the Hebrew *Bible*, or in the writings of the Jewish historian Josephus who—as a former Galilean rebel leader against the Romans—had personally fortified the towns of Galilee.[50] Almost certainly "Nazarene" referred, instead, to a Jewish/Christian sect that was later identified with the Ebionites, or "The Poor Ones."[51]

Another rendering of this word is "Nazorean," which means "keeper"— either Keeper of the Law, or Keeper of the Secrets.[52] It has been mentioned previously that the Nazorean sect may have produced both *The Gospel of the Ebionites* and *The Gospel of the Nazoreans*. Robert Eisenman, in *James the Brother of Jesus*, goes even further in suggesting a connection between these sects and the Essenes, as well as the Naassenes—the "heretics" which claimed to have received Jesus' teachings from James through Mary Magdalene.[53] In calling Jesus a Nazarene, was Mark's young man— an initiate into the mysteries of the kingdom of God—passing on a secret Nazarene teaching to the three women in the empty tomb?

...the existence of a town called Nazareth during Jesus' time has never been confirmed.

The young man tells the women that Jesus wasn't where they had expected him to be. He had been there, but no longer. He had "risen." The Greek word the young man uses for "risen" is "egeiro," but that word does not have to be translated as "resurrection from the dead." It literally means "to awaken from sleep." If we were to translate Mark's passage with this understanding, then his message might have been that Jesus was now fully *awake* in the Buddhist sense of the term.

After his enlightenment, the historical Buddha was asked not, "Who are you?" but "What are you?" And his reply was, "I am awake." Would it be fair to understand Jesus' "resurrection" in this way? Certainly many early Christians interpreted Jesus' resurrection in this manner:

> The Savior swallowed up death ... for he put aside the world which is perishing (the material world is transitory). He transformed [himself] into an imperishable Aeon and raised himself up, having swallowed the visible by the invisible, and he gave us the way of our immortality. Then, indeed, as the Apostle said, 'We suffered with him, and arose with him, and we went to heaven with him.' Now if we are manifest in this world wearing him, we are that one's beams, and we are embraced by him until our setting, that is to say, our death in this life. We are drawn to heaven by him, like beams by the sun, not being restrained by anything. This is the spiritual resurrection which swallows the psychic in the same way as the fleshly.

> ... the resurrection ... is truth which stands firm. It is the revelation of what is, and transformation of things, and a transition into newness. For imperishability [descends] upon the perishable; the light flows down upon the darkness, swallowing it up... Therefore, do not ... live in conformity with this flesh for the sake of unanimity, but flee from the divisions and the fetters, and already you have the resurrection.[54]

Like the women prophets of Corinth, the Christians who read works like *The Treatise on the Resurrection* (another work discovered at Nag Hammadi) believed in a "realized eschatology." The believer—who knows that death is inevitable—should consider him or herself to be dead while alive, and already existing in the resurrected state. One's release from the material realm comes through the realization that the Savior and the believer are one.[55]

In the end, it matters little whether Mark intended his story of the resurrection to be understood on a literal or on an esoteric level. Since corpses do not come back to life, Mark was writing mythology. Some Christians chose to interpret that myth one way, while other Christians chose to interpret it in another.

GOING BEFORE YOU INTO GALILEE

Mark's young man in the empty tomb then tells the women what they should do with the new information they have acquired. Or, perhaps, he is telling them what to do with their new understanding about life and death. In either case, they are to tell others what they have experienced, and tell the disciples *and* Peter that Jesus is going before them into Galilee where they can expect to see him.

"Going before you to Galilee" is a very strange and confusing statement. If Jesus is risen, and his risen form is going to Galilee (do ghosts have to walk?), then surely Jesus will reach the other disciples before the women do, in which case there is no point in returning to Galilee with their message.

The young man's statement reflects an earlier statement by Jesus in *Mark* 14:28 where Jesus says, "But after I am raised up, I will go before you to Galilee." Here, the statement makes even less sense. If Jesus is going to rise from the dead, what difference does it make where the disciples see him? But since both passages in Mark have Jesus say, "I will go *before* you," I think the word "before" is the key to understanding Mark's meaning.

"Proago," the Greek word for "go before," normally means to "go before" in the sense of "leading the way." Since both of Mark's references about "going before" the disciples to Galilee are tied to Jesus' resurrected state, the implication is that, while Jesus had led the disciples during his life, he will continue to lead them after his death. Where can they expect to find him: In a very familiar place—precisely where they already are.

In Mark's narrative of the resurrection, even the women are not gifted with a vision of the risen Jesus at the place of his burial, which is *in Jerusalem*. They will only be able to see him, the young man tells them, *in Galilee*. For Mark, perhaps, Jerusalem represented a city of violence, disbelief, death and burial—the city Jesus cried over. Galilee, on the other hand, represented future hope and promise.

If we interpret Mark's statement esoterically, then Jerusalem is a metaphor for the lower, illusory, realm of material existence. Jesus' spirit is now no longer compatible with that realm of existence. Jesus is now pure spirit, and spirit can only be found among the living. So the women are told to return to the land of the living where they will find Jesus.

In Mark's passion narrative, the evangelist tells us that some of Jesus' female disciples—especially Mary Magdalene, Mary, the mother of James and Joses, and Salome (a woman who appears only in Mark's Gospel)—were especially linked to Jesus through his Galilean mission.[56] It was here that they, along with many other women, followed Jesus and ministered to him.

> ...*their ministry, their apostolate, is not to the world at large, but specifically to the male disciples!*

So the women are instructed to return to their ministry. Their ministry is no longer dependent on Jesus' physical presence, but Jesus will support them nonetheless. Jesus—and their ministry—awaits them as always. But their ministry, their apostolate, is not to the world at large, but specifically to the male disciples!

THE ENDINGS OF MARK

It is right at this point where Mark's original Gospel breaks off (16:8). Instead of returning to Galilee to inform the male disciples of what they had seen and heard, "they went out and fled from the tomb; for trembling and astonishment had come upon them; and they said nothing to any one, for they were afraid."

The writings of Clement of Rome, Origen, Eusebius and Jerome demonstrate that these early Church fathers knew nothing of any ending to *Mark* beyond 16:8.[57] The oldest extant Greek manuscripts of *Mark* also have nothing beyond 16:8.[58]

But later Christians saw a problem with Mark's incomplete ending. It was not sufficiently "Christian." Sometime around the middle of the second century an additional ending began to appear in hand-copied manuscripts, and this ending attempted to harmonize *Mark* with the later Gospels of *Matthew, Luke,* and *John*.[59]

Actually, there were at least two alternative endings to *Mark* circulating in Christendom—a short one, and the more familiar long version. The shorter ending reads:

> But they reported briefly to Peter and those with him all that they had been told. And after this, Jesus himself set out by means of them, from east to west, the sacred and imperishable proclamation of eternal salvation.[60]

It is interesting to compare this appendage in some ancient manuscripts with the ending of the *Sophia* (Wisdom) *of Jesus Christ*:

> [And the disciples] began to preach [the] gospel of God, [the] eternal, imperishable [Spirit].[61]

Some scholars believe that the *Sophia* was composed as early as the second half of the first century.[62] If this were the case, then it is possible that the author of the shorter Markan ending used *Sophia* as a model for his own work. "Eternal, imperishable Spirit" became the more orthodox "Sacred and imperishable proclamation of eternal *salvation*."

The longer ending to *Mark*'s Gospel, comprising 16:9-20, is the ending most Christians are familiar with; because in most versions of the New Testament, it is included as if it were part of the original *Gospel of Mark*. In academia, these verses are known as "Pseudo-Mark."

Here I quote only verses 9 through 14 from Pseudo-Mark, since the remaining verses are not relevant to the resurrection story. The following is a literal translation from the Greek:

> Now having risen early [the] first [day] of the week he appeared first to Mary the Magdalene, from whom he had cast out seven demons. She having gone told [it] to those who had been with him, [who were] grieving and weeping. And they having heard that he is alive and has been seen by her disbelieved [it]. And after these things he was manifested in another form to two of them as they walked, going into [the] country; and they having gone told [it] to the rest; neither did they believe them. Afterwards as the eleven reclined [at table] he was manifested and reproached their unbelief and hardness of heart, because they had not believed those who had seen him arisen.

ORIGINAL AND SUBSEQUENT TRADITIONS

This addendum to the original *Gospel of Mark* is interesting for a number of reasons, but mainly for what it implies about the tradition of Mary Magdalene. The author confirms Mary Magdalene as the first person to experience the risen Jesus. The other women are entirely missing in this story, which adds even more emphasis to Mary's role.

If these verses were added to Mark sometime after the middle of the second century, then they affirm that popular belief still held that Mary Magdalene had been the first disciple to have an experience of the risen Jesus. Peter does not even receive an honorable mention here.

As in *The Gospel of Mary*, the disciples were weeping and grieving, but they do not allow themselves to be comforted by either Mary's report, or the report of two other disciples. To me, this phraseology suggests three early traditions: the first believing tradition centered around Mary Magdalene, the second believing tradition centered around some anonymous male followers of Jesus, and a third *unbe-*

lieving community of disciples which initially included Peter. Since Peter is repeatedly accused of disbelief throughout *The Gospel of Mark*, Peter's reputation may have been earned after the death of Jesus, not before. Peter may have been viewed as faithless, in general, because he did not come to believe in a risen Jesus for quite some time. Eventually he began to have visions of Jesus himself, and it is possible that those experiences resulted from the power of suggestion.

Pseudo-Mark tells us that the risen Jesus finally manifested himself to the eleven—a group that may, or may not, have included Peter. But he appeared only because these disciples refused to believe the word of others. The first thing Jesus does when he appears is to upbraid the men for their disbelief and continuing hardness of heart.

So the ending of canonical *Mark* in which Mary Magdalene and the other women do not report to Peter and the eleven—as well as the two spurious endings in which they do make contact—all agree *that the core group of male disciples did not immediately adopt a resurrection faith*.

The scenario proposed by Mark suggests that the following happened: According to the original ending of *Mark*, the women (formally) told no one of their Easter experience—ever. The women never had direct contact with the male disciples, yet history suggests that the men heard rumors about the women's experiences. Then, after the passage of time, and perhaps through the power of suggestion, the male disciples began to have experiences of the risen Jesus themselves. The men finally came to believe what the women had believed for some time: that Jesus had somehow transcended death. In Mark's scenario, as well as every other one, the matriarchal resurrection tradition preceded the patriarchal, and was—in some way—the *catalyst* for that tradition.

Before we move on to the other Gospel accounts of the resurrection, we need to note how the idea of the resurrection itself was treated by Pseudo-Mark. Nowhere in this appendage to Mark's Gospel does the author suggest that Jesus rose from the dead in a physical body. Rather, Jesus *"appeared"* to Mary Magdalene. Jesus *manifested* himself in *"an-*

other form" to two other disciples. And Jesus *"was manifested"* in the presence of the eleven.

The Greek word used for both *"appeared"* and *"manifested"* is, in each case, "phaino," which literally means "to reveal". Even though second century orthodox patriarchs like Tertullian were adamant about the physical resurrection of Jesus, Pseudo-Mark offers clear evidence that other second-century Christians—perhaps a majority—had yet to adopt such an idea. That, in turn, suggests that the original empty tomb narrative was not written as a response to an evolving belief in the physical resurrection of Jesus.

As Antoinette Wire suggested, the empty tomb story involving women could not have developed after a patriarchal-resurrection tradition was already in place. I believe that Mark's resurrection narrative was based on an early legend having to do with Mary Magdalene (and possibly other women), and that tradition had nothing to do with an empty tomb. Mark invented the empty tomb concept for narrative purposes, but intended his audience to understand that the empty tomb was a metaphor, its sole purpose to suggest that Jesus no longer existed among the dead, but among the living.

IN SUMMARY:

♦ Only women witnessed the crucifixion of Jesus, and all other elements of Mark's crucifixion story were the inventions of Mark himself.

♦ Women did not go to the tomb of Jesus for the purpose of performing burial rites.

♦ The young man in white in Mark's empty tomb story was not an angel, but possibly an initiate into the mysteries of the kingdom of God. The secret version of Mark's Gospel connects this man with the man in the Garden of Gethsemane who ran away naked when Jesus was arrested.

♦ The secret version of Mark's Gospel claims that Jesus initiated others into the mysteries of the kingdom of God.

♦ The earliest known version of Mark's Gospel contains no appearance stories.

♦ Early Gospel accounts of the resurrection were contradictory, and indicate a wide range of Christian beliefs about what "resurrection" actually meant. The earliest Christians, however, did not believe in the physical resurrection of Jesus. As recorded in the Gospels, the earliest resurrection experiences were in the form of apparitions, visions, and revelations.

♦ The legend about Jesus' resurrection began as a matriarchal tradition.

X. Mary Magdalene
According to *Matthew*

THE CRUCIFIXION AND RESURRECTION
IN *MATTHEW*

Matthew copied Mark's crucifixion/resurrection story, but embellished it with many more details, not the least of which was his notation that at the moment of Jesus' death, there was an earthquake which caused tombs to open and "saints" to rise from the dead, causing fright among those to whom they appeared.[1] While this text seems to be evidence that Matthew believed in the idea of physical resurrection, his real purpose in creating this strange scenario was to suggest something else altogether.

At the time Matthew wrote his Gospel—toward the end of the first century—the Roman persecution of Christians was in full swing. For Christians, such rabid and unwarranted attacks were a signal that the predicted apocalypse had begun. Matthew's resurrected "saints"— Christians rising from the grave decades before there *were* any Christians—served Matthew's purpose of announcing the beginning of the apocalypse, both to other Christians, and to the Romans.

As far as Matthew was concerned, the Romans should be scared to death of the impending doom, so he turned them into confessors at the scene of the crucifixion:

> Now when the centurion, and they that were with him, watching Jesus, saw the earthquake, and those things that took place, they feared greatly, saying, 'Truly, this was God's son.'[2]

Matthew followed Mark in placing Mary Magdalene at the crucifixion scene, and he also retained Mary, the mother of James and Joseph, as one of the other women.[3] But Matthew removed Salome from the group of three and replaced her with the "mother of the sons of Zebedee."

...Matthew— along with Luke and John— edited Salome out of early Christian history.

By the end of the first century, Salome had fallen into disgrace by virtue of being associated with various heretical sects, not the least of which was the Carpocratians, who appealed to her as an authority.[4] Thus, Matthew—along with Luke and John—edited Salome out of early Christian history.

As in *Mark*, Matthew has Joseph of Arimathea enter the scene immediately following the mention of the women at the crucifixion. But Matthew's Joseph is not just a seeker of the kingdom of God, he is an actual disciple of Jesus. And when Joseph goes to Pilate to beg the body of Jesus, he succeeds—not because of his religious and political influence—but because he was a wealthy man (27:57). In telling the story in this way, Matthew was able to identify Joseph with the anonymous rich man—in 6:26—who walked away dejected after Jesus told him that it was necessary for him to give up his wealth in order to enter the kingdom of God.[5] Thus, in addition to telling the story of Jesus' burial, Matthew's Joseph story was meant to convey that—while it might be difficult for a rich person to enter the kingdom—it was not impossible.

Again, in contrast to Mark, Matthew does not have Mary Magdalene "and the other Mary" follow Joseph to the tomb, at a distance, or in secret. Since Joseph is supposedly a disciple of Jesus now, there is no need for the women to fear him. And while Joseph and the women never exchange words, as Joseph completes the burial of Jesus, Mary "and the other Mary" are present and "sitting there opposite the sepulcher."[6]

Even though the women are present at the burial of Jesus, Matthew does not claim that they performed any burial rites. Perhaps Matthew meant the reader to infer that women performed their duties in this respect, but the issue itself does not seem to be important to this evangelist. Thus, when the two Marys appear again at the tomb on Easter morning, they are not carrying oils and spices.

To combat late first-century rumors that Jesus' body was stolen from the tomb by his disciples, Matthew next invented a story in which Jesus' Jewish enemies went to Pilate with the request that he place guards at the tomb to prevent this very thing. The ever-accommodating Pilate sends soldiers to seal the tomb entrance, and to guard it around the clock. Matthew's message is simple and to the point: with all this security, nothing but an act of God would allow Jesus to come forth from the tomb.

Matthew's resurrection event begins with another earthquake, after which an angel—"whose countenance was like lightening, and *his* raiment white as snow"—descends from heaven in order to roll the stone away from the entrance of Jesus' tomb. The Roman guards are understandably scared half to death by all this supernatural activity, as are Mary Magdalene and "the other Mary" who suddenly appear on the scene.

BELIEVERS AND UNBELIEVERS

The angel has no advice for the guards, but tells the women not to be afraid. He then instructs them—as Mark's young man did—to tell the disciples what they have seen and heard. But Matthew adds a sense of urgency to this request. The angel tells the women to *"go quickly"*!

Matthew then reports that the women did, in fact, "go quickly." But what was Matthew's reason for requiring haste on the part of the women? I believe he contrived this demand for haste in order to suggest (unlike Mark) that very little time passed between the women's resurrection experience and subsequent experiences of the male disciples.

Matthew directly addresses Mark's abrupt ending where the women never report to the male disciples at all. Matthew *suggests* that the women made their report, and that they did so very soon after having their Easter experience. Matthew's male disciples are therefore able to begin having experiences of the risen Jesus very soon after the crucifixion. Matthew "corrects" Mark's Gospel by allowing for an early patriarchal resurrection tradition.

To make sure that the women understood the angel's instructions and the need for haste in informing the male disciples, Matthew has Jesus meet them on their way back to Galilee. While the angel had instructed the women only to go and tell Jesus' "disciples," the risen Jesus is more specific: the women are to go and tell his "brethren." It seems that Matthew is reinforcing the idea that the women are little more than subservient messengers by having them fall to the ground before the risen Jesus, take hold of his feet and worship him.[7] At the same time, however, Matthew implies that the women specifically needed to go to the "brethren," because these men will never be able to "get it" unless they do.

Matthew's next narrative element is an anti-Semitic fiction in which the Roman guards who witnessed the supernatural events of the resurrection returned to Jerusalem and informed the "chief priests" of all that had happened. Members of the religious "council" of elders then bribed the guards with "much money" in order to ensure their silence. The terms of the bribe further required that the Roman guards spread a rumor that Jesus' disciples had stolen his corpse. Matthew tells us that, "this report is spread abroad among the Jews until the present day."[8]

Matthew was apparently so intent on attacking the anti-Christian Jews of his day, that he forgot to add a story in which Mary Magdalene, and "the other Mary" actually *do* report to the male disciples. It is left to the reader to assume that the women actually did what they were *twice* instructed to do. There is not, however, any necessary reason to assume that they actually did as instructed. Why was Matthew not more specific on this point?

For all of this, it is surprising that none of the male disciples in Matthew's Gospel receive individual appearances of the risen Jesus. Peter is not mentioned at all, and Jesus appears only once, and that appearance is to "the eleven" as a group. Even then he appears only in the context of his ascension into heaven.

Even more surprising is Matthew's notation at the end of his Gospel that—even in the *presence* of the risen Jesus—some of the eleven still "doubted."[9] What I think we can legitimately infer from such a footnote is that at least some of Jesus' *original* followers *never* adopted a resurrection faith. There were, in other words, early followers of Jesus who continued to follow his teachings, but never became "Christians."

THE ENDINGS TO *MATTHEW*

There is a problem with the ending of Matthew's Gospel, however. It seems to end, most naturally, at 28:15: " ... this report is spread abroad by the Jews until the present day." The remaining verses (16-20)—which have to do with Jesus appearing to "the eleven"—seem quite awkward and out of context with the preceding verses, the entire section appearing as if it has just been dropped into place, with no real connection. In fact, these five verses seem to have come from another source, and may have not been part of the original Gospel.

Helmut Koester confirms that verses 16-20 came from a separate tradition, and that they were heavily redacted by the author of *Matthew*.[10] Yet Koester is reluctant to propose that someone other than the author of Matthew wrote the verses, or that they were added to an earlier version of Matthew.

To maintain this stance, however, Koester has to ignore the testimony of some ancient authorities which include Papias of Hierapolis, Eusebius, and Origen. According to these orthodox patriarchs, the Gospel of Matthew had originally been written in Hebrew or Aramaic, and only later translated into Greek.[11] We cannot get into the debate on this subject here, but it is at least worth noting that if there had been a prior translation of Matthew—or at least an earlier version of the Gospel—it may not have included verses 16-20.

Is it so impossible that an original version of Matthew in Aramaic or Hebrew once existed? Scholars have always maintained that all of the New Testament was originally written in Greek. They have also always maintained that Jesus and his disciples never wrote anything because they were illiterate. But why are they so sure about this? Morton Smith has pointed out that "Literacy was common even among the lower classes in the Roman world."[12]

Smith is one scholar who believed that there *were* written documents generated by early followers of Jesus, and that the loss of *all* of those writings—by the vagaries of history—seems very unlikely. "So what became of their writings?", Smith asks. "Most likely they were suppressed."[13]

> If Matthew 28:16-20 is spurious, then Matthew's Gospel, like Mark's, lacked a patriarchal resurrection tradition.

What concerns us more directly here, however, is the possibility that original Matthew lacked a story about Jesus appearing to the male disciples! If Matthew 28:16-20 is spurious, then Matthew's Gospel, like Mark's, lacked a *patriarchal* resurrection tradition. Again, both Gospels reported that Mary Magdalene was commissioned to "go and tell" the male disciples of her experience, but neither Gospel states that she ever actually did so! Even the redacted ending to Matthew's Gospel is not a real appearance story, but a mythological story about Jesus' ascension into heaven.

Aside from these considerations, Matthew's Gospel again supports the thesis that the story about Mary Magdalene was the earliest and best preserved resurrection tradition. Matthew also states that Mary was the first—and perhaps only—disciple to receive an appearance of the risen Jesus (outside of visions and "revelations").

It should also be pointed out that Matthew records not one, but two, early traditions about Mary. Matthew repeats Mark's empty tomb story, but he also records an entirely separate tradition in which Mary receives an appearance of the resurrected Jesus some time *after* the Easter event itself.

What is even more interesting is that this appearance story immediately follows the departure of Mary Magdalene and "the other Mary" from the empty tomb—"with fear and great joy." On their way to tell the other disciples, Jesus meets the women on the road. Is it possible that this story originally belonged to Mark's Gospel as well, but was later edited out? Certainly Mark's ending is suspiciously abrupt, and it seems evident that something is missing. Since both Matthew and Pseudo-Mark "corrected" the abbreviated ending of Mark in the same way—with an appearance of Jesus to Mary Magdalene—it seems quite likely that the original version of Mark (now lost to us) contained this story as well.

As for Peter, Matthew apparently did not feel compelled to include him in his resurrection scenario at all. Unlike Luke, Matthew was not interested in rehabilitating Peter's reputation by favoring him with a resurrection appearance. Peter denied Jesus after his arrest, so that was the end of Peter as far as Matthew was concerned.

IN SUMMARY:

- The author of Matthew's Gospel edited Salome out of his list of women who witnessed the crucifixion and resurrection because her name had become associated with heretical Christian sects.

- Joseph of Arimathea in *Matthew* was upgraded to an actual disciple of Jesus, and Mark's young man in white at the empty tomb was upgraded to angelic status.

- In Matthew's Gospel, Mary Magdalene and "the other Mary" do not come to the tomb of Jesus on Easter morning with the intent of preparing Jesus' body for burial. Matthew does not give us a reason for their presence.

- Matthew's Gospel, like Mark's contains a spurious ending that provides a basis for a patriarchal resurrection tradition.

- Mary and "the other Mary" are the only disciples to receive an individual appearance of the risen Jesus.

- Matthew's original ending does not specify that the women reported their experiences to the male disciples.

- Jesus' appearance to Mary Magdalene in Matthew's Gospel may have been a story original to Mark's Gospel that was later excised, then restored by Pseudo-Mark.

XI. Mary Magdalene According to *Luke*

A s we discussed earlier, Luke not only attempted to diminish Mary Magdalene's importance in his Gospel by inventing the story of her "seven demons," he also made her anonymous in his crucifixion and resurrection narratives.

In Luke's Gospel, Mary Magdalene appears for one purpose only: to report the crucifixion and resurrection events to "the eleven," to "all of the rest," and to "the apostles."[1] What both Mark and Matthew's Gospels failed to do—to definitively link Mary's resurrection tradition with a later patriarchal tradition—was finally accomplished by Luke:

> And they remembered these words, and returned from the tomb and related all these things to the eleven and to all the rest. Now it was Mary Magdalene and Joanna and Mary the mother of James, and all the rest with them, who told the apostles these things.[2]

In Luke's first resurrection story (24:1-12), the women (who now also include additional, but anonymous, female disciples) ostensibly tell everyone associated with Jesus about their discovery of an empty tomb and about their subsequent visionary experiences. Luke begrudgingly admits that the earliest resurrection faith was a faith exclusive to women. But

Luke still withholds a commissioning story, so that women of his time, and in the future, could not use this story as a mandate for preaching and teaching in the Church.[3]

Luke also lessened the importance of the women by claiming that the male disciples did not believe their testimony: "But these words seemed like idle tales, and they did not believe them."[4] Luke's first resurrection narrative has the women introduce resurrection *hope*, but he also makes it clear that the men were not ready to come to faith on the basis of second-hand information delivered by women whose testimony was unreliable.

In his second resurrection narrative (24:13-35) Luke tells the story of two disciples on their way to Emmaus who are joined by a stranger who later turns out to be Jesus in disguise. The mysterious disciple, Cleopas— who appears nowhere else in the Gospels—and a second anonymous disciple, relate to the stranger all the events that had just taken place in Jerusalem. Their teacher had been crucified, but what happened after that was truly wondrous:

> And certain women amongst us, having been to the tomb, and when they did not find his body, came to us and said that they had also seen a vision of angels which said to them that he was alive.[5]

This testimony in Luke's account of two disciples meeting (but not recognizing) Jesus (24:13:35) echoes a similar story in Pseudo-Mark (the long ending attached to Mark's Gospel):

> After this he (Jesus) appeared in another form to two of them as they were walking into the country. And they went back and told the rest, but they did not believe them.[6]

Interestingly, Pseudo-Mark's version of this story does not specify whether the anonymous disciples were male or female. Either way, their report was also rejected (16:11).

Pseudo-Mark later echoed Luke's claim that initial reports of the resurrection by women were given no credence by the male disciples. These men, at least in the beginning, did not have the Easter faith of Jesus' female disciples. But while Luke may have intended to demean the credibility of women, his report only supports the thesis that the earliest resurrection tradition was a tradition exclusive to women!

In Pseudo-Mark, the testimony of two anonymous disciples was rejected by Jesus' inner circle.[7] In *Matthew*, "some" of the disciples "doubted."[8] Luke reported that the male disciples *did not* believe the women,[9] and in John's Gospel, it is Thomas who represents the "doubter" among the Jesus people.[10] There is a strong early tradition, then, that maintains that while the resurrection faith of women was early, the faith of men was not.

But why would any of the evangelists have reported such disbelief on the part of Jesus' male disciples? Certainly it is not a flattering picture, and I doubt very much that if the men's lack of faith had lasted only a few days—as all of the Gospel accounts seem to imply—then such an embarrassing footnote would not have been reported at all. More likely, early disbelief continued for quite some time, and was so much a part of Christian tradition, that the evangelists could not altogether ignore it. Instead, they truncated time in the process of mythologizing the evolution of the Easter event itself.

There is another element to Luke's road to Emmaus story that strengthens this argument. Luke, like every other Gospel author, made the traditional connection between the empty tomb legend and Mary Magdalene's visions. But in the telling of this story, Luke reveals the inherent problem with the empty tomb part of Mary's tradition. The two disciples on their way to Emmaus meet up with a stranger who later turns out to be Jesus. The disciples tell the stranger:

> And certain women among us astonished us when,
> having been to the tomb early, did not find his body.
> They came to us saying that they had also seen a vision

of angels, who said that he was alive. And certain of them who were with us went to the tomb, and found it as the women had said; but they did not see him.[11]

...the discovery of an empty tomb was a secondary, and ultimately meaningless, story element.

This passage is testimony to Christian resurrection faith at the time Luke wrote his Gospel, and it has four main elements: 1) the women discovered an empty tomb; 2) the women had one or more visions which convinced them that Jesus had transcended death; 3) male disciples confirmed the existence of an empty tomb; and 4) this confirmation did *not* lead to faith as it had for the women.

In terms of the myth itself, then, the women's discovery of an empty tomb acted as a catalyst for visions that convinced them that Jesus was alive. The *same* discovery on the part of the men, however, did *not* have this effect. *The transformative event, therefore, was not the discovery of an empty tomb, but the visionary experiences that followed it, and only women had those visionary experiences at first.* In reality, the empty tomb itself has always been irrelevant to Christian faith.

With this in mind, we can reread all the other Gospel accounts of the resurrection and realize that the discovery of an empty tomb was a secondary, and ultimately meaningless, story element. Resurrection faith developed, not as a result of material evidence, but from inner spiritual transformation on the part of the believer.

In *Matthew, Mark, Luke* and *John*—in each and every case—Mary and the other women came to believe that Jesus was alive, not because they found his tomb empty, but because they experienced his living presence in some manner. This suggests to me that *the earliest resurrection tradition having to do with Mary Magdalene was originally independent from the later tradition about an empty tomb.* It seems highly likely that the empty tomb legend, whenever it was invented, was grafted onto Mary Magdalene's tradition as a matter of narrative convenience.

Where does all this evidence leave us? I believe it allows us to propose a new hypothesis for the origins of faith in the resurrection of Jesus. It allows for the possibility that the *original* resurrection tradition was one in which only women had visions of a living Jesus. At some point, rumors about women having these experiences reached other groups of Jesus' disciples. At first these rumors were dismissed out of hand because they originated with women. As those rumors continued to build, however, they finally reached critical mass within the larger Jesus community. Through the power of suggestion, *some* male disciples of Jesus also began to have visions of Jesus. Later still, when Christians like Mark and Luke felt compelled to justify resurrection faith on the basis of historical events, the empty tomb legend was invented and appended to the resurrection legend about Mary Magdalene.

Assuming, for the sake of argument that this scenario represents historical fact, it certainly would have left Luke with a problem. As a promoter of patriarchal Christianity, he did not want his audience to come to the conclusion that Christian faith originated in the company of women.

Luke therefore had to take pains to diminish the importance of women. He did this, first, by suggesting that Mary Magdalene's visions were not altogether credible because she had once been possessed by demons. Secondly, Luke erased Mary Magdalene, by name, from the crucifixion scene. Thirdly, he insisted that the male disciples of Jesus did not find any value in the women's post-crucifixion visions.

Finally, Luke invented—or, perhaps, accurately reported—other resurrection traditions that included only men. After his Emmaus story, Luke tells another story in which Jesus appeared directly to the male disciples, insisted on his physicality, and then commissioned the men to go forth and preach in his name (24:36-53).

Luke further diminished the importance of women by claiming that when they arrived at the empty tomb on Easter morning they were met, not by a young man in white, and not by an angel, but by "two *men*" in "shining garments" (24:1-4). Stating that these two men wore "shining

211

garments" was Luke's way of intimating that these men had heavenly credentials without directly saying so.

Luke could not state that the men were angels because his audience knew that angels were androgynous. Luke needed his messengers to be masculine because that allowed him to go one step further in denigrating women: When the women came into the presence of these men they "bowed their faces to the ground." The women showed their submissiveness by assuming a submissive posture. In ancient societies, falling prostate was a gesture of respect from an inferior to a superior.[12]

The women then rise and go tell the other disciples what they had seen and heard. Unfortunately, they meet general skepticism. Peter, however, is somewhat less skeptical and goes to the tomb to see for himself. When he finds the tomb empty, he "returns home...marveling" at what happened (24:12).

There are several problems with this verse however: 1) Peter was not in Jerusalem, he was in Galilee; 2) Peter could not have "returned home" (which the author of this passage suggested to be nearby), because his home was in Capernaum in Galilee; and 3) Some early manuscripts of Luke's Gospel do not include this story.[13] The reference *Bible* I use, for instance, leaves out verse 12 altogether. No doubt this passage was a scribal addition. It was not original to Luke's Gospel, but was probably based on John 20:3-10.[14]

The same scribe who edited Luke at 24:12 may also have inserted another verse, this time in Luke's road to Emmaus story. Near the end of an otherwise smooth narrative, a disciple states "The Lord has risen indeed, and has appeared to Simon" (24:34). The insertion has no other purpose than to assert Peter's status as an apostle who had received an individual appearance of the risen Jesus, and is otherwise completely out of place.

In a final appearance story (24:36-43) Luke has the risen Jesus appear to "the eleven" as a group. This story is obviously of late construction since here Jesus maintains that his resurrected body is not a spiritual form, but a physical one. To prove this, Jesus asks the disciples for food to eat.

Luke may have drawn on Greek drama in inventing this story. Plato, in his dialogue *Gorgias*, has Socrates say: "If anyone has been a sturdy rogue, and bore traces of his stripes in scars on his body ... then after death too his body has these marks visible on it."[15] More than anything else, this story reflects Luke's own beliefs and the beliefs of some Christians sometime around the beginning of the second century. As such, it is a proclamation of faith, not a report of historical facts.[16]

In a final appearance story (24:36-43) Luke has the risen Jesus appear to "the eleven" as a group. This story is obviously of late construction since here Jesus maintains that his resurrected body is not a spiritual form, but a physical one.

Luke's three resurrection stories represent the early evolution of orthodox Christian thought on this subject. Initially, Jesus appeared to Mary Magdalene as an apparition. Later, men like Paul had visions of Jesus. Still later Christians saw the risen Jesus as a divine figure who could be recognized in other human beings. Finally, as the Christian myth became literalized, the faithful came to believe that Jesus had actually risen from the dead in a physical body.

The spiritual nature of the resurrection—so evident in the traditions of Mary Magdalene and the Corinthian women prophets—eventually became vestigial in orthodox Christianity. The early patriarchs of orthodoxy refused to base the validity of their central tenet of faith on the ecstatic experiences of women. The matriarchal resurrection faith was gradually, and thoroughly, eclipsed.

IN SUMMARY:

- The author of *Luke* attempted to diminish the importance of Mary Magdalene and her resurrection tradition by inventing a story about her "seven demons," not naming her as a witness to the crucifixion, denying her an apostolic commission, having her prostrate herself before two masculine heavenly messengers, and by claiming that the male disciples of Jesus did not believe her testimony.

- *Luke* was the first Gospel to clearly state that the women who witnessed the resurrection made direct contact with the male disciples of Jesus.

- *Luke* provides further evidence that many of Jesus' original disciples did not believe in his resurrection.

- A later scribe inserted a Petrine resurrection tradition into the *Gospel of Luke*.

- *Luke* was the first Gospel to include an appearance story that claimed that Jesus rose from the dead in a physical body.

- The original Easter faith was not based on the empty tomb legend, but on the experience of Jesus' living presence.

XII. Mary Magdalene in the *Gospel of John*

GENERAL CONSIDERATIONS

T*he Gospel According to John* is thought to have been written sometime around the beginning of the second century, and has traditionally been seen as the latest of the canonical Gospels. But if Luke's Gospel was written as late as 120 C.E.[1], then it is possible that John's Gospel is earlier than Luke's.

Helmut Koester believes that John's Gospel went through several stages of composition, and that its earliest draft may have come into existence around the *middle* of the *first* century.[2] If Koester is correct, then the final version of John's Gospel attempted to address a widely diverse Christian audience over a substantial period of time.

John's Gospel, three canonical epistles attributed to him, the canonical *Book of Revelations*, the apocryphal *Acts of John* and *The Apocryphon of John* all evolved out of Johannine Christianity and a body of believers who Raymond Brown refers to as the *Community of the Beloved Disciple*.[3]

The Johannine community was originally founded around the mysterious "disciple whom Jesus loved," and it developed a unique Christology over

215

a period of seventy years. The Johannine community took issue with Jewish Christians on the one hand, and those of a Gnostic persuasion on the other—even though part of the community eventually became Gnostic.

As a whole, John's Gospel itself was considered heretical by many orthodox Christians of the second century. Part of the reason for this view was that the author(s) of John often used Gnostic vocabulary and imagery, if not theology. Terms like "logos" (word), "Sophia" (Wisdom), "bride," "bridegroom" and "bridal chamber," were all terms commonly used by Gnostic Christians.

For the most part, however, the author of *John* used Gnostic terminology to express an orthodox point of view. Perhaps John intended to beat Gnostic Christians at their own game by subverting their theological language. Even if he did, we need to remember that John's Gospel was written during a time when such language was common coin, and before "orthodox" and "heretical" theologies were clearly defined.

MARY AND THE CRUCIFIXION IN *JOHN*

Mark claimed—and Matthew and Luke did not contradict—that the female disciples of Jesus watched his crucifixion "from afar." The author of John's Gospel, however, wanted the crucifixion of Jesus to be an up-close-and-personal event. To this end, he placed the women at the very foot of the cross along with "the disciple whom Jesus loved" (traditionally associated with the disciple John, brother of James and Salome, and son of Zebedee).

John, in fact, assembled quite a little crowd around the cross: Mary, Jesus' mother, his mother's sister, Mary the wife of Clopas, Mary Magdalene, and the "beloved disciple." All but one of these disciples are identified by name, but the identity of the "disciple whom Jesus loved" remains a mystery. Christians have always been mystified and intrigued by the beloved disciple, and understandably so. The "disciple whom Jesus loved" is mentioned numerous times in John's Gospel, and yet is never given a name.

Prurient interest in the sex lives of Jesus and Mary Magdalene have led some theorists outside the academic community to propose that the "disciple whom Jesus loved" was Mary Magdalene. Certainly this is a provocative suggestion, and the argument actually has a few things in its favor, not the least of which was the author's sense of mystery. John writes:

> Jesus therefore seeing his mother, and the disciple whom he loved standing by says to his mother, 'Woman, behold thy *son.*' Then he says to the disciple, 'Behold thy mother.' And from that hour the disciple took her to *his* own home.[4]

It seems clear enough that Jesus was referring to a man, not a woman, in this text, since he uses "uios," the Greek word for "son" in referring to the beloved disciple. "Uios" is commonly used in referring to men throughout the New Testament, but "uios" also has a more extended meaning. It can refer to someone who is *not* a direct offspring or descendent, but is adopted as a *spiritual* "son."

Since John is writing about spiritual adoption, "uios" could, technically, refer to either a man or a woman.

"Uios," as a matter of fact, is used in this sense several times in the New Testament,[5] and this is also how John is using the word as well.[6] Since John is writing about spiritual adoption, "uios" could, technically, refer to either a man or a woman.

"Uios" is also often used in the New Testament in a non-gendered sense—as in the "*sons* of God", "*son* of man", etc. So, if we were to consider only John's use of the term at the crucifixion scene, the argument that the beloved disciple was a man is not entirely compelling.

Then there is the way that John constructs the two sentences in question: "Standing by the cross were his mother, his mother's sister, Mary the wife of Clopas, and Mary Magdalene." In the first sentence, John names four people, and they are all women. He does not name a fifth person, and he certainly doesn't name any man. If John had wanted his audience to understand that there was, in fact, a fifth member of this group—whether male or female—then why did he not mention that person in this sentence? And if we wanted a man at the foot of the cross, why did he not give him a name?

Immediately after naming Mary Magdalene, John goes on in the next sentence to say, "When Jesus saw his mother, and the disciple whom he loved standing there, he said to his mother, behold your 'uios' ..." The sentence makes perfect sense if Mary Magdalene was the "uios," but no sense at all if Jesus is addressing a fifth person, and a man—someone who has just appeared, without introduction, out of thin air.

This is hardly evidence enough to make a serious case for Mary Magdalene being the beloved disciple, however. And, as we will see in a moment, such a case can be easily contradicted by other evidence. In the end, the identity of the "beloved disciple" remains a mystery.

MARY MAGDALENE AND THE RESURRECTION IN *JOHN*

John, like the other evangelists, claimed that after Jesus died on the cross, Joseph of Arimathea claimed his body. John, like Matthew, identifies Joseph as a disciple of Jesus, but in his version of events, Joseph does not take Jesus' body to the tomb by himself, but is assisted by a certain Nicodemus—a man who "had first come to Jesus at night."[7]

Why did Nicodemus come to Jesus at night? John tells us that Nicodemus was a leading Pharisee, so the assumption is that he came to Jesus under the cover of darkness so that he would not be seen by his peers.

Nicodemus is introduced for the first time in John's Gospel at 3:1, where we are informed that he was a Pharisee who considered Jesus to be a man of God. He came to Jesus—at night—to question him on the matter of the kingdom of God, and the necessity of being "born again." It is interesting to note in passing, that both the nocturnal visit and the subject matter of that visit suggest that Nicodemus might have come to Jesus to be initiated into the mysteries of the kingdom.

Yet Nicodemus—since he appears in no other Gospel—was probably a Johannine fiction.[8] While John probably invented Nicodemus in order to address the Pharisees (later known as rabbis) of his own time, Nicodemus' presence at Jesus' burial also solved two problems for John—one of which had to do with Mary Magdalene.

In this Gospel, it is Nicodemus—not Mary or any other woman—who brought "myrrh and aloes" to the tomb in order to prepare Jesus' corpse for burial.[9] John thus eliminates the need to embalm Jesus as the reason for Mary's presence at the tomb on Easter morning. In John's story, Mary went to the tomb simply to grieve for Jesus.

John noted that in Mark's and Luke's accounts, the women who came to prepare Jesus' corpse actually failed in their mission—if only because the tomb was empty when they arrived. In the case of Jesus, the Jewish funerary customs of washing, anointing, and wrapping the corpse had not taken place, and John sought to correct this oversight by having Nicodemus perform these duties—even though these duties were traditionally performed by women.

There must have been some good reason why the author of John did not want Mary to play the traditional role of a common woman performing the burial rights for a loved one. In fact, in John's Gospel, Mary Magdalene had a much different role to play.

This is not an insignificant observation. John agrees with Matthew's Gospel in having Mary Magdalene appear on Easter morning *without* oils and spices, and *without* any intent to prepare the corpse of Jesus. Mary, here, is not one of many women, not even one of several. She has been singled out as the sole witness to the Christian myth of origin—as the interpreter of events and their meaning.

Unlike every other Gospel, there is no young man or angel to greet Mary—no one at all to explain how or why the stone had been moved or why the tomb is empty. Mary immediately came to her own conclusion: someone had *stolen* the body of Jesus.

Panicked by this possibility, Mary then runs to inform the other disciples (who are still in Jerusalem, and have not returned to Galilee) about the grave robbery. The first two disciples she runs into are Peter and *"the other disciple whom Jesus loved.*"[10] In this story, Mary Magdalene and the "beloved disciple" are clearly not the same person.

Hearing Mary's report, Peter—along with the beloved disciple—run to the tomb to see for themselves if it is, in fact, empty. The beloved disciple runs faster than Peter and reaches the tomb first. The tomb is empty, and only the burial clothes remain. Peter is typically puzzled by all of this, but the beloved disciple immediately "believes." Whatever the men's state of mind, both of them return "home" without knowing what had happened to Jesus.

But just as Peter's resurrection experience in Luke was a later scribal addition, this story in *John* is also a later scribal addition.[11] If we remove John 20:2-10 from the text, the narrative flows smoothly: In 20:42 Mary discovers the empty tomb. In 20:11 the story continues as Mary is weeping because she thinks Jesus' body has been stolen. Ann Graham Brock states: "The discontinuity in sequence and the two seams between v. 1 and v. 2 and between v. 10 and v. 11 strongly suggest that the scene of Peter and the other disciple running to the tomb is an interpolation."[12] Once again, a Petrine resurrection tradition has been *forced* into a Gospel in which it did not formerly exist.

HER MASTERS VOICE: JOHN'S TREATMENT OF WOMEN

When Mary stops weeping, she decides to enter the empty tomb and immediately has an angelic vision. She sees two angels seated in the tomb: one at the head of where Jesus had lain, and one at the foot—the two positions where Jews traditionally placed candles.[13]

Mary hears the angels ask her why she is weeping, and she explains that she is crying because someone has taken away the body of her Lord. Then immediately, Mary's attention is pulled elsewhere. Still in visionary consciousness, Mary turns around and sees Jesus, but the image is apparently unclear because she mistakes the apparition for the gardener. Jesus, like the angels, asks Mary why she is weeping.

She once again explains and wants to know if he—the gardener—has removed the body.

Instead of answering Mary's question, something wonderful happens. Jesus has only to say her name: "Mary," and immediately Mary's eyes are opened. In an instant, Mary recognizes the "gardener" as her Lord.

A miracle has taken place—a moment of illumination. Mary is like a Zen Buddhist monk who suddenly achieves enlightenment by hearing the sound of a single word, a falling drop of water, a touch of the Zen master, or while gazing at a dew drop on the petal of a rose. Hearing a single word, Mary Magdalene is instantly transported into the living presence of her teacher.

> *Mary is like a Zen Buddhist monk who suddenly achieves enlightenment by hearing the sound of a single word...*

This image is important. The author of John expected his readers to understand that Mary was a superior disciple due to her unique ability to hear her master's voice. John, in fact, wants his readers to make a connection between Mary's epiphany and his earlier story about Jesus as the "good shepherd":

> The sheep hear his voice, and he calls his sheep by name,
> and leads them out. And when he puts forth his own sheep,
> he goes before them, and the sheep follow him; for they know
> his voice.[14]

John wants his audience to recognize that Mary is among Jesus' chosen few because of her innate ability to comprehend great spiritual truths. John wanted to extend this honor to other women as well. While in Matthew's Gospel (16:16), it is Peter who recognizes Jesus as the Christ, in *John* 11:27 the person who proclaims "You are the Christ, the Son of God" is a woman: Martha, sister of Mary and Lazarus.

John honors women's spiritual understanding again in his story of the

Samaritan woman who in 4:29 proclaims to her brothers and sisters: "Come, see a man who told me all that I ever did. Can this be the Christ?" It was through this woman's faith, and most especially through her *word*—her action as an *apostle*—that her fellow Samaritans also come to believe in Jesus.

While men can certainly come to faith on their own, John goes out of his way to emphasize that women are particularly capable of understanding Jesus, and that they are often responsible for prompting faith in men. John honors Jesus' mother, Mary, in just this way. Whereas other Gospels deemphasized or denigrated Mary of Nazareth's role in Jesus' ministry, John clearly saw the mother of Jesus as his willing and able disciple from the very beginning. John honors Jesus' mother to such an extent that he places her at the very foot of the cross, then gives her over to the care and protection of the beloved disciple.

On the subject of women as primary disciples of Jesus in John's Gospel, Raymond Brown states:

> Another proof that women could be intimate disciples of Jesus is found in ... the allegorical parable of the Good Shepherd (where) John compares the disciples of Jesus to sheep who know their shepherd's voice when he calls them by name ... This description is fulfilled in the appearance of the risen Jesus to Mary Magdalene as she recognizes him when he calls her by her name... The point that Mary Magdalene can belong to Jesus' sheep is all the more important since in 10:3-5 the sheep are twice identified as 'his own,' the almost technical expression used at the beginning of the Last Supper: 'Having loved his own who were in the world, he loved them to the end.'...It is clear that John has no hesitation in placing a woman in the same category of relationship to Jesus as the Twelve who are included in 'his own' in 13:1.[15]

The author of *John* seems to have come from a Christian community that welcomed women as apostles. It is Mary Magdalene, not Simon

Peter, who receives an appearance of risen Jesus. The interpolation in Luke's Gospel: "The Lord has risen indeed, and appeared to Simon" is countered by John in 20:18: "Mary Magdalene went and said to the disciples, 'I have seen the Lord.'"

Raymond Brown suggests that this Johannine viewpoint concerning women as apostles and teachers may have been promoted by a group of heterodox Johannine secessionists who gradually drifted toward a more Gnostic theology, and "… that it was probably John's portrait of Mary Magdalene that sparked the Gnostic Gospels to make her the chief recipient of post-resurrectional revelation and the rival of Peter."[16]

Given John's favorable treatment of women in his narrative—and of Mary Magdalene in particular (and especially because of several important theological parallels) there may have been some connection between Johannine Christians and those Christians who used the *Gospel of Mary*. The theology these two Christian groups held in common include belief in the pre-existence of the soul, realized eschatology, the individual's essential union with the Divine Principal (or Word), the thesis of sinlessness and the quest for individual perfection.[17]

Given these factors, and those mentioned earlier, perhaps we should not altogether reject the possibility that some Johannine Christians considered Mary Magdalene to be "the disciple whom Jesus loved." The Johannine schismatics who became Gnostic Christians may have been the very Christians responsible for The *Gospel According to Mary*. This is pure speculation on my part, but perhaps it is worth considering.

MARY'S VISION

While many of the details of John's story concerning Jesus' appearance to Mary Magdalene may be mythological, it seems certain that the historical Mary Magdalene had an experience of the risen Jesus not unlike the one described in *John*.[18] All of John's claims seem to ring true: Mary was alone at the time of her vision. She was in a state of grief at the time of her vision. And she had not gone to the tomb seeking to anoint Jesus' corpse.

Raymond Brown agrees that it is historically likely that Mary had the first vision of a living Jesus after his crucifixion.[19] Mary's experience—whatever it was—acted as a catalyst for the faith of others.

After Mary's recognition, Jesus gives her instructions:

> But touch me not, for I have not yet ascended to my Father; but go to my brethren and say to them, "I go to my Father; and to my God, and your God."[20]

Mary's experience—whatever it was—acted as a catalyst for the faith of others...

There is nothing in Jesus' instruction that indicate that he will go to the other disciples himself. In fact, this is Jesus' first, and last, revelation. Jesus does not instruct Mary to go tell the other disciples that they, too, will soon see him. Instead, she is merely to tell them, as she does in 20:18, "I have seen the Lord." Mary is the only witness to the resurrection, and she will always be the only witness because Jesus is returning to whence he came.

The author of *John* or, more likely, the redactors of *John*, added three other appearance stories to this Gospel: 20:19-23, 20:24-31and 21:1-25. But none of these stories logically follow Jesus' appearance to Mary, since Jesus had already dematerialized. These later additions to John's Gospel are—not surprisingly—patriarchal traditions. Moreover, they suggest the physicality of Jesus' resurrection. All of these elements suggest that these traditions represent later redactions to John's Gospel.[21]

There is one more important element to John's narrative about Mary Magdalene that deserves mention. In John's Gospel, Mary Magdalene is not just the sole witness to Jesus' resurrection, she is also the only witness to his *ascension*! John's narrative contains both elements, and this is highly unusual.

Mark's Gospel contains no ascension story. Matthew's Gospel contains no ascension story. Outside of the Marian tradition in *John*, ascension narratives exist only in Luke's Gospel, and in Pseudo-Mark. Since Luke attempted to diminish the importance of Mary Magdalene elsewhere in his Gospel, it is possible that he also invented his ascension narrative to counteract a Marian ascension tradition. And since Luke's and Pseudo-Mark's ascension stories are almost identical, it is likely that Pseudo-Mark copied *Luke*.

IN SUMMARY:

♦ The identity of the "disciple whom Jesus loved" is unknown, but the possibility exists that the beloved disciple was Mary Magdalene.

♦ *The Gospel of John* uses Gnostic vocabulary and imagery, but uses it to defend an orthodox point of view.

♦ John's crucifixion scene is not historical. His Marian resurrection narrative, on the other hand, may have been based on historical tradition.

♦ John's Gospel was favorable to women.

♦ Mary's resurrection tradition in John is also an ascension tradition, and probably predated the patriarchal ascension traditions in Luke and Pseudo-Mark.

XIII. Mary Magdalene in Apocryphal Literature

THE GOSPEL OF PETER

For all of the appearance stories in the canonical Gospels, there is not a single story about the resurrection itself. There is no scenario in which Jesus gets up and walks out of the tomb. This detail tells us a great deal. Early stories about Jesus' resurrection did not need to be accompanied by an empty tomb narrative because early Christians did not believe that Jesus rose in a physical body.

Later Christians, however, must have puzzled over the absence of a Gospel tradition in which Jesus' body was resuscitated. The evangelist who wrote *The Gospel According to Peter*—or later redacted it—recognized this problem and attempted to solve it.

THE CROSS THAT WALKED AND TALKED

A partial manuscript of a Gospel attributed to Simon Peter was discovered late in the nineteenth century in a monk's grave at Achmim, Egypt.[1] *The Gospel of Peter* contains an elaborate reworking of the pas-

> *While Luke...refused to name the women who witnessed the crucifixion, the author of Peter's Gospel went one step further and eliminated the female witnesses altogether!*

sion and empty tomb traditions, even though many scholars now see a common resurrection tradition underlying both Peter's Gospel and the resurrection tradition in the canonical Gospels.[2]

Given the fantastical nature of the narrative in the extant manuscript of *Peter*, the Gospel (in its present form) must have been written well into the second century. Other factors point to a late date as well. While Luke, for instance, refused to name the women who witnessed the crucifixion, the author of Peter's Gospel went one step further and eliminated female witnesses altogether!

Joseph of Arimathea again appears in Peter's Gospel to claim Jesus' corpse. But *Peter* adds a new detail to the story: After Joseph washed Jesus' body and wrapped it in a shroud, he laid it in his *own* tomb called, conveniently, "Joseph's Garden."

Like the canonical authors, Peter states that a large stone was rolled in front of the entrance to the tomb. But to make certain nobody could get in or out of the tomb without supernatural assistance, the author of this Gospel manifested Roman guards to secure the tomb entrance with "seven seals"—the highest level of Roman security. What happens next is worthy of a Hollywood script:

> Early, at first light on the Sabbath, a crowd came from Jerusalem and the surrounding countryside to see the sealed tomb. But during the night before the Lord's day dawned, while the soldiers were on guard, two by two during each watch, a loud noise came from the sky, and they saw the skies open up and two men come down from there in a burst of light and approach the tomb. The stone that had been pushed against the entrance began to roll by itself and moved away to one side; the tomb

opened up and both young men went inside.

Now when these soldiers saw this, they roused the centurion from his sleep, along with the elders. (Remember, they were also there keeping watch.) While they were explaining what they had seen, again they see three men leaving the tomb, two supporting the third, and a cross was following them. The heads of the two reached up to the sky, while the head of the third, whom they led by the hand, reached beyond the skies. And they heard a voice from the skies that said, 'Have you preached to those who sleep?' And an answer was heard from the cross: 'Yes!'[3]

While this part of Peter's resurrection narrative is fictive, his treatment of Mary Magdalene (whom he identifies as "a disciple of the Lord") at least sounds plausible. As in *Matthew* and *John*, Mary does not go to the tomb on Easter morning carrying oils and spices, since Joseph had already prepared Jesus' corpse for burial. Mary goes to the tomb for only one purpose: to grieve.

The author of *Peter* also does not attempt to name the other women who went with Mary to the tomb. By simply identifying them as Mary's "friends," this evangelist is honestly admitting that he didn't know who these other women were.

Peter explains that Mary and her friends had not gone to the tomb of Jesus earlier because they were afraid of milling crowds of "enraged Judeans." The formal burial process had been interrupted by this, so the women "did not perform at the tomb of the Lord what women are accustomed to do for their loved ones who die." They had yet to "weep and beat (their) breasts."

That the women had not performed their burial duties is likely, but the reason for that negligence is not. The reference to "enraged Judeans" cannot be a historical note about the Easter story, since the Jews had no reason to be enraged over Jesus—dead or alive. This bit of anti-Semitism (like all such stories in the various Gospels) points to a later time when early Christianity came into conflict with rabbinical Judaism.

The next narrative element in Peter's Gospel is almost identical to Mark's version of the story:

> And they went and found the tomb open. They went up to it, stooped down, and saw a young man sitting there (in) the middle of the tomb; he was handsome and wore a splendid robe. He said to them, 'Why have you come? Who are you looking for? Surely not the one who was crucified? He is risen and gone. If you don't believe it, stoop down and see the place where they laid him, for he is not here. He has risen and gone back to the place he was sent from.' Then the women fled in fear.[4]

Unlike Mark, Peter's young man does not tell the women that they will see Jesus back in Galilee. They will not see him at all, in fact, because he had "gone back to the place he was sent from." Neither does the young man commission the women to tell the male disciples about Jesus' resurrection. While the existence of an early matriarchal resurrection tradition is confirmed by *Peter*, the author does not attempt to connect that tradition to any other one. As in *Mark*, the women tell no one of their experiences, so this part of Peter's resurrection account is very primitive.

According to Helmut Koester,

> ... all gospels were dependent upon one and the same basic account of the suffering, crucifixion, death, and burial of Jesus. But this account ended with the discovery of the empty tomb. With respect to the stories of Jesus' appearances, each of the extant gospels of the canon used different traditions of epiphany stories which they appended to the one common passion account. This also applies to the Gospel of Peter.[5]

Koester is stating that there were several, different, resurrection traditions in which various people claimed to have seen the risen Jesus. But there was only one tradition about the empty tomb. If the empty tomb story was relatively late in development, then the various appearances of Jesus to individuals—especially his appearance to Mary Magdalene—*predated* the Easter story of the empty tomb.

There are still problems with this theory, however. If the empty tomb tradition was late, why—in both *Mark* and *Peter*—do the women who come to the tomb run away in fear? Neither narrative gives any reason for the women's fear. And the fear existed in spite of the fact that the women were given good news: Jesus had risen!

Could it be that that these references to hysterical women—a tradition used by the authors of both *Mark* and *Peter*—were originally constructed in order to suppress a matriarchal resurrection tradition? And, could it be that the authors of Pseudo-Mark, *Matthew* and *John* were more sympathetic to an independent matriarchal tradition, and attempted to correct this false note in the myth of the empty tomb?

The text of *Peter* breaks off after just two more verses. The first verse informs us that "the twelve" were grieving over the death of Jesus, while the second states that Peter, Andrew and Levi were preparing to go fishing. The rest of Peter's Gospel is, unfortunately, lost to us.

As with Mark's Gospel, the all-important ending to the story is left to the reader's imagination. Most scholars assume that the original text of *Peter* must have included stories about the risen Jesus appearing to his disciples, but there is no way to substantiate this.

Why all these problems with the endings of the Gospels? The endings of two Gospels entirely disappeared, while the endings of the other Gospels show signs of being tampered with. What was the original conclusion of the Easter story that the later Church didn't want its readers to see? Unfortunately, we will probably never know the answer to that question.

MARY REPLACED

As time passed, the patriarchs of orthodoxy escalated their war against the historical tradition of Mary Magdalene by doing what Luke had done—alter the master story of the crucifixion and resurrection of Jesus in order to diminish the importance of Mary. Various apocryphal texts such as the *Epistula Apostolorum* rewrote the Christian myth of origin so that Mary appeared to be just one of several women—all of them equally ineffective. Finally, in an effort to find a "final solution" for the Mary problem, even more shameless Church fathers erased Mary Magdalene from the story altogether.

The Epistula Apostulorum

The *Epistula Apostolorum* contains a resurrection story, but it is essentially a dialogue between Jesus and his disciples that takes place after the resurrection. Most likely composed around the middle of the second century,[6] this "letter of the apostles" presents yet another version of the resurrection legend involving Mary Magdalene, and contains especially interesting changes and additions. There is both an Ethiopic and Coptic version of this work. Here, we will address the Ethiopic.

In this spin on the empty tomb tradition, it is Sarah, Martha and Mary Magdalene who come to the tomb and find it empty. Jesus then appears to the women, and tells them, "Let one of you go to your brothers and say, 'Come, our master has risen from the dead.'"[7] Mary is the first to go, but the male disciples dismiss her without cause: "What have we to do with you, O woman?"

Mary returns and tells Jesus that the men did not believe her, so Jesus sends Sarah with the same message and instructions. The male disciples are even more hostile to Sarah and accuse her of lying to them.

Sarah reports her lack of success to Jesus, so he decides that he will have to go to the men himself. Rather than going alone, however, Jesus takes the women with him on this third mission. This way there will be strength in numbers, and Jesus will be able to vindicate the women's witness and testimony by appearing with them in the same place at the same time.

Still the men refused to believe. They see Jesus, but they are certain that they are seeing a ghost. And if Jesus is a ghost, then he cannot be real. For this group of male disciples, the spiritual realm does not exist.

The Letter of the Apostles provides additional support for the hypothesis that a resurrection tradition involving women predated a patriarchal tradition.

By now, Jesus is altogether put out with these hardheaded, faithless men, and says to Peter, "I am your teacher whom you, Peter, denied three times before the cock crowed, and now do you deny me again?"

Ultimately, Jesus has to trick the men by telling them that what they are seeing is his flesh-and-blood body, not a ghost. Being materialists, the men finally believe in the resurrection.

It might appear that the author of this document is promoting belief in the physical resurrection of Jesus, but he is actually making the opposite point. He is criticizing those Christians who cannot believe in Jesus as spirit, and he is chiding those who don't even trust their own spiritual insight.

On the one hand, the author of the *Epistula* diminished Mary Magdalene's importance in the resurrection story by making her just one of several, seemingly ineffective, women. But—whether the author intended to do so or not—the *Letter of the Apostles* praises the women for their spiritual insight and honors them as apostles to the apostles. Here, too, the author pits Simon Peter against Mary Magdalene, and it is Mary—because of her faith—who once again proves to be the superior disciple.

The Acts of Philip

The fourth-century *Acts of Philip* features three central figures: Mary Magdalene, Philip, and Bartholomew. It is actually Mary Magdalene who emerges as the central figure in the second half of the text, and here she plays the same role as she does in *The Gospel of Mary* and the Manichean Psalms—as comforter, and as one who encourages the faith of others.[8] But Mary's abilities in this work far exceed her talent for calming the fears of other disciples.

Mary stands by the side of Jesus as he assigns apostolic missions to each of the male disciples. It is Mary who holds the register that lists the countries the disciples are to go. It is Mary who prepares the bread and salt and presides over the breaking of the bread.[9]

Jesus gives Mary Magdalene the task of traveling with Philip on his apostolic mission because he is weak while she is strong. Because of her inner strength, Mary is able to console and encourage Philip, and Jesus' trust in her is evidenced in his words: "I know that you are good and courageous and blessed among women."[10]

So far, so good. But three other versions of the document also exist, written in Coptic, Ethiopic, and Arabic. In these later reworkings of *The Acts of Philip*, Mary has been replaced by Peter! Peter is the companion of Philip. Peter is the one who stands by Jesus' side when the apostolates are allocated. And it is Peter who plays the role of teacher and comforter. [11]

MARY REPLACED IN OTHER ANCIENT TEXTS

The *Acta Thaddaei, Diatessaron, Quaestiones et responsiones ad Orthodoxos, Didascalia Apostolorum,* and the Coptic *Book of the Resurrection of Jesus Christ*

In the Greek text known as the *Acta Thaddaei*, it is Jesus' mother, Mary, who is first to receive an appearance of the risen Jesus. Not surprisingly, this same text is highly favorable to Peter—making him out as a bastion of faith and first among the apostles.[12]

In Ephrem's commentary on Tatian's *Diatessaron* (an early harmony of the four canonical Gospels), Mary Magdalene has once again been replaced by Mary, Jesus' mother. Ann Brock states that "Those texts that conflate the figure of Mary, the mother, with that of Mary Magdalene appear to be achieving a deliberate and systematic 'superimposition' of the Marys. Ephrem, for instance, represents Jesus' mother as taking the place of Mary Magdalene in the garden four times in his commentary. . ."[13]

Theodoret's *Quaestiones et responsiones ad Orthodoxos* retells the story from the *Gospel of John* in which Jesus tells Mary Magdalene not to touch him in his resurrected state. But in Theodoret's version of the story, Mary Magdalene is once again replaced by Mary, Jesus' mother. And in the *Didascalia Apostolorum*, as well as in homilies of the Church father, Chrysostom, Mary Magdalene is replaced with Jesus' mother and becomes, instead, "the other Mary."[14]

In a single ancient fragment written in Coptic and known as Revillout Fragment 14, Mary Magdalene is again replaced by Mary, the mother, at the scene of Jesus' resurrection. And it is Mary, the mother, who is commissioned to go and tell Jesus' brethren of his resurrection.[15]

In the Coptic *Book of the Resurrection of Jesus Christ* by Bartholomew the apostle, the author also substitutes Mary, the mother, for Mary Magdalene at the resurrection scene. It is Jesus' mother who asks the gardener if he has taken away the body of Jesus, and he replies to her: "Oh my sister, what is [the meaning of] the words you speak, O you holy virgin, the mother of the Christ?" The author also has the gardener—who is given the name, Philogenes—refer to Peter as the "the great interpreter of Jesus."[16]

It is no coincidence that in those texts where Mary Magdalene has been replaced with the mother of Jesus, Peter is also made the primary and faultless disciple of Jesus. I do not think that "conspiracy" is too strong a word to use in describing the later Church's concerted effort to undermine the tradition of Mary Magdalene and to obfuscate the true history of early Christianity.

In rewriting the master story, the authors of such texts as those discussed above were able to obscure the importance of Mary Magdalene, elevate Peter to the status of Jesus' primary disciple, and elevate a woman who was *not* a virgin—either before or after the birth of Jesus—to the status of perpetual virgin and mother of God.

IN SUMMARY:

- The author of the *Gospel According to Peter* removed women as witnesses to the crucifixion.

- A common crucifixion/resurrection tradition lies behind all Gospel accounts and ends with the empty tomb. Stories about Jesus appearing to his disciples came from separate traditions.

- In the *Epistula Apostolorum's* account of the resurrection, Jesus appeared to his female disciples first, while the male disciples refused to believe in the validity of the women's experience. They rejected, as well, *their own* visionary experiences of the risen Jesus.

- Mary Magdalene's superiority as a disciple is once again confirmed by her ready acceptance of Jesus' *spiritual* resurrection. Simon Peter is portrayed as an adversary, and as a materialist who rejected the reality of the spiritual realm.

- Many authors of early apocryphal literature reworked the canonical crucifixion/resurrection legend in order to diminish the role played by Mary Magdalene. Other authors went even further by writing her out of the story altogether.

XIV. The Matriarchal Tradition

With the single exception of the apostle, Paul, virtually all other resurrection traditions have a single common denominator: Mary Magdalene. The major texts we have examined all make it clear that Mary's historical tradition stood at the very center of early Christian faith.

We cannot know just what Mary Magdalene experienced after the death of Jesus, but it would appear that her experience had a profound effect on other followers of Jesus. To one degree or another, the evangelists who wrote the canonical Gospels attempted to deemphasize this fact. Paul entirely ignored it. And the later patriarchs of the Church denied it altogether. Still, the fact remains: the experience of Mary Magdalene—whatever the nature of that experience—provided the major catalyst for the Christian claim that Jesus continued to live on after his crucifixion.

If this much is true, then the following may be true as well: The resurrection stories about Jesus began as a matriarchal tradition, and all subsequent traditions—those that included men—were founded on an overwhelming influence of that tradition. Mary's story, after all, is not embedded within the various patriarchal resurrection traditions. Mary's story stands alone and, in placement, always precedes other stories.

If this were the case, historically, then the commissioning stories involving Mary Magdalene probably have no literal historical basis. Those stories were probably nothing more than a narrative device used by Mark (and copied by Matthew, Luke and John) to connect an early, entirely independent, matriarchal resurrection tradition with a variety of later resurrection traditions involving men.

Since none of the Gospels connect Mary Magdalene with Simon Peter or, for that matter, any of the male disciples (none of the canonical Gospels include any dialog between Mary and other disciples) there is no necessary reason to believe that Mary Magdalene was ever part of the same group of disciples that included Simon Peter. Rather, much of the evidence points in the opposite direction.

There is no evidence in the "sayings"-source Gospels (*Q* and *Thomas*) to suggest that Jesus' earliest followers gave any theological meaning to his crucifixion, much less to rumors that he had appeared to a woman known as Mary Magdalene after his death. It was Paul—the self-appointed apostle of Christ who rejected the historical Jesus and his teachings—who imbued those events with meaning, inventing Christianity in the process.

If Simon Peter had originally been part of a Q community—which certainly seems possible—then his reputation for having denied Jesus may have been based on his early disbelief of Mary Magdalene's Easter experience (whether or not he ever came into physical contact with Mary herself). Whatever Peter eventually came to believe about the resurrection of Jesus must have been quite different from what Mary Magdalene believed, and this led to conflict between the followers of Peter and the followers of Mary. As Karen King points out, "The competition between Peter and Mary . . . had its roots in the pre-Pauline and pre-gospel tradition."[1]

Is it possible that Mary Magdalene and Simon Peter were never members of the same group of disciples? At the time of Jesus' crucifixion, the author of Mark's master story admits that there were two different groups of disciples, each residing in two widely separated locales. One group of disciples was made up of women, and this group was in Jerusalem. These women witnessed the crucifixion of Jesus, and one or more members of the group had a religious experience of a living Jesus after he was dead. A second group of disciples, consisting mostly of men, were in hiding in Galilee, and they remained there for an undetermined period of time.

Among the first group of disciples, one woman—Mary Magdalene—had some kind of extraordinary religious experience that convinced her that the crucifixion was not the end of Jesus. Her experience, perhaps, included a vision of heavenly beings. It may also have included a vivid apparition of Jesus in a spiritual body. Whatever Mary Magdalene's experience was, it was so real, and so strange, and so wonderful, and so impossible, and so insane, and so glorious and so confusing that in the beginning, Mary was reluctant to talk about it with anyone outside of her own circle of female friends. At some point, however, Mary's heart became so full with joy in the knowledge that her rabbi was alive—in spite of the fact that he was dead—that she began to proclaim from the rooftops what she now believed was true.

Meanwhile, the group of disciples in Galilee was trying to live with the shame of having deserted their teacher in his greatest hour of need. When Jesus did not return to Galilee himself, this group of disciples assumed—correctly—that he had been executed. All that was left for these men to do now was to grieve the death of their teacher and live with their own guilt.

Now we come to the critical juncture as far as the sequence of historical events is concerned. If Mary Magdalene and other female disciples of Jesus actually were part of the Galilean community—as the master story insists—it is at this point (after an indeterminate period of time) that they returned home to inform the men of their experiences in Jerusalem. Or, if the women following Mary Magdalene represented a different group of disciples who were, perhaps, based in Jerusalem—rumors of Mary's experiences reached the ears of the men in Galilee—and most especially the ears of Simon Peter. In either scenario, the Galilean disciples probably did not put much stock in the testimony of "hysterical" women. The men

> *Most scholars seriously doubt that there ever was a special group of twelve male disciples which followed Jesus everywhere he went.*

did not have any extraordinary experiences of a risen Jesus themselves, so whatever the women experienced, it all seemed meaningless to them at the time.

Most scholars seriously doubt that there ever was a special group of twelve male disciples which followed Jesus everywhere he went. Certainly some of Jesus' disciples became itinerants and did follow Jesus from town to town. But other disciples, like Lazarus and his sisters Mary and Martha, were householders; and these disciples came out to hear Jesus only when he was in their area.

Which sort of disciple was Mary Magdalene? Since it was uncommon for a woman to physically follow an itinerant rabbi around the countryside, the statistical odds are in favor of Mary being a householder, not an itinerant. But with no evidence to guide us in either direction, we must leave this an open question.

What is true, however, is that while there is no historical evidence to suggest that Mary Magdalene and other women ever made a journey to Galilee after Jesus' crucifixion, there *is* historical evidence that confirms that *the male disciples returned to Jerusalem*!

Paul's letter to the Galatians tells us that Peter and John, along with Jesus' brother James (who had not been a disciple during Jesus' lifetime), were the leaders of a firmly established Jesus community in Jerusalem—founded sometime during the years that followed Jesus' crucifixion. We have to wonder why—if Jesus' main ministry had been in Galilee, and if his main disciples were native Galileans and had homes and families in Galilee—they did not remain in Galilee. Why did these men desert the Galilean mission and return to the scene of the crime?

These former disciples of Jesus did not just return to Jerusalem for a visit. They set up a permanent mission there. And while we don't know just when they did this, it must have been after a considerable length of time because, early on, they still had reason to fear for their own lives.

Unfortunately, none of this evidence suggests a motive for establishing the first "church" in Jerusalem.

Perhaps the Jesus people set up a mission in Jerusalem simply because that city was the center of Israel's religious life. But is it possible that Peter and John returned to Jerusalem in order to confirm or deny reports about the crucified Jesus appearing to a woman called Mary Magdalene? Certainly these men did not have any visions of a risen Jesus until they did, in fact, come in contact with Mary; and both Luke and John's Gospels claim that they had their visions in Jerusalem, not in Galilee.

If there were, in fact, at least two different groups of Jesus people, and they both had separate resurrection traditions about Jesus, this would certainly have presented a problem for the author of the first narrative Gospel (*Mark*) who was, we must remember, a Hellenistic Christian writing from Rome, and not a member of the Jesus movement. His challenge was to establish a "Christian," patriarchal resurrection tradition without ignoring the matriarchal tradition that was popular common lore. He met this challenge by making Mary Magdalene a Galilean disciple, and by inventing a commissioning story in which Mary Magdalene was tasked with informing the Galilean disciples of her Easter experience.

This entire scenario is a radical proposition, certainly. And it is a hypothesis, not a demonstrable fact. But I do not think that we can automatically assume that a specific female disciple—Mary Magdalene—initiated contact with Simon Peter in Galilee sometime after Jesus' crucifixion. *The Gospel of Mark*, we must remember, ended without Mary Magdalene and the other women reporting anything to anyone.

Matthew's Gospel claims that Mary and the other women were instructed to go tell the other disciples, but Matthew failed to invent a story in which they actually did so. Only the later Gospels of *Luke* and *John* have stories in which the women made contact, and this leads one to suspect that these authors were "correcting" earlier Gospels. One of these stories, in fact, is not original to the Gospel, but is an interpolation!

In the *Gospel of John*, there are not one, but two instances in which Mary Magdalene tells her story to other disciples (20:2-10 and 20:18).

One story is not original to *John*. It was artificially inserted into John's narrative by a later redactor.[2]

Scholars have noted that there are two seams in this story: one between verses 1 and 2; and one between verses 10 and 11. In the following example, the original text is indicated in bold face, and the interpolation in italics:

> 1 **Now on the first day of the week Mary Magdalene came to the tomb early, while it was still dark, and saw that the stone had been taken away from the tomb.** 2 *So she ran, and went to Simon Peter and the other disciple, the one who Jesus loved, and said to them, "They have taken the Lord out of the tomb, and we do not know where they have laid him." 3 Peter then* came out with the other disciple, and they went toward the tomb. *4 They both ran, but the other disciple outran Peter and reached the tomb first; 5 And stooping to look in, he saw the linen cloths lying there, but he did not go in. 6 Then Simon Peter came, following him, and went into the tomb; he saw the linen cloths lying, 7 and the napkin, which had been on his head, not lying with the linen cloths but rolled up in a place by itself. 8 Then the other disciple, who reached the tomb first, also went in, and he saw and believed; 9 for as yet they did not know the scripture, that he must rise from the dead. 10 Then the disciples went back to their homes.* 11 **But Mary stood weeping outside the tomb, and as she wept she stooped to look into the tomb; and she saw two angels in white ...**

If we remove verses 2-10, then the story reads smoothly:

> Now on the first day of the week Mary Magdalene came to the tomb early, while it was still dark, and saw that the stone had been taken away from the tomb. Mary stood weeping outside the tomb, and as she wept she stooped to look into the tomb; and she saw two angels in white ...

So there is just one instance in John's original Gospel where Mary speaks to other disciples, and it is the conclusion of the original story about Mary that begins at 20:1 and ends at 20:18 (without verses 2-10). Mary makes a simple statement of faith: "Mary Magdalene went and said to the disciples 'I have seen the lord'." Here, Peter is not mentioned, and the "eleven" are not mentioned. Neither are the disciples who heard Mary's statement of faith named or identified by gender, or by place. There is, in other words, no reason to suppose that Mary communicated with Peter or with the Galilean disciples or, for that matter, with men.

In the end, only Luke's Gospel insists that Mary Magdalene (and two other women) actually made contact with "the eleven." And yet Luke dismisses the meeting as unproductive and irrelevant. The male disciples did not believe the women, so there was no point to their interaction.

Luke had to admit that the "core" group of disciples who had followed Jesus did not immediately adopt a faith in his resurrection. But while this was (or should have been) an embarrassing admission for a Christian, it allowed Luke to sever all connections between the matriarchal and patriarchal resurrection traditions. It allowed him to put to rest, once and for all, all implications that women had inspired the faith of men.

There is...no reason to suppose that Mary communicated with Peter or with the Galilean disciples or, for that matter, with men.

In 24:34, Luke attributes Mary's statement of faith in John's Gospel ("I have seen the Lord") to Peter: "The Lord is risen indeed and has appeared to Simon!" Luke successfully erased Mary as first witness of the resurrection, erased her statement of faith, transferred a matriarchal resurrection tradition to the patriarchs, and burnished Peter's tarnished reputation as someone who had denied Jesus by making him the first disciple to witness his teacher's resurrection. It took Luke to finally write a Gospel that was politically correct for the new Christian age of the second century. The original matriarchal tradition of Mary Magdalene soon ceased to exist—as did women's influence in the Church.

ECHOES OF MARY'S TRADITION

Earlier I raised the possibility that a "community" of Mary may once have existed. But since we had no direct evidence for such a community, I also pointed out that there was little more that could be said about the subject. Since I wrote those words, however, new research has come to my attention, and this additional information allows us to revisit this subject.

Up until this point I have said little about another early Christian work that was discovered during the nineteenth century. *The Training of the Lord Through the Twelve Disciples*—better known as the *Didache*—came to light in 1873, in Istanbul, and is a training manual for converts to an early Jesus community. While the theology of the Didache might be labeled "Christian," it seems to have very little in common with the theology of Paul's early Christ cult. Those who trained novices in the Way of Life had little interest in a theology about Jesus and were more concerned with practical holiness and the faith *of* Jesus.[3]

Like the first layer of *The Gospel of Q* and *The Gospel of Thomas*, the *Didache* is entirely silent on the issue of Jesus dying for our sins, is disinterested in theology about Jesus' resurrection and ascension into heaven, and does not elevate Jesus to the status of son of God—much less THE Son of God.[4]

While these "non-Christian" elements of the *Didache* in themselves suggest an early date of composition, until recently most scholars considered the *Didache* to be a work of the second century. In a recently published work,[5] however, Aaron Milavec—a scholar who has worked on this text for many years—argues persuasively for a date around the middle of the *first* century.

If the *Didache* is, in fact, an early work, then it provides us with important information about one of the very first Jesus communities. What is of special interest to us is the *Didache*'s position on women as community teachers and leaders. Like Gnostic Christians, the *Didache* communities—at the very least—trained women and supported women as mentors of other women. And these women taught on the same terms as men did—in direct contrast with Paul's churches. Milavec states:

> When women are not trained in Torah, it follows that they must rely on what their fathers, their brothers, and their husbands tell them about it. In effect, they must then be admonished to "be obedient" to their men since they have no skill in discernment within themselves. In the *Didache* communities, the textual evidence shows that the Way of Life addressed both the issues of women and the issues of men and that a gender-inclusive language was used throughout. In such a community, as in the case of many elective gentile associations, women were called on not only to train other women but also to correct backsliders (no matter what their sex or rank), to lead daily prayers, to offer first fruits, to prophesy, and even to officiate at the Eucharistic meals. Female novices, accordingly, came to honor their spiritual mothers 'as the Lord'.[6]

If early Jesus communities were egalitarian in nature, then it is highly likely that at least some of Jesus' own groups of disciples treated women as equals. Given this knowledge, it is certainly not hard to imagine Mary Magdalene as a teacher and leader—either within a *Didache* community—or within a community of her own.

In *The Resurrection of Mary Magdalene*, Jane Schaberg goes so far as to suggest that there may have been a "Magdalene Christianity," just as there was a Pauline, Thomasine, Johannine, and Petrine Christianity:

> If we can brave our ways (sic) through the charge of 'sheer fantasy!,' and the anger of professors jabbing pens on paper, we may come to know more about the role of women in apocalyptic and mystical groups. Even if we are not able to locate its center(s), we will be able to imagine more clearly a Magdalene group or groups continuing to exist and create, on

the basis of wo/men's insight, revelation, and leadership. Examination of the rivalry posed by Petrine (and perhaps James) traditions will give us a fuller picture of the struggle of and for early Christian egalitarianism.[7]

Still, Schaberg recognizes that the patriarchal enclaves of academia will continue to resist evidence that suggests that women were important founders of the Christian tradition. In this regard, the present situation is not altogether unlike the one faced by those who followed Mary Magdalene during the first and second centuries: "I see Magdalene Christianity as disconcerting, demanding, and horribly vulnerable. It attempted the impossible. It represented wo/men's empowering speech, and sanity."[8]

IN SUMMARY:

♦ There is no evidence in the earliest Gospels (*Q* and *Thomas*) to suggest that the disciples of the historical Jesus gave any theological significance to the final events in his life and death. The crucifixion of Jesus, and his alleged resurrection (common themes of those mystery religions that featured dying and resurrected god/men), were symbolic cosmic events important only to the early Hellenistic Christ cults which co-opted the historical Jesus for their own theological purposes.

♦ There is insufficient evidence in the canonical Gospels to support the Christian thesis that Mary Magdalene and Simon Peter belonged to the same group of Jesus people. Likewise, there is insufficient evidence to support the claim that Mary Magdalene made contact with the Galilean disciples of Jesus after his death.

♦ A foundational matriarchal resurrection tradition existed independently from all other such traditions, and was associated with Mary Magdalene and other women disciples of Jesus. This tradition was systematically eliminated from the Christian mythos by revisionist "historians," such as the author of *The Gospel According to Luke.*

Conclusion

THE VIRGIN MARY: MARY OF NAZARETH OR MARY OF MAGDALA?

As orthodox Christianity gradually evolved into the Roman Catholic Church, it eventually recognized that, in eradicating the divine feminine from its theology, it had lost a certain amount of leverage over women in the Church by denying them a feminine object of devotion. But the only woman historically prominent enough and worthy enough to become such an object—Mary Magdalene—was far too dangerous a figure to consider. The patriarchs, instead, chose a woman who had played only a marginal role in the ministry of Jesus: his mother. In *Born of a Woman*, former Anglican bishop, John Shelby Spong, points out that,

> … when placed beside Mary Magdalene, Mary the mother of Jesus is a pale, shadowy figure in the Gospel accounts. But in time this early record was countered and the woman who appeared to have been at Jesus' side during his earthly life was removed…Real feminine power was suppressed, and a woman who was manageable took that place in the tradition.[1]

249

In order to create a semi-divine figure in the person of Jesus' mother—and attract women away from other mystery religions in which godmen were often born of virgins[2]—the Church made Mary of Nazareth a perpetual and immaculate virgin. Certainly this sleight of hand by the early Church was one of its more dazzling acts of misdirection given the fact that the Gospel record makes it very clear that Jesus' mother was most certainly *not* a virgin. Jesus himself, it seems, was conceived out of wedlock, and his mother went on to produce a clan of siblings—again apparently without benefit of a husband.[3]

In reality, it was Mary Magdalene, not Jesus' mother, who was viewed as a virgin by many early Christians. In *Dialogue of the Savior*, for instance, Jesus explains to Mary Magdalene that all those who come from truth do not die, while all those born of women do. In other words, everything in the material universe has a beginning and an end—while the non-material spirit is eternal.

In order to create a semi-divine figure in the person of Jesus' mother...the Church made Mary of Nazareth a perpetual and immaculate virgin.

Mary Magdalene then asks the Savior why she, specifically, has come to this place (the material world), and Jesus states, "You have come to reveal the greatness of the revealer." Ann Brock points out here that Jesus is making it clear that Mary's purpose in life is not to procreate—because whatever comes from procreation dies. Mary's purpose, like the purpose of Jesus himself, is to reveal spiritual truth to others.[4]

This was certainly not the message the Church wanted to convey, so it found it necessary to have Mary of Magdala and Mary of Nazareth trade places. The non-virgin Mary was transformed into the the virginal mother of God, while the real virgin Mary was reinvented as a whore.

Since many early Christians thought of Mary Magdalene as Jesus' spiritual consort—as well as an incarnation of Sophia, or divine Wisdom—Mary of Magdala could easily have evolved into a Christian Goddess figure. With the reinvented Mary of Nazareth, however, there was no danger that the mother of God would ever become God the Mother.[5]

THE MARY OF HISTORY

As we come to the end of Mary's story, we have occasion to reflect upon what we have gained by taking this intellectual and spiritual journey. We began with a simple question: Who was this woman from Magdala? We have learned that, if nothing else, there are no simple or absolute answers.

While we may never know just who the historical Mary Magdalene was, we do know who she was not. She was not a prostitute. She was not a penitent sinner. She was probably never possessed by "demons," psychological or otherwise.

At a minimum we do know that the historical Mary was a prominent disciple of Jesus. She remained faithfully by his side to the very end, witnessing his crucifixion. She had a profound experience of a "living" Jesus after his death, and her experience ultimately convinced other disciples that her experience was valid.

If Mary was part of an entourage of disciples who followed Jesus from town to town, then Mary had taken up the itinerant life along with Jesus. If Mary followed Jesus' teachings—and all indications are that she did—she was probably celibate like Jesus as well.

The multiple attestations to Mary in ancient texts, and the prominence of her tradition in early Christianity, further suggests that Mary Magdalene was considered an apostle and a holy woman by nearly all early Christians. Many Christians also saw her as a teacher, a leader and a visionary.

It seems likely that a community was founded in Mary's name, and that it emphasized the teachings of Jesus rather than theology about him. This brought her tradition into conflict with other Christian movements which were based around men like Simon Peter and Paul.

The importance of Mary Magdalene as a standard bearer for women's liberation during the early years of Christianity should also not be over-looked. The Gospel written in Mary's name clearly contains women's theology and further supports the liberation theology of the Corinthian women prophets.[6]

The Mary who appears in the Gospel attributed to her was solidly based on canonical tradition.[7] This tradition represented her as "an exemplary disciple, a witness to the ministry of Jesus, a visionary of the glorified Jesus, and someone traditionally in contest with Peter," all of which "made her the only figure who could play all the roles required to convey the message and meaning of the Gospel of Mary."[8]

MARY "THE GREAT"?

In referring to Mary, the trend today among scholars and lay persons alike is to call her "Mary of Magdala" rather than "Mary Magdalene." Conventional wisdom considers "Magdalene" to mean "the one who is from Magdala," so the contemporary appellation "of Magdala" seems less awkward than "Mary, the one who is from Magdala."

But there is a problem with this name. No one has ever been able to identify a town (supposedly on the shores of the Sea of Galilee) called Magdala.[9] The Jewish historian, Josephus—a native of Galilee—never mentions a town of Magdala in any of his writings. The name does not appear in any Hebrew scriptures, nor is it mentioned in the New Testament itself. Just as "Jesus, the Nazarene" does *not* mean "Jesus of Nazareth," "Magdalene," too, may refer to something other than Mary's hometown.

At least one scholar has suggested that the author of Mark's Gospel created the name from the Hebrew word, "magdal," which means "large" or "great."[10] Just as Mohandas Karamchand Gandhi was commonly referred to as Mahatma ("great soul") Gandhi, Mary may have been known far and wide as "Mary the Great." After all that we have learned about Mary Magdalene, such an honorary appellation would seem more than fitting.

THE BELOVED DISCIPLE—
MARY AS JESUS' SUCCESSOR

Jane Schaberg in *The Resurrection of Mary Magdalene* makes a strong case for the possibility that Mary Magdalene was considered Jesus' successor (or, at the very least, *a* successor) by members of the early Johannine community. Although Mary's succession tradition was obscured in the *Gospel of John* (either by the author, or by a later redactor), Schaberg believes that clues to this tradition still exist in John's placement of women at the foot of Jesus' cross (19:25-27), and in the story of the risen Jesus commissioning Mary as the first apostle (20:17-18).

As I did earlier in chapter XII, Schaberg questions the identity of the "disciple whom Jesus loved." Like me, Schaberg is troubled by the mathematics of *John's* crucifixion scene. Schaberg—and others before her—argue that a male witness is not indicated in this passage. In other words, the Beloved Disciple was not standing *next* to the women at the cross, the "disciple whom Jesus loved" *was* one of the women—and that woman was most likely Mary Magdalene. By hinting at an unidentified male presence, however, the evangelist who wrote *John* attempted to obscure the identity of this figure.[11]

As the reader will recall, in John's version of the crucifixion scene, Jesus puts the future care and keeping of his mother into the hands of the Beloved Disciple. Schaberg believes that this is a veiled reference to Jesus transferring his authority to this disciple. Even though the scene is mythological, it indicates that members of the Johannine community considered its founder to have been the rightful heir to Jesus.

If Mary was the Beloved Disciple, then Mary—not the disciple, John—could have been the founder of the Johannine community. And for this reason, or so the argument goes, the evangelist who wrote the Gospel attributed to John, tried to obscure the true identity of "the disciple whom Jesus loved."

There are all manner of problems associated with this hypothesis, but it is a provocative enough theory to deserve serious attention. Schaber warns, however, that we cannot be too literal here. She points out that the "disciple whom Jesus loved" was both a literary device and a paradigm suggesting the "ideal disciple" of the Johannine community. Mary may have been seen as *one* of those ideal disciples—but there were, perhaps, others.[12]

Still, the parallels between the tradition of the Beloved Disciple and the tradition of Mary Magdalene are striking. As far as the early Johannine community was concerned, the Beloved Disciple was an apostle above all others. He (or she) was the disciple Jesus especially favored, and the one to whom he passed on his teaching tradition—a viewpoint shared by the author of *The Gospel of Mary*.

John's Gospel is very favorable to Mary Magdalene while, at the same time, Peter is subordinated to the Beloved Disciple throughout the text. This suggests that the Johannine tradition was in conflict with the Petrine tradition—just as Mary Magdalene's tradition was.

Additionally *The Gospel of Mary* contains all of the basic elements of *John's* Easter story. In the (surviving) opening scene of *The Gospel of Mary*, the action takes place between the time Jesus was resurrected and the time he ascended into heaven. Mary then has a vision of Jesus in this ascended state. She conveys the meaning of that vision to the other disciples, and attempts to convince the men (especially Peter) of the validity of her vision.

Certainly it seems possible that at some early point, the Johannine and Marian traditions were one and the same. If they were, then Mary was certainly a founder—or *the* founder—of the community, and her followers would have seen her as both the Beloved Disciple, and the rightful heir to Jesus' wisdom tradition.

As we discussed previously, the Johannine community split apart at some point around the end of the first century. One group aligned itself with the orthodox Church, the other with Gnostic Christianity. It would not take a great deal of the imagination to suppose that the "sectarians" who split off from the Johannine community were Marian Christians, and were ultimately responsible for writing *The Gospel According to*

Mary in order to preserve her tradition.

According to Schaberg, the second indicator that some Johannine Christians saw Mary Magdalene as Jesus' successor can be found in *John's* commissioning story (20:17-18). When Jesus appears to Mary Magdalene after his crucifixion, he tells Mary that because he is in the process of "ascending to my Father and your Father, to my God and your God" he will be making no other appearances. Mary is the only disciple who will ever see him in his resurrected state, and because of this it will be entirely up to her to convince Jesus' "brethren" that he has risen and returned to the place from whence he came.

The male disciples cannot come to Easter faith unless Mary herself creates that faith within them. *The responsibility for the survival of Jesus' tradition is placed squarely on the shoulders of Mary Magdalene.* The male disciples have no such responsibility. Schaberg states:

> Note that the commission of Mary Magdalene here does not contain a promise that the disciples will see the risen Jesus. In fact, she is just to inform them that he is going. If the text is read on its own, apart from the subsequent Johannine scenes, it is clear that they will not see him, 'but are only relayed Jesus' farewell.' Her role then, is not a preliminary or transitional one. In any work that may have ended with this scene, Mary Magdalene would be the only guarantor of the vindication of Jesus, and this is the final message. That message implicitly says who she is, as well who they are as 'brothers'; it does not empower them for a worldwide mission.[13]

But how important, historically, is John's commissioning story in relationship to those promoted by the authors of Mark's and Matthew's Gospels? In my opinion, John's story—or at least the form of the story that stands behind it—comes closest to the original Marian resurrection legend. As far as Matthew's Gospel is concerned, Schaberg concurs, as does C.F. Dodd. Schaberg states, "He (Dodd) judges—as I do—the Johannine appearance to Mary Magdalene better preserved than the shorter Matthean appearance to the women."[14] As to Mark—or at least to Pseudo-Mark—Schaberg suggests that this author may not have known about the tradition used by John. At the same time, she is careful to point out that it is equally possible that the author of *John* turned a simple visionary story into a succession narrative.[15]

In the end, the succession tradition of Mary Magdalene—or, as Schaberg has it, Magdalene Christianity—could not survive within the patriarchal framework of the patriarchal branch of Christianity which produced the canonical Gospels.

TOWARD A NEW MYTHOLOGY OF MARY

We have learned that the image of Mary Magdalene as penitent sinner was not based on historical reality. I have argued, similarly, that there is no historical evidence to support the notion that Jesus and Mary had a romantic relationship. Such images of Mary Magdalene were, and are, used (intentionally or unintentionally) to obscure Mary's true importance to the foundation of Christianity. Such images also continue to support the subordination of women—the patriarchal desire that women should remain "in their place."

Even the popular contemporary belief (based on another falsehood produced by the author of *Luke*) that Mary and other women were financial backers of Jesus' mission subordinates women and subverts Jesus' egalitarian message. Women may be supporters by nature, but that does not define who they are.

We tend to make the best of myths that are handed down to us, however. The mythology of Mary Magdalene as a penitent sinner, while historically inaccurate, was at least useful to Christian women who lived in pre-Enlightenment times. The image of Mary as a penitent inspired Christian women for centuries, offering hope (and, in their minds, salvation) to those who led less than perfect lives.

In modern times, it seems to be useful for some people to think of

Jesus and Mary as lovers. For many, such a belief humanizes these historical figures and makes them more accessible. Even those who believe that Mary provided monetary backing for Jesus' ministry are encouraged by the thought of her financial independence as a woman.

All of these myths can be given a useful spin. But they do not represent history, and they are often debilitating as well. Without the Church's specter of the "sin of Eve" hanging over the heads of today's enlightened women, the penitent Mary is no longer a useful role model. The image of Mary as wife and mother—not that there is anything wrong with those roles—does nothing to support the hopes and dreams of contemporary women who refuse to think of themselves any longer as "weak vessels."

If Mary Magdalene is to be mythologized—as she always will be—why not imagine her to be the person early Christians believed her to be? By their accounts, she was a woman of great strength, indomitable courage, unshakable faith, and unending compassion. She was a teacher of wisdom, a spiritual athlete, and a visionary. She was, and is, a woman who is truly worthy of respect and reverence.

Mary Magdalene's true value as a woman, and as a human being, cannot be measured only by her devotional relationship to Jesus, either. One may appreciate Mary for being a model disciple, but her memory is best served by thinking of her as a disciple who ultimately became a master herself.

Rather than thinking of Mary as sitting at Jesus' feet, and instead of imagining Jesus and Mary hand in hand, it seems far more useful—and accurate—to think of this man and this woman standing side by side. Side by side, but not too close together—"For the pillars of the temple stand apart, and the oak tree and the cypress grow not in each other's shadow."[16]

THE THEOLOGY OF MARY AND THE CHURCH'S "FINAL SOLUTION"

The theology associated with Mary Magdalene can be summed up as follows: The resurrection of Jesus was a spiritual, not physical, event. The resurrection of Christians in Christ is a present, not future, reality. The body is not the true self, and the individual soul is immortal, since it is part of the All. There is no such thing as original sin, and the true God did not condemn humanity for breaking *His* laws. Rather, ignorance is the root of all evil and leads to the death of the spirit.

Jesus was Christ and Savior, not because he saved humanity from sin, but because he came to dispel human ignorance. Salvation is attained by gaining gnosis, or knowledge of the true divinity of the Self, and by overcoming attachment to the cravings of the flesh and the temptations of the material world. Finally, the kingdom of God is not the rule of God on earth yet to come. The kingdom is a state of consciousness—the ability to see God in all beings and in every aspect of life.

In challenging such theological principals—all common to Eastern philosophy—early Church fathers such as Irenaeus called those who believed such things "absolutely foolish and stupid people." The believers, in turn, maintained that Irenaeus could not recognize such teachings as being true because he had not advanced beyond a naïve level of spiritual understanding.[17]

Save for a single historical event, Christians might still be debating these issues today. But this was not to be. On October 28, 312 C. E., the new Roman emperor, Constantine, had a dream in which he saw the cross of Christ leading his Roman legions to victory over all those in the empire who challenged his authority and the unity of the empire. Constantine converted to Christianity, but it was Christianity in the orthodox mold.

The Roman emperor ended the centuries-long persecution of Christians, but only against those Christians who accepted the theology of the Catholic Church. In 324 C.E., Constantine ordered all heretics and schismatics to stop meeting—even if they met in private homes—and demanded that they surrender their churches and property to the Catholic Church.[18]

The emperor's Christian revolution was, at the same time, anti-Semitic. Constantine abridged the legal rights of Jews, and even forbade them from entering Jerusalem—save for the one day each year on which they mourned the loss of their holy city. He further ordered that Jews were not to seek or accept converts to Judaism, and "prescribed that any Jew who attempted forcibly to prevent conversion from Judaism to Christianity should be burned alive."[19]

As a result of Constantine's war on heretics and schismatics, the theology of Christians such as those who read the *Gospel According to Mary* was obliterated from Christianity for all time. Feminine power within the Christian faith was finally and thoroughly suppressed. The feminine understanding of God was condemned as heresy. And the God of Christianity, along with its clergy, became exclusively male.

The Church Universal in the East followed the same course. When his third rival was lynched in 361 C.E., Athanasius became Bishop of Alexandria for the third and last time, and immediately set about consolidating his power and establishing his authority over "holy men" such as those monks who lived in monasteries founded by Pachomius.

In 367 C.E., Athanasius wrote an Easter letter that mandated a Christian canon that determined the twenty-seven books of the New Testament. All of the churches under his control were to henceforth cleanse themselves of all "apocryphal books" which were "empty and polluted."[20]

One of the monks who read Athanasius' letter in his monastery near Nag Hammadi decided to defy the Bishop's order. Removing more than fifty books from the monastery library, he hid them in a jar and buried them in the hot Egyptian soil near the cliff where Muhammad 'Ali would find them sixteen-hundred years later.[21]

Endnotes

PREFACE

1 A favorite designation used by Jesus to refer to Mary Magdalene in the fourth century text, *Pistis Sophia*.

2 Quoted in Jean Doresse, *The Secret Books of the Egyptian Gnostics*, MJF Books, New York, 1958, first English edition published by Inner Traditions International, 1986, p. 42.

3 His complete title in logion 1 of *The Gospel of Thomas* is Didymus Judas Thomas. Only Judas is a proper name; Didymus means "twin" in Greek, and Thomas is the word for "twin" in Aramaic. Judas (not Iscariot) was the disciple, Thomas, of Gospel tradition. The "twin" reference implies that Thomas was the (spiritual) twin of Jesus. A number of early works were attributed to this disciple, including the *Gospel of Thomas, Thomas the Contender*, and the *Acts of Thomas*. *The Gospel according to Thomas* is now considered by most scholars as the "fifth" Gospel because it contains sayings that can be traced to the historical Jesus, but which are not found in any of the canonical Gospels of the New Testament.

4 Coptic, as a written language, was strictly limited to Egyptian Christian usage, and was generally used to translate documents originally written in Greek.

5 The modern book was actually the invention of early Christians, and virtually all early Christian manuscripts were in the form of codices, not scrolls.

6 Sansnos is identified in Codex VII as a monk who was in charge of the monastery cattle. He was probably responsible for the creation of the leather cover of this codex.

7 Most scholars would agree that the codices of the *Nag Hammadi Library* were probably buried in haste in order to preserve them from being destroyed during Constantine's purge of "heretics" during the fourth century C.E.

8 Dr. Carl Reinhardt, who purchased what is now known as the Berlin Codex, and which contained *The Gospel According to Mary*, speculated that the antiquities dealer who sold him the manuscripts had originally acquired them from someone who had plundered the gravesites of Achmim.

9 Based on Robinson's Introduction to *The Nag Hammadi Library in English*, see 10 below, pp. 19—22.

10 This narrative is based on Karen L. King's reconstruction of events in *The Gospel of Mary of Magdala*, Santa Rosa, California, Polebridge Press, 2003, pp 7—12.

11 James M. Robinson, General Editor, *The Apocryphon of John, The Nag Hammadi Library in English*, revised, first paperback edition, New York, HarperCollins, 1990, p. 123. The dramatization is based on Robinson's Introduction, pp. 7—24, and on John Dart and Ray Reigert's, Unearthing the Lost Words of Jesus, Berkeley, Seastone / Ulysses Press, 1993, pp. 3—9.

THE CRUCIFIXION OF MARY MAGDALENE

INTRODUCTION

[1] *The Random House College Dictionary*, New York, Random House, 1980 edition, p 628.

[2] *Luke* 7:37; and Robert W. Funk and the Jesus Seminar, *The Acts of Jesus*, New York, HarperCollins, 1998, p. 477.

[3] In the Gospels of *Matthew* and *John*, as well as in Pseudo-Mark (the redacted ending of the Gospel of Mark).

[4] See Chapter II, "The Suppressed Tradition: Mary as Apostola Apostolorum."

[5] Quoted by Susan Haskins in *Mary Magdalene in Myth and Metaphor*, New York, Berkeley Publishing Group, 1993, p. 385.

[6] Ibid.

[7] Ibid, p. 12.

[8] Hans Jonas, *The Gnostic Religion*, Second Edition, Boston, Beacon Hill, 1958.

[9] Haskins, p. 11.

[10] With the exception of the *Gospel of John* in which "the disciple whom Jesus loved", presumed to be a man, was also present.

[11] The *Pistis Sophia*

[12] *The Gospel of Mary*

[13] *The Gospel of Philip*

[14] *Dialogue of the Savior*

[15] Quoted in *Time magazine*, December 22, 2003, p. 61.

[16] Gerd Lüdemann, *Heretics*, Kentucky, first American edition, Westminster John Knox Press, 1996, p. 219.

[17] King, *The Gospel According to Mary of Magdala*, p. 62.

[18] *The Gospel According to Mary*, King translation of BG 8502, 9:28-29.

[19] *The Gospel of Eve*, quoted in Doresse, p. 42.

[20] *The Gospel According to Thomas*, Logion 77.

CHAPTER ONE

[1] Simon Magus, or Simon the Magician, is mentioned in *Acts* 8:9-24 where he is baptized by Philip and later runs afoul of Simon Peter. Many scholars consider Simon (whose followers were referred to as Simonists) the founder of Gnosticism itself. Nicolaus appears in *Acts* 6:6, where he is elected as one of the first seven deacons of the Jerusalem Church. Though not all scholars agree, Nicolaus is considered by some to be the founder of the Nicolatians, Christians who were condemned by the author of the New Testament *Book of Revelations*. For a brief overview on the subject of Simon and Nicolaus see Doresse, Chapter 1.

[2] See Gregory J. Riley, *One Jesus, Many Christs*, New York, HarperCollins, 1989.

[3] Elaine Pagels, *Beyond Belief: The Secret Gospel of Thomas*, New York, Random House, 2003, p. 181.

4 King, *The Gospel of Mary of Magdala*, p, 155.
5 No one summed up Semitic religious thought about the gulf that exists between humanity and God better than Martin Buber in his work, *I and Thou*. Perhaps the text best representing the concept of I *am* Thou is the Bagavad Gita.
6 King, *The Gospel of Mary of Magdala* p. 3.
7 In *The Gospel of Mary of Magdala*, Karen King offers all three texts in a parallel format.
8 Robert Funk, Roy Hoover, *The Five Gospels*, New York, Macmillan Publishing Company, 1993, p. 9.
9 Ibid, p. 8.
10 The words of the Roman emperor, Julian (later dubbed "the Apostate"), who temporarily reversed Constantine's policy. Julian, Ep. Lii (to the people of Bostra, 362 C.E.) in Henry Bettenson, *Documents of the Christian Church*, Second Edition, London, Oxford University Press, 1963, pp. 27-28.
11 King, *The Gospel of Mary of Magdala*, p. 6.
12 *A Dictionary of Early Christian Beliefs*, Peabody, Mass, Hendrickson Publishers, 1998, pp. xv-xix.
13 *New Testament Apocrypha*, Wilhelm Schneemelcher, editor, Revised edition, Louisville, Kentucky, Westminster/ John Knox Press, 1991, Vol. I., p.390.
14 Ibid.
15 Ibid.
16 Ann Graham Brock, *Mary Magdalene, the First Apostle: The Struggle for Authority*, Cambridge, Mass, Harvard University Press, 2003, p. 86.
17 *Pistis Sophia*, I, 17:9, in G.R.S. Mead, *Pistis Sophia*, Garber Communications, 1984.
18 1:1, Ibid, p. 1.
19 Ibid, p. xlvi.
20 Ibid, p. xlv.
21 *Pis. Soph.*1.36, Brock translation, p. 87.
22 *Pis. Soph.* 4.146, Ibid.
23 2.72, Ibid.
24 The *Gospel of Thomas*, Logion 114.
25 The *Gospel of Mary* 10:1-10.
26 King, *The Gospel of Mary of Magdala*, p. 7.
27 Ibid, p. 8.
28 Ibid, pp. 8-11.
29 Although other books on *The Gospel According to Mary* were published earlier, Karen King's *The Gospel of Mary of Magdala* represents the first complete scholarly analysis of this work.
30 *The Nag Hammadi Library in English*, p. 526.
31 Ibid, p. 24.
32 Karen King's address to The Jesus Seminar (Westar Institute), October, 2003.
33 Introduction to *The Sophia of Jesus Christ, The Nag Hammadi Library in English*, p. 222
34 For a comprehensive overview of this subject, see Brock, *Mary Magdalene, the First Apostle – the Struggle for Authority*.

[35] Introduction to *The Sophia of Jesus Christ*, *The Nag Hammadi Library in English*, p. 221.

[36] Karen King, address to the Jesus Seminar, October, 2003.

[37] *The Sophia of Jesus Christ*, *The Nag Hammadi Library in English*, p. 243.

[38] Ibid, pp. 222-243.

[39] Introduction to *Dialogue of the Savior*, *The Nag Hammadi Library in English*, p. 243.

[40] *Dialogue of the Savior*, Ibid, p. 252.

[41] Ibid.

[42] Ibid, p. 253.

[43] Ibid, p. 248.

[44] Ibid, p. 251.

[45] Introduction to *The Gospel According to Philip*, The Nag Hammadi Library in English, p 141.

[46] King, *The Gospel of Mary of Magdala*, p. 114.

[47] *The (Ffirst) Apocalypse of James*, *The Nag Hammadi Library in English*, p. 267.

[48] King, *The Gospel of Mary of Magdala*, p. 143.

[49] Funk, Hoover, *The Five Gospels*, p. 470.

[50] See Helmut Koester, *Ancient Christian Gospels*, Harrisburg, Pennsylvania, Trinity Press International, 1990, pp. 75 - 124.

[51] Ibid, p. 85.

[52] Ibid, p. 86.

[53] Karen King, *What is Gnosticism?*, Cambridge, Mass., Harvard University Press, 2003, p. 111.

[54] Ibid, pp. 111-112.

[55] King, *The Gospel of Mary of Magdala*, p. 173.

[56] Burton L. Mack, *Who Wrote the New Testament?*, San Francisco, Harper San Francisco, 1989, pp. 150-151.

[57] Riley, p. 17.

[58] Francis Legge, *Forerunners and Rivals of Christianity*, New York, University Books, 1964, p. vi.

CHAPTER TWO

[1] In *Matthew* and *John*, Mary is first to receive an appearance of Jesus, as well as in the "long" ending of Mark's Gospel (16:9-20), if not in the original ending. See below, note 49,

[2] Raymond Brown, *An Introduction to the New Testament*, New York, Doubleday, 1997, pp. 267 - 268.

[3] *The Complete Gospels*, Robert J. Miller, Editor, Sonoma, 1994, p. 115.

[4] See Richard I. Pervo, "Dating Acts," and Joseph B. Tyson, "The Date of Acts: A Reconsideration," (papers presented at the semi annual meeting of the Westar Institute, Santa Rosa, CA, October 19, 2002); see also Joseph B Tyson, "The Date of Canonical Luke", paper presented to the same body, Fall meeting, 2003.

⁵ See Brock, Chapter 2.
⁶ The same reference appears in *Mark* 16:9, but it was copied from Luke and was not part of the original ending of Mark's Gospel.
⁷ King, *The Gospel of Mary of Magdala*, p. 142.
⁸ John Shelby Spong, *Born of a Woman*, San Francisco, HarperSanFrancisco, 1992, p. 8.
⁹ *I Corinthians* 15:35.
¹⁰ Elaine Pagels, *The Gnostic Gospels*, New York, Random House, 1981, p. 76.
¹¹ Ibid.
¹² *Matthew* 28:16-20 is the only true commissioning of men story.
¹³ See also, *Ephesians* 5:24.
¹⁴ For much of Christian history the name "Junia" in Romans 16:7 was translated using the masculine nominative of the name, so that the text read "Junias", which is incorrect. See Brock p. 146, Beverly Brooten in Brock, n. 10; Elisabeth Schüssler Fiorrenza, *In Memory of Her*, New York, Crossroad, 1986, p. 172; and King, *The Gospel of Mary of Magdala*, p. 176.
¹⁵ *I Timothy* 2:11-15.
¹⁶ Haskins, p. 62.
¹⁷ Halvor Moxnes, "Lost in Translation", Santa Rosa, The Fourth R, Westar Institute, Vol. 17, no. 6, p. 6.
¹⁸ Antoinette Clark Wire, *The Corinthian Women Prophets*, Eugene, Or., Wipf and Stock Publishers, 1990, p. 83.
¹⁹ *I Cor.* 4:21.
²⁰ F.F. Bruce, *Jesus and Christian Origins Outside the New Testament*, Grand Rapids, William B. Eerdmans Publishing Co, 1974, p. 200.
²¹ Everett Furguson, *Backgrounds of Early Christianity*, Grand Rapids, William B. Eerdmans Publishing, second edition, 1993, pp. 179 – 180.
²² Ibid, p. 292.
²³ *I Cor.* 3:1-2.
²⁴ Wire, p. 181.
²⁵ *I Cor.* 7:1-16.
²⁶ *I Cor.* 11:2-16.
²⁷ *I Cor.* 14:34-40.
²⁸ *I Cor.* 14:37.
²⁹ Wire, p. 160,
³⁰ Ibid, p. 181.
³¹ Ibid, pp 117 – 118.
³² Ibid, p. 139.
³³ Ibid, pp. 174 – 176.
³⁴ Ibid, p.14.
³⁵ *I Cor.* 14:33-36.
³⁶ Wire, pp. 156 – 157.
³⁷ Ibid, p. 158.
³⁸ *I Cor.* 14:37.
³⁹ *II Corinthians* 11:4; 11:12-13.
⁴⁰ Previously, scholars had assigned a late second century date to *Mary*, but Karen

King in an address to the Jesus Seminar in October, 2003 has suggested 125 C.E. as a date for the construction of this Gospel. Robert J Miller and Robert W. Funk, in the introduction to *The Gospel of Mary* in *The Complete Gospels*, (p. 360) have suggested the possibility of an even earlier date.

[41] *The Gospel According to Mary*, POxy 3525, 5:4-10 (King translation), *The Gospel of Mary of Magdala*, p. 15.

[42] Ibid, pp 86 – 87.

[43] *The Gospel According to Mary*, BG 8502, 6:1-2, King, *The Gospel of Mary of Magdala*, p. 15.

[44] Ibid, 6:3.

[45] Ibid, 10:1-5, p. 17.

[46] Ibid.

[47] King, *The Gospel of Mary of Magdala*, p. 87.

[48] Ibid.

[49] Early manuscripts of Mark's Gospel exist that do not contain 16:9-20, making it certain that those verses were added at a later date in order to bring Mark's Gospel into harmony with the other canonical Gospels. Almost certainly the additional verses were inspired by Luke's Gospel because the redactor of *Mark* included Luke's reference to Mary Magdalene's "seven demons", a parallel to Luke's road to Emmaus story, as well as Jesus' ascension into heaven – all of which, many scholars now believe, were Lukan inventions.

CHAPTER THREE

[1] *Romans* 16:7. Also see: Brock, pp. 146 – 147 and n. 10 – 13m, pp. 151 – 152.

[2] *Zondervan's Bible Dictionary*, Grand Rapids, Zondervan, 1993, p. 48

[3] *John* 20:17. It is Jesus himself who tells Mary to "go and tell" his *brethren*.

[4] Brock, p. 161.

[5] Ibid, pp. 63 – 64.

[6] *Mark* 14:50.

[7] *Mark* 14:26 and 15:7.

[8] Robert W. Funk and The Jesus Seminar, *The Acts of Jesus*, San Francisco, HarperSanFrancisco, HarperCollins, 1998, pp. 466 – 467.

[9] Gerd Lüdemann, *What Really Happened to Jesus?*, Louisville, Westminster John Knox Press, 1995, p. 27.

[10] *Luke* 24:9-10.

[11] *Galatians* 1:18-10.

[12] *Luke* 24:10-11.

[13] *Luke* 24:48-49.

[14] *The Acts of Jesus*, p. 495.

[15] Ferguson, p. 563.

[16] From Origen's *Contra Celsum*, quoted in Brock, p. 170.

[17] Miller / Funk, p. 3.

ENDNOTES

CHAPTER FOUR

[1] Brock, p. 168.

[2] Rosemary Ruther, *Women – Church*, San Francisco, Harper and Row, 1985, p. 286 n. 1.

[3] Uta Ranke-Heinemann, *Putting Away Childish Things*, San Francisco, HarperSanFrancisco, 1994, pp. 137 – 138.

[4] Tertullian, *De Culta feminarum* 1.1.

[5] King, *The Gospel of Mary of Magdala*, p. 65.

[6] Pagels, *The Gnostic Gospels*, pp. 35 – 36. For a full study of this subject see also Elaine Pagels, *Adam, Eve, and the Serpent*, New York, Random House, 1988.

[7] Pagels, *Adam, Eve, and the Serpent*, p.64.

[8] Genesis 1:26.

[9] Michael Grant, *The History of Ancient Israel*, New York, Charles Scribner's Sons, 1984, p. 43.

[10] Ibid.

[11] Ibid, p. 24.

[12] See, Raphael Patai, *The Hebrew Goddess*, New York, Avon Discus, 1978, and Saul M. Olyan, *Asherah and the Cult of Yahweh in Israel*, Society of Biblical literature, Monograph series 34, Atlanta, Scholars Press, 1988.

[13] Ibid.

[14] Grant, p. 174.

[15] Elizabeth Schüssler Fiorenza, *In Memory of Her*, New York, Crossroad, 1986, p. 133.

[16] Robert Price, "Anastasis at the Areopagus", seminar paper for the Westar Institute, Santa Rosa, Fall 2003; on the subject of the Hebrew Goddess see Patai, pp. 38 – 39; and Olyan, pp. 70 – 74.

[17] Fiorenza, pp. 132 – 133.

[18] Ibid, p. 134.

[19] Ibid, p. 133.

[20] Pagels, *The Gnostic Gospels*, pp. 58 – 59.

[21] Lüdemann, *Heretics*, p. 159.

[22] Ibid, see Chap. 6.

[23] Tertullian, *De Virginibus velandis*, 9, quoted in Brock, p. 103.

[24] Brock, pp. 1 – 2.

[25] Raymond Brown, *The Community of the Beloved Disciple*, New York, Paulist Press, 1979, p. 189.

[26] Augustine, Tractate 121, commentary on *John* 20:10-29.

[27] Haskins, P. 93.

[28] Pope Gregory the Great, Homily. XXXIII, PL LXXVI, col. 1180.

[29] Brock, p. 168 n.

[30] *II Cor.* 11:13.

[31] Elaine Pagels, *The Origin of Satan*, New York, Random House, 1996, p.155.

[32] Gregory of Antioch, quoted in Brock, p. 15.

CHAPTER FIVE

1   *I Cor.* 15:5-8.
2   Ibid, 15:9
3   The dating of such material is imprecise, and scholars often differ. Raymond Brown, for instance, assigns Paul's first letter to the later part of the fifth decade, while other scholars prefer an earlier date. Even so, virtually all scholars agree that *I Corinthians* was written sometime during the 50s.
4   *I Cor.* 7:1.
5   *I Cor.* 11:3.
6   *I Cor.* 11:5.
7   *I Cor.* 11:9.
8   *I Cor.* 14:34.
9   *I Cor.* 14:35.
10 Paul in *Galations* 1:16 merely says that "God's son was revealed to me". In *II Corinthians* 12:2-3, he talks of being caught up into the "third heaven". The author of *Luke/Acts* mythologized Paul's conversion experience in his well known "road to Damascus story" in *Acts* 9:1-9.
11 Geza Vermes, *The Changing Face of Jesus*, New York, Penguin Compass, 2002, p.72.
12 A. N. Wilson, *Paul, the Mind of the Apostle*, New York, W. W. Norton & Co., 1997, p. 69.
13 Vermes, p. 75.
14 *Galatians* 2:5-6.
15 Lüdemann, *Heretics*, p. 94.
16 *Galatians* 1:8-9.
17 *Philippians* 3:2
18 *Philippians* 1:17.
19 Paul's authentic letters include *Romans, I* and *II Corinthians, Galatians, Philippians, I Thessalonians,* and *Philemon* (this last being to an individual).
20 *I Cor.* 9:1-2.
21 *II Cor.* 12:16.
22 *II Cor.* 11:1-5.
23 Lüdemann, *Heretics*, p. 88.
24 *II Cor.* 12:1-14.
25 *II Cor.* 11:19.
26 *Gal.* 1:6-9.
27 *Gal.* 1:11-12.
28 *Gal.* 1:16-17.
29 *Gal.* 2:5-6.
30 Vermes, P. 75.
31 *II Cor.* 6:8.
32 Lüdemann, *Heretics*, p. 94.
33 Wire, P. 53.
34 *I Cor.* 14:36.
35 Wire, p. 53.

[36] Ibid.

[37] Wire, p. 156.

[38] *I Cor.* 11:16.

[39] Wire, 221.

[40] Ibid.

[41] *I Cor.* 14:37.

[42] Ibid, p. 156.

[43] *I Cor.* 15:1-58.

[44] See Wire, Chapter 8: "Women Risen to New Life in Christ".

[45] Vermes, p. 91.

[46] See Wire, Chapter 8.

[47] Ibid, p. 161.

[48] Ibid.

[49] Ibid, pp. 161 – 162.

[50] Wire, p. 162.

[51] *I Cor.* 15:40-50.

[52] Wire, p. 233.

[53] Ibid, p. 160.

[54] *The Gospel of Philip, The Nag Hammadi Library in English*, p. 153.

[55] *The Treatise on the Resurrection, The Nag Hammadi Library in English*, p. 56.

[56] *Gal.* 3:8.

[57] *I Cor.* 4:8.

[58] Wire, p. 176.

[59] The Nazirites were not a Jewish "sect", but a consecrated order. The Nazirite vows required vegetarianism, abstention from wine, and a prohibition of the use of the razor. Other famous Biblical Nazirites were Samson, Samuel, and John the Baptist.

[60] Eusebius, *Ecclesiastical History*, I.II.XXIII.

[61] Robert Eisenman, *James the Brother of Jesus*, New York, Penguin Books, 1997, p. 415.

[62] Lüdemann, *Heretics*, p. 57.

[63] Wilson, p. 33.

[64] *Gal.* 2:1-14.

[65] Lüdemann, *Heretics*, p. 59.

[66] Ibid, p. 44.

[67] So called because they are falsely attributed to Clement, the early second century bishop of Rome. The earliest strata of these writing dates from the second century, the latest from the fourth century (Lüdemann, *Heretics*, p. 57). Because these documents paint Paul in a very bad light they have, in modern times, been largely ignored, even suppressed.

[68] Eisenman, pp. XXIX, XXX, 146m 278 ff.

[69] Lüdemann, *Heretics*, p. 57.

[70] Eisenman, pp. 588-589.

[71] *Acts* 21:26-36; 24:5-9.

[72] Lüdemann, *Heretics*, p. 59.

[73] *Homilies* XVII 19, 1-7, in Lüdemann, *Heretics,* p. 58.
[74] Lüdemann, *Heretics,* p. 59.

CHAPTER SIX

[1] *The Infancy Gospel of Thomas,* 3:1 – 4:1, *The Apocryphal New Testament,* Oxford, Clarendon Press, 1975, p. 50.
[2] *The Book of the Cock, Ibid,* p. 150.
[3] Edgar Hennecke, On: *The Questions of Mary, New Testament Apocrypha,* Vol. I, p. 390.
[4] G.R.S. Mead, Introduction to the *Pistis Sophia,* p. 34.
[5] Hennecke, *New Testament Apocrypha,* Vol. I, p. 339.
[6] Eusebius, *Ecclesiastical History,* III. XXVIII.6 – XXXIX.4, Vol. 1, *Loeb Classical Library,* Cambridge, Harvard University Press, 1974, p. 267.
[7] Brock, p. 125.
[8] Ibid., pp. 125 -126.
[9] Coptic Psalm-book II, see Hennecke, *New Testament Apocrypha,* 1963 edition, Vol. 1, pp. 353-354.
[10] Manichean Psalter CCXLVI 54. 8-55. 13.
[11] Jonas, p. 230.
[12] Manichean Psalter, CCXXIII 9:31-10:19.
[13] Jonas, pp. 231 – 232.
[14] Revillout fragment K1,v, *New Testament Apocrapha,* Vol. 1, pp. 555 – 556.
[15] *Epistula Apostolorum,* 10:38, Ibid, p. 255.
[16] *The Acts of Pilate,* XIII, Ibid, p. 514.
[17] In the Coptic, Ethiopic, and Arabic versions of the *Acts of Philip*; in the *Acta Thaddaei,* in the *Diatessaron,* in the *Quaestiones et responsiones ad Orthodoxos,* in the *Didascalia Apostolorum,* in the homilies of Chrysostom, in the Coptic version of the *Book of the Resurrection of Jesus Christ.* See Conclusion.
[18] Brock, p. 141.
[19] Ibid, p. 142.
[20] Fiorenza, p. 274.
[21] Hennecke, *New Testament Apocrypha,* Vol. I, p. 362.
[22] Fiorenza, Ibid, p. 274.
[23] Ibid.
[24] *Gal.* 3:28.
[25] Fiorenza, p. 277.
[26] Ibid.
[27] Ibid.
[28] Pagels, *The Gnostic Gospels,* p. 59.
[29] Ibid, p. 58.
[30] Ibid, p. 59.
[31] From the writings of the Naassenes, quoted in Hippolytus, *Refutations* 5.6.

[32] Ferguson, p. 280.
[33] Robert Price, "Anastasis at the Areopagus", Westar Institute conference, October 2003, Seminar papers, p. 227.
[34] Ibid.
[35] Ibid, p. 232.
[36] *Pistis Sophia* in *New Testament Apocrypha*, Vol. 1, p. 362.
[37] Pagels, *The Gnostic Gospels*, pp. 21-22.
[38] *Pis. Soph.* p. 366.
[39] Brock, p. 93.
[40] *Pis. Soph.* multiple references.
[41] *The Gospel of Philip*, 65:34
[42] *Pis. Soph.* Ibid, 1.17.
[43] *Dialogue of the Savior*, 20.2, Miller / Funk, *The Complete Gospels*, p. 353.
[44] *Pis. Soph.* I, 17:9-14., in Mead.
[45] Ibid, I 19:1-5.
[46] Ibid, I 61:2-4.
[47] Dan Brown, *The Da Vinci Code*, New York, Doubleday, 2003, p. 246.
[48] *The Gospel of Philip*, *The Nag Hammadi Library in English*, p. 148.
[49] Karen King, Address to the Jesus Seminar, October, 2003.
[50] *Philip*, 58:30 – 59:5, *The Nag Hammadi Library in English*, p. 145.
[51] *Philip* 63:30-64 – 64:10, Ibid, p. 148.
[52] *The Gospel of Mary*, Papyrus Oxyrhynchus 3525, 5:4-8, King, *The Gospel of Mary of Magdala*, pp. 14 – 15.
[53] *Philip*, *The Nag Hammadi Library in English*, p. 151.
[54] Fiorenza, p. 275.
[55] *Philip*, *The Nag Hammadi Library in English*, p. 158.
[56] Doresse, p. 50.
[57] *I Cor.* 9:4-5.
[58] Clement of Alexandria (c. 180 C.E.95) E 2.390, 391.
[59] John Dominic Crossan, *The Historical Jesus*, San Francisco, HarperSanFrancisco, 1992, p. 335.
[60] *I Cor.* 7:7.
[61] *I Cor.* 7:32-34.
[62] *I Cor.* 7:20.
[63] Wire, p. 181.
[64] Wire, p. 183.
[65] *I Cor.* 7:4-5.
[66] Wire, P. 181.
[67] *Luke* 20:34-35; *Matthew* 22:30
[68] *Matthew* 19:11-12.
[69] *The Book of John the Evangelist*, *The Apocryphal New Testament*, p. 191.
[70] Vermes, p. 162, 272.
[71] Ibid, p. 272,
[72] Halvor Moxnes, "Lost in Translation – What happened to the eunuchs in Matthew 19:12?", Santa Rosa, The Westar Institute, The Fourth R, Volume 17,

No. 6, p. 8.
[73] Funk / Miller, *The Five Gospels*, p. 220.
[74] Moxnes, p. 7.
[75] William F. Arndt, F. Wilbur Gingrich, *A Greek-English Lexicon of the New Testament*, Chicago, University of Chicago Press, 1957, pp. 324 – 325.
[76] Moxnes, p. 7.
[77] Tertullian, *On Monogamy*, 3.1, Moxnes, Ibid.
[78] Moxnes, p. 7.
[79] Pagels, *Adam, Eve, and the Serpent*, pp. 14 – 15.
[80] Ibid, p. 16.
[81] Moxnes, p. 6.
[82] Price, "The Da Vinci Fraud", "The Fourth R," Vol. 17, No. 1.

CHAPTER SEVEN

[1] Burton Mack, *Who Wrote the New Testament? The Making of the Christian Myth*, San Francisco, HarperSanFrancisco, 1995, p. 201.
[2] Ibid, p. 205.
[3] Wilson, p. 107.
[4] Ibid, p. 106.
[5] Eusebius, *Ecclesiastical History*, II, xiv.
[6] *Acts* 12:1-17.
[7] *Gal.* 1:18-19.
[8] Burton Mack, *A Myth of Innocence, Mark and Christian Origins*, Philadelphia, Fortress Press, 1991, p.88.
[9] *Gal.* 2:1-10.
[10] *Gal* 2:11.
[11] *Gal.* 2:11-14.
[12] Most scholars consider "the twelve" to be a narrative fiction. See Mack, *A Myth of Innocence*, pp. 78 – 80.
[13] *Mark* 8:33; *Matthew* 16:23.
[14] Mack, *A Myth of Innocence*, p. 90.
[15] The group of some one hundred scholars known as the Jesus Seminar, in Funk/the Jesus Seminar, *The Acts of Jesus*, p. 149
[16] *John* 18:10.
[17] Brown, *An Introduction to the New Testament*, p. 292.
[18] *I Cor.* 5:1-5.
[19] The Greek word, "olethros" as used here specifically in the sense of "The handing over to Satan will result in this sinner's death", William F. Arndt and F. Wilber Gingrich, *A Greek / English Lexicon of the New Testament*, Chicago, Cambridge University Press, 1957 p. 566.
[20] *I Cor.* 6:1-3.
[21] Justin Martyr, *Apologia*, I, 6.
[22] Wilson, p. 107.
[23] *Mark* 1:16-17.

[24] *John* 1:35.
[25] Funk / The Jesus Seminar, pp. 368 – 369.
[26] *Acts* 1:21-22,
[27] *John* 4:2.
[28] Burton Mack, *The Lost Gospel, The Book of Q & Christian Origins*, San Francisco, HarperSanFrancisco, 1993, pp. 73 – 80.
[29] Koester, pp. 162 – 163.
[30] Ibid, pp. 135 – 136.
[31] The *Gospel of the Nazaraeans*, Jerome, adv. Pelag. III 2, *New Testament Apocrypha*, p. 160.
[32] Joan E. Taylor, *The Immerser: John the Baptist within Second Temple Judaism*, Grand Rapids, William B. Eerdmans, 1997, p. 263.
[33] W. Barnes Tatum, *John the Baptist and Jesus*, Sonoma, Polebridge Press, 1994, p. 166.
[34] Brock, p. 77.
[35] *Pis. Soph.* I, Chap. 36, in Mead, P. 47.
[36] *Pis. Soph.* II, Chap. 2, 161, in Mead, P. 175.
[37] Brock, p. 104.
[38] Ibid, p. 102.
[39] Ibid, p. 37.
[40] Ibid, p. 39.
[41] Compare *Mark* 15:41; *Matthew* 27:55; *Luke* 8:3.
[42] Brock p. 33.
[43] Ibid, pp. 63 – 64.
[44] *John* 20:3-8.
[45] Brock p. 57.
[46] *John* 11:27a, Brock, p. 43.
[47] Pagels, *The Gnostic Gospels*, p. 9.
[48] Karl Holl, In Pagels, *The Gnostic Gospels*, p. 11.

CHAPTER EIGHT

[1] *John* 20:11-13.
[2] Mead, *Pistis Sophia*, V, pp. 300 & 314.
[3] *Mark* 14:72.
[4] *Luke* 19:43-44.
[5] *The Gospel of Thomas*, 69a.
[6] From (The Hymn of Jesus, 42) *The Acts of John, New Testament Apocrypha* Vol. II, p. 231.
[7] From *The Apocryphon of James, The Complete Gospels*, p 337.
[8] Ibid.
[9] From *Thomas the Contender, The Nag Hammadi Library in English*, p. 207.
[10] *The Gospel of Mary*, P. Oxy. 5:4-9, King, *The Gospel of Mary of Magdala*, pp. 14 – 15.
[11] King, *The Gospel of Mary of Magdala*, pp. 122 – 123.

[12] *Matt.* 9-13, 12.7, *Mark* 12:33.
[13] *Mark* 14:55-59; see also John Dominic Crossan, *Who Killed Jesus?*, San Francisco, HarperSanFrancisco, 1991, pp. 108 – 109.
[14] Eisenman, pp. 452 – 453 ff.
[15] *Mary* 3:1-14.
[16] King, *The Gospel of Mary of Magdala*, p. 122.
[17] Ibid.
[18] Ibid, p. 124.
[19] Ibid, p. 127.
[20] *Mary* 2:2-5.
[21] *Luke* 17:20-21.
[22] Stephen Mitchell, *The Gospel According to Jesus*, New York, HarperCollins, 1991, p. 146.
[23] C. H. Dodd, *The Parables of the Kingdom*, New York, Charles Scribner's Sons, 1961, pp. 62 f.
[24] *Thomas* 3:1-3.
[25] *Thomas* 113.
[26] *Dialogue of the Savior* 9:3a.
[27] *Mary* 3:3-7.
[28] Dodd, Ibid.
[29] The Greek word, "mysterion" can be translated variously as "secret", "secret rite", "secret teaching", or "mystery". This was the word generally used by the Greeks and Romans in referring to their mystery religions. Ref: William F. Arndt, F. Wilbur Gingrich, pp. 531-532.
[30] *Mark* 4:11-12; *Matthew* 13: 11; *Luke* 8:10.
[31] *John* 3:3; 3:5.
[32] The Jesus Seminar, Red Letter Edition, *The Parables of Jesus*, Santa Rosa, Polebridge Press, 1988, pp. 18-19.
[33] *Mary* 4:8.
[34] King, *The Gospel of Mary of Magdala*, pp. 100-102.
[35] Ibid, p. 61.
[36] Ibid, pp. 61-62.
[37] *Mary* 10:9-10.
[38] King, *The Gospel of Mary of Magdala*, p. 173.
[39] Mary R. Thompson, *Mary of Magdala*, New York, Paulist Press, 1995, p. 117.

CHAPTER NINE

[1] See below, *The Endings of Mark.*
[2] Gerd Lüdemann, *What Really Happened to Jesus?*, Louisville, Westminster John Knox Press, 1995, p. 25.
[3] See: Robert M. Price, "Mary Magdalene, Gnostic Apostle", Grail 6.1, 1990, pp 54 – 71. in King, *The Gospel of Mary of Magdala*, n. 13: 61, 71.
[4] Brock, p. 170. This was a serious enough charge that Origen, in his *Contra*

Celsum, had to refute Celsus at length.

⁵ Brock, 103.

⁶ Ibid. p. 69.

⁷ *Matt.* 27:56.

⁸ *Luke* 23:49.

⁹ *John* 19:25.

¹⁰ *Luke* 8:3.

¹¹ Josephus in John Dominic Crossan, *The Birth of Christianity*, San Francisco, HarperSanFrancisco, 1989, p. 543.

¹² Ibid. See also Jerry M. Landay, *Silent Cities, Sacred Stones*, New York, McCall Publishing Company, 1971, pp. 207-208.

¹³ Lüdemann, *What Really Happened to Jesus?*, p. 23.

¹⁴ Funk/The Jesus Seminar, p. 160.

¹⁵ *Mark* 15:43.

¹⁶ *Jonah* 1:17; *Hosea* 6:2.

¹⁷ *Mark* 15:43.

¹⁸ Funk and the Jesus Seminar, *The Acts of Jesus*, p. 159.

¹⁹ Ibid, pp. 159 – 160.

²⁰ John Dominic Crossan, *Who Killed Jesus?*, San Francisco, HarperSanFrancisco, 1995, pp. 160 – 163.

²¹ Embassy to Gaius 302, in Crossan, *Who Killed Jesus?*, p. 148.

²² Ibid.

²³ Funk and the Jesus Seminar, *The Acts of Jesus*, p. 158.

²⁴ *Mark* 16:1.

²⁵ Funk and the Jesus Seminar, *The Acts of Jesus*, p. 161.

²⁶ *Mark* 16:5.

²⁷ *Mark* 16:5-6.

²⁸ *Mark* 14:51-52.

²⁹ See Morton Smith, *The Secret Gospel*, New York, Harper and Row, 1973.

³⁰ Charles W. Hedrick with Nikolaos Olympiou, in the article, "Secret Mark, New Photographs, New Witnesses", Santa Rosa, Westar Institute, "The Fourth R", Volume 13, number 5, September – October 2000, pp. 3 – 11.

³¹ In Smith, pp. 16 – 17.

³² Ibid, p. 17.

³³ Koester, p. 296.

³⁴ See Lüdemann, *What Really Happened to Jesus?*, p. 27.

³⁵ Miller / Funk, *The Complete Gospels*, p. 410.

³⁶ Ibid, p. 411.

³⁷ Riley, p. 121.

³⁸ Ibid, p. 93.

³⁹ See Smith, Chapters 11 and 12.

⁴⁰ Miller/Funk, *The Complete Gospels*, p. 411.

⁴¹ Salome (who appears only in Mark's Gospel) is present in both instances, and the two other women who tried to visit Jesus in Jericho could both have been "Marys" – Mary of Bethany, and Jesus' mother, Mary.

[42] *Mark* 4:11.
[43] Smith, p. 105.
[44] Ibid.
[45] Ibid, p. 106.
[46] Doresse, p. 14 n.
[47] Ibid, p. 270.
[48] *Homilies*, in *The New Testament Apocrypha*, Vol. II, p. 545.
[49] Ibid.
[50] Eisenman, n., p. 1001.
[51] Ibid, pp. 35 – 36.
[52] Ibid, p. 841.
[53] Ibid, p. 27.
[54] *The Treatise on the Resurrection, The Nag Hammadi Library in English*, pp. 54 – 56.
[55] Introduction to *The Treatise on the Resurrection, The Nag Hammadi Library in English*, p. 53.
[56] *The New Oxford Annotated Bible*, notes on *Mark*, p. 1239.
[57] Miller / Funk, *The Complete Gospels*, p. 453.
[58] Daryl D. Schmidt, *The Gospel of Mark*, Sonoma, Polebridge Press, 1990, p. 152.
[59] Ibid.
[60] Miller / Funk, *The Complete Gospels*, p. 453.
[61] *The Sophia of Jesus Christ*, in *The Nag Hammadi Library in English*, p. 243.
[62] Ibid, introduction, p. 221.

CHAPTER TEN

[1] *Matt.* 27:52-53.
[2] *Matt.* 28:54.
[3] *Matt.* 27:54.
[4] Smith, p. 70.
[5] *Matt.* 16:26
[6] *Matt.* 28:61.
[7] *Matt.* 28:9.
[8] *Matt.* 28:15.
[9] *Matt.* 28:17.
[10] Koester, p 330.
[11] Koester, pp. 316ff.
[12] Smith, p. 131.
[13] Ibid.

ENDNOTES

CHAPTER ELEVEN

1 *Luke* 24:9-10.
2 *Luke* 24:8-10.
3 Brock, p. 165.
4 *Luke* 24:11.
5 *Luke* 24:22-23.
6 *Mark* 16:12.
7 *Mark* 16:12.
8 *Matt* 28:17.
9 *Luke* 24:11.
10 *John* 20:24-29.
11 *Luke* 24:22-24.
12 Funk and the Jesus Seminar, *The Acts of Jesus*, p. 470.
13 Funk/Miller, *The Complete Gospels*, p. 172.
14 Funk and the Jesus Seminar, *The Acts of Jesus*, p. 470.
15 Plato, Gorgias, quoted in Funk and the Jesus Seminar, *The Acts of Jesus*, p. 486.
16 Ibid.

CHAPTER TWELVE

1 Koester, p. 334.
2 Ibid, p. 267.
3 See: Raymond Brown, *The Community of the Beloved Disciple*.
4 *John* 19:26-27.
5 *Matt.* 1:20; Matt 27:9l; *Luke* 1:16.
6 *A Greek / English Lexicon of the New Testament*, p. 841.
7 *John* 19:39.
8 Funk / The Jesus Seminar, *The Acts of Jesus*, p. 439.
9 *John* 19:39-40.
10 *John* 20:2.
11 See Brock, p. 57.
12 Ibid.
13 Ferguson, p. 228.
14 *John* 10:3-4.
15 Brown, *The Community of the Beloved Disciple*, p. 192.
16 Ibid, p. 154.
17 See Brown, *The Community of the Beloved Disciple*, pp. 124 – 127; 151.
18 While the Fellows of the Jesus Seminar agreed, for the most part, that John's narrative was not historical, they overwhelmingly agreed that Mary Magdalene probably did have a vision of the risen Jesus similar to that described by John. See, Robert Funk and the Jesus Seminar, *The Acts of Jesus*, pp. 478 – 479.
19 Brown, *The Community of the Beloved Disciple*, p. 189n.

[20] *John* 20:17.

[21] See Lüdemann, *What Really Happened to Jesus?*, pp. 67 – 78.

CHAPTER THIRTEEN

[1] Miller/Funk, *The Complete Gospels*, p. 399.

[2] Ibid., pp. 399-400.

[3] *Peter* 9:1-10:5.

[4] *Peter* 13:1-3.

[5] Koester, p. 231.

[6] *New Testament Apocrypha*, Vol. I, p. 251.

[7] *Epistula Apostolorum* 10:38-39, in *New Testament Apocrypha*, Vol. I, p. 255.

[8] Brock, p. 124.

[9] Ibid, p. 125.

[10] Ibid.

[11] Ibid, pp. 124 – 127.

[12] Ibid, pp. 127 – 128.

[13] Ibid, p. 130.

[14] Ibid, pp. 130 – 131.

[15] Ibid, p. 132.

[16] Ibid, pp. 134 – 135.

CHAPTER FOURTEEN

[1] King, *The Gospel of Mary of Magdala*, p. 176.

[2] Brock, p. 57.

[3] Aaron Milavec, in an interview with *The Fourth R*, Vol. 18, no. 3, Santa Rosa, Polebridge Press, May-June 2005, pp-7-8.

[4] Ibid, p. 8

[5] Aaron Milavec, *The Didache*, Liturgical Press, 2005.

[6] Milavec, *The Fourth R* interview, p. 11.

[7] Jane Schaberg, *The Resurrection of Mary Magdalene*, New York, The Continuum International Publishing Group, 2004, pp. 347-348.

[8] Ibid, p.349.

CONCLUSION

1 John Shelby Spong, *Born of a Woman*, San Francisco, HarperSanFrancisco, 1992, p. 207.

2 Among those savior-gods born of virgins were Krishna, Hercules, Quetzalcoatl, Bacchus and Hesus. But the tradition of miraculous births applied to figures in the Hebrew *Bible*. Isaac, Jacob, Rueben, Joseph, Samson and Samuel were all born to women who were "barren". These women were infertile, but were finally able to conceive through intercourse with their husbands after God intervened and removed their "barrenness". (See Robert Miller, "Thinking Straight About the Virgin Birth", Sonoma, The Fourth R, Polebridge Press, 2001, Vol. 14, No. 6, p. 6.

3 The Joseph of the nativity stories is a shadowy figure who probably did not exist. In any event, Joseph was considered an elderly man when he took the young Mary—with child—as a wife, and could not have produced children. Moreover Joseph is never mentioned outside the mythical stories of Jesus' birth (and Luke's fiction about the twelve-year-old Jesus). The Gospels are clear that Jesus had brothers and sisters, but no father is ever mentioned. The very fact that Jesus is identified with his mother, rather than with a father, would have been a rare and scandalous aberration in Jewish culture during the first century. Indeed, many scholars have proposed that the story of Mary being with child by the Holy Spirit was invented specifically to counteract common knowledge that Jesus had been an illegitimate child.

4 Brock in King, *The Gospel of Mary of Magdala*, p. 147.

5 Pagels, *The Gnostic Gospels*, p. 50.

6 King, *The Gospel of Mary of Magdala*, p. 185.

7 Brock, p. 171.

8 King, *The Gospel of Mary of Magdala*, p. 187.

9 Spong, p. 196.

10 Dale Miller and Patricia Miller, *The Gospel of Mark as Midrash on Earlier Jewish and New Testament Literature*, Lewiston, New York, Edwin Mellen Press, 1990, p. 370., referenced by Spong, p. 196,

11 Schaberg, p. 334.

12 Ibid, p. 344.

13 Ibid, p. 319.

14 Ibid, p. 318.

15 Ibid, p.345.

16 Kahlil Gibran, *The Prophet*, New York, Alfred A. Knopf, 1926, p. 17.

17 Elaine Pagels, *Beyond Belief, The Secret Gospel of Thomas*, New York, Random House, 2003, p. 159.

18 Ibid, p. 174.

19 Ibid, p. 170.

20 Ibid, pp. 176 – 177.

21 Ibid.

Bibliography

Arndt, William F., and F. Wilber Gingrich. *A Greek-English Lexicon of the New Testament and Other Early Christian Literature*. Chicago: University of Chicago Press, 1957.

Bercot, David W. *A Dictionary of Early Christian Beliefs*. Peabody, Mass: Hendrickson Publishers, 1998.

Bettenson, Henry. *Documents of the Christian Church*. Second edition. London: Oxford University Press, 1963.

Brock, Ann Graham. *Mary Magdalene, the First Apostle—The Struggle for Authority*. Cambridge, Mass: Harvard University Press, 2003.

Brown, Raymond. *The Community of the Beloved Disciple*. New York: Paulist Press, 1979.

_____*An Introduction to the New Testament*. New York: Doubleday, 1997.

Bruce, F.F. *Jesus and Christian Origins Outside the New Testament*. Grand Rapids: William B. Eerdmans, 1974.

Crossan, John Dominic. *The Birth of Christianity—Discovering What Happened in the Years Immediately After the Execution of Jesus*. San Francisco: HarperSanFrancisco, 1989.

_____*Who Killed Jesus?* San Francisco: HarperSanFrancisco, 1991.

Dart, John and Reigert, Ray. *Unearthing the Lost Words of Jesus*. Berkeley: Seastone / Ulysses Press, 1993.

Dodd, C. H. *The Parables of the Kingdom*. New York: Charles Scribner's Sons, 1961.

Doresse, Jean. *The Secret Books of the Egyptian Gnostics*. New York: MJF Books, 1958.

Eisenman, Robert. *James the Brother of Jesus*. New York: Penguin Books, 1997.

Eusiebius. *Ecclesiastical History*. Loeb Classical Library, Cambridge: Harvard University Press, 1974.

Ferguson, Edward. *Backgrounds of Early Christianity*. Second edition. Grand Rapids: William B. Eerdmans Publishing, 1993.

Fiorenza, Elizabeth Schussler. *In Memory of Her*. New York: Crossroad, 1986.

Funk, Robert W., and Roy Hoover. *The Five Gospels*. New York: Macmillan Publishing Company, 1993.

Funk, Robert W., and The Jesus Seminar. *The Acts of Jesus*. San Francisco: HarperSanFrancisco, 1998.

Gibran, Kahlil. *The Prophet*. New York: Alfred A. Knof, 1926.

Grant, Michael. *The History of Ancient Israel*. New York: Charles Scribner's Sons, 1984.

Haskins, Susan. *Mary Magdalene in Myth and Metaphor*. New York: Berkeley Publishing Group, 1993.

Hedrick, Charles W., and Nikolaos Olympiou. "Secret Mark, New Photographs, New Witnesses". *The Fourth R*. Volume 13, Number 5, September—October, 2000.

Hennecke, Edgar and Wilhelm Schneemelcher. *New Testament Apocrypha*. Two volumes. Revised English edition. Louisville: Westminster/John Knox Press, 1991.

James, M.R., Editor. *The Apocryphal New Testament*. Second edition. London: Oxford University Press, 1976.

Jesus Seminar, The. *The Parables of Jesus*. Santa Rosa: Polebridge Press, 1988.

Jonas, Hans. *The Gnostic Religion*. Boston: Beacon Hill, 1958.

King, Karen. *What is Gnosticism?* Cambridge: Harvard University Press, 2003.

_____*The Gospel of Mary of Magdala—Jesus and the First Woman Apostle*. Santa Rosa: Polebridge Press, 2003.

Kloppenberg, John S., Marvin W. Meyer, Stephen J. Patterson, Michael G. Steinhauser. *Q-Thomas Reader*. Sonoma: Polbridge Press, 1990.

Koester, Helmut. *Ancient Christian Gospels*. Harrisburg, Pennsylvania: Trinity Press International, 1990.

Landay, Jerry M. *Silent Cities, Sacred Stones*. New York: McCall Publishing Company, 1971.

Legge, Francis. *Forerunners and Rivals of Christianity*. New York: University Books, 1964.

Lüdemann, Gerd. *What Really Happened to Jesus?—A Historical Approach to the Resurrection*. Louisville: Westminster John Knox Press, 1995.

_____*Heretics—The Other Side of Christianity*. First American edition. Louisville: Westminster John Knox Press, 1996.

Mack, Burton. *Who Wrote the New Testament?* San Francisco: HarperSanFrancisco, 1989.

_____*A Myth of Innocence—Mark and Christian Origins*. Philadelphia: Fortress Press, 1991.

_____*The Lost Gospel—The Book of Q & Christian Origins*. San Francisco: HarperSanFrancisco, 1993.

Mead, G.R.S. *Pistis Sophia—A Gnostic Gospel*. U.S.A.: Garber Communications, 1984.

Miller, Robert J., Editor, Foreword by Robert F. Funk. *The Complete Gospels*. Sonoma: Polebridge Press, 1994.

Mitchell, Stephen. *The Gospel According to Jesus*. New York: HarperCollins, 1991.

Moxnes, Halvor. "Lost in Translation". *The Fourth R*, Vol. 17, No. 6. Sonoma: Polebridge Press, December, 2004.

Olyan, Saul M. *Asherah and the Cult of Yahweh in Israel*, Society of Biblical Literature, Monograph series 34, Atlanta, Scholars Press, 1988.

Pagels, Elaine. *The Gnostic Gospels*. New York: Random House, 1981.

_____*Adam, Eve and the Serpent*. New York: Random House, 1988.

_____*The Origin of Satan*. New York: Random House, 1996.

_____*Beyond Belief—The Secret Gospel of Thomas*. New York: Random House, 2003.

Patai, Raphael. *The Hebrew Goddess*. New York: Avon Discus, 1978.

Pervo, Richard I. "Dating Acts". Seminar paper for the Jesus Seminar—Westar Institute. Santa Rosa, CA: October, 2002.

Price, Robert, "Anastasis at the Areopagus". Seminar paper for the Jesus Seminar—Westar Institute. Santa Rosa: October, 2003.

_____"The Da Vinci Fraud". *The Fourth R*. Sonoma: Westar Institute, Vol. 17, No. 1, January—February, 2004.

Ranke-Heinemann, Uta. *Putting Away Childish Things*. San Francisco: HarperSanFrancisco. 1994.

Riley, Gregory J. *One Jesus, Many Christs*. New York: HarperCollins, 1989.

Robinson, James M., General Editor. *The Nag Hammadi Library*, Revised edition. San Francisco: HarperSanFrancisco, 1990.

Schaberg, Jane. *The Resurrection of Mary Magdalene, Legends, Apocrypha, and the Christian Testament*. New York, The Continuum International Publishing Group Inc., 2002.

Schmidt, Daryl. *The Gospel of Mark*. Sonoma: Polebridge Press, 1990.

Smith, Morton. *The Secret Gospel of Mark*. New York: Harper and Row, 1973.

Spong, John Shelby. *Born of a Woman*. San Francisco: HarperSanFrancisco, 1992.

Tatum, W. Barnes. *John the Baptist and Jesus*. Sonoma: Polebridge Press, 1994.

Taylor, Joan E. *The Immerser: John the Baptist Within Second Temple Juidaism*. Grand Rapids: William B. Eerdmans, 1997.

Thompson, Mary R. *Mary of Magdala*. New York: Paulist Press, 1995.

Tyson, Joseph B. "The Date of Canonical Luke". Seminar paper for the Jesus Seminar—Westar Institute, Santa Rosa, Oct. 2003.

Vermes, Geza. *The Changing Face of Jesus*. New York: Penquin Compass, 2002.

Wilson, A. N. *Paul, the Mind of the Apostle*. New York: W. W. Norton & Co., 1997.

Wire, Antoinette Clark. *The Corinthian Women Prophets*. Eugene, Oregon: Wipf and Stock Publishers.

Names, Terms, and Sources

Acts of Philip A fourth century Greek text that has survived only in fragmentary form. Philip the apostle is the hero of the story, but is aided, supported and comforted by his traveling companion, Mary Magdalene. A later Coptic version of this text replaced Mary Magdalene with Simon Peter.

Acts of the Apostles Written by the author of *The Gospel of Luke* (see *Luke* below), *Acts* purports to be a history of the early Church. In fact, *Acts* is a revisionist polemic supporting the traditions of Peter and Paul. Only the first 15 chapters can be attributed to the original author. The rest of *Acts* was written by a different hand.

Achmim An ancient town in upper Egypt, situated along the Nile river some one hundred miles north of Nag Hammadi.

Alexandria One of the greatest learning centers of the ancient world; home of the largest library of all antiquity; seat of power for the orthodox Church in the East; produced some of the most influential patriarchs of the early Church.

Androgyny A state of being that is inclusive of both male and female qualities and characteristics.

Anastasis Literally, "the resurrection". Also a woman's proper name.

Angel A messenger from God.

Angelophany An epiphany, or direct awareness, of an angelic being.

Anthropomorphic Having the nature or characteristics of humans.

Antioch A Hellenistic city in Syria founded by Antiochus I, and capital of the Selucid empire, then a city in the Roman province of Galatia. Mentioned in *Acts of the Apostles,* and in Paul's letter to the Galatians. Antioch was an early headquarters for the Christ cult, and it was here that Paul verbally attacked Simon Peter.

Apostle (Gr. Apostolos) One who is sent out; a delegate or envoy; an honored believer with a special function; one who proclaimed the gospel.

Apocalypse/Apocalypticism A scriptural text focusing on the events that will take place at the end of time. The belief that the old world in which evil prevails is about to end, and will be replaced by a new world in which humanity will be entirely obedient to God's will and laws.

Apocalypse of James (*first*) Coptic Christian text discovered at Nag Hammadi in 1945, and attributed to James the Just, Jesus' brother and leader of the early Jesus movement.

Apocrypha/apocryphal Literally: hidden. In practical use, refers generally to early Christian scripture not included in the New Testament canon.

Apologist/apologetics A defense of, or arguments for, certain beliefs.

Aramaic The common tongue of northern Palestine during the time of Jesus.

Athanasius Fourth century orthodox bishop of Alexandria; ordered the destruction of all heretical Christian texts which probably led to burial of the *Nag Hammadi Library*.

Askew Codex, The (See: *Pistis Sophia*)

Athenagoras Greek philosopher and early apologist for orthodox Christianity.

Augustine (354-430) A major orthodox theologian, bishop, and defender of oxthodox faith against heresy.

Avatar God in human form who appears in different guises during special periods of history.

Bagavad Gita, The A holy book (especially for the Advaita Vedanta school of Hinduism) which is part of the Hindu epic, *Ramayana*, in which the avatar Krishna dialogues with Arguna about the illusory nature of reality, and the essential divine nature of every human being. Krishna tells Arjuna: "Tat tvam asi", "thou art that". That is, the Atman (Self) is Brahman (God).

Bartholomew Attributed in all four canonical Gospels of the New Testament as having been one of Jesus' twelve male disciples. Since he is mentioned nowhere else in the New Testament, it is not likely that he was an actual, historical, person. In Gnostic Christian texts, however, Bartholomew is often included in a small group of advanced disciples along with Matthew, Mary Magdalene, John, Philip and Thomas.

B.C.E./C. E. "Before the Common Era"/"Common Era." Secular dating nomenclature now preferred in the sciences and in the field of Biblical scholarship. Equivalent to B.C./A.D.

Berlin Codex Shorthand for Codex Berolinensis 8502. Written in Coptic on papyrus sheets and bound together as a book, the Berlin Codex was discovered in 1896 at an antiquities market in Cairo, Egypt, by Dr. Carl Reinhardt. The Codex was written some time during the fifth century and contains four separate works: *The Gospel of Mary*, the *Apocryphon of John*, the *Sophia of Jesus Christ*, and the *Act of Peter*.

Bitumen An asphalt substance used as cement or mortar. Bitumen was used to seal the earthenware pot containing the Nag Hammadi Library.

Bodhisattva In Buddhism, a buddha or enlightened being who renounces final entry into the state of Nirvana until all sentient beings have been saved (enlightened).

Canon/canonical In Christianity, the official collection of authorized texts selected for inclusion in the New Testament. Various early Christian groups compiled their own canon collection of sacred scripture. The Roman Catholic canon was not officially closed until 1546 C.E., at the Council of Trent.

Carpocratians Followers of Carpocrates, an early Gnostic Christian teacher from Alexandria during the first half of the second century.

Celsus Second century Roman philosopher and critic of Christianity who maintained that Christian faith had been founded on nothing more than the testimony of an "hysterical woman". Celsus' anti-christian rhetoric and accusations were apparently influential enough that the great Church father, Origen, felt compelled to write a defense in a book titled, *Against Celsus*.

Chenoboskia Ancient name for a town in the Nag Hammadi region of Egypt.

Christology Teachings and theology about Jesus as the Messiah or Christ.

Christophany An epiphany in which Jesus appears (see **Epiphany** below)

Clement of Alexandria Second century Church father and head of a school for Christian converts in Alexandria, Egypt. Clement wrote many works of theology and significant letters, one of which contains an excerpt from the *Secret Gospel of Mark*.

Clement of Rome (Clement I) Early second century bishop of the Church at Rome. Clement, like Paul before him, threatened the Corinthian church with excommunication or worse if the members of that church did not stop its drift towards heresy. The Pseudo-Clementines were "heretical" works falsely attributed to Clement of Rome.

Cleopas Mentioned in *Luke* 24:18 as one of two disciples who met the resurrected Jesus on the road to Emmaus. Otherwise, nothing is known about him.

Codex A collection of papyrus pages, with writing on both sides, bound together as a book. Invented by early Christians, this book method of preserving texts replaced the more ancient scroll—which contained writing on only one side of the papyrus.

Constantine Fourth century Roman emperor, and the first to become a Christian. Constantine ended the Roman persecutions of orthodox Christians, but continued to persecute those Christians who would not accept the Catholic form of the faith. Constantine extended his power, and the reach of the Empire, by swelling his Roman legions with Christian soldiers. Primarily responsible for convening the Church's famous Council of Nicea. Constantine—while remaining faithful to the orthodox cause—did not officially become a Christian (was baptized) until he was on his death bed.

Coptic The form of Egyptian language in use at the time Christianity was introduced to that country. Virtually all Egyptian Christian texts were written using Coptic (which employed the Greek alphabet).

Corinth A major Greek city in which the apostle Paul founded an important, but wayward, Christian congregation.

Daimon A Greek word originally meaning "spirit energies", and having a positive connotation. With its usage in the New Testament, however, the word came to mean "evil spirits" or negative forces.

Dialogue of the Savior Discovered at Nag Hammadi in 1945, *Dialogue of the Savior* purports to be a question and answer session between the risen Jesus and Mary Magdalene, Judas (not Iscariot) and Matthew. *Dialogue of the Savior* is thought to have been written sometime during the second century C.E. Only one, badly damaged, manuscript is extant.

Demiurge An aspect of the (inferior) creator-god. Designer of the left-hand things, i.e. the world of matter.

Didache (*The Teachings of the Twelve Apostles*) Discovered in 1875, the *Didache* is a manual of instruction for Christian life and communal living. Portions of the Didache date to the first century C.E., and reflect the teachings of Jewish Christianity. Unlike Paul, those Christians who compiled this text did not see Jesus as the son of God. Its authors also promoted equality between men and women. Women in this community were allowed to teach, prophecy, and even officiate in the distribution of the Eucharist.

Diatessaron Composed around the year 172 C.E., the *Diatessaron* is the earliest known "harmony" of the four New Testament Gospels. Attributed to Tatian, the *Diatessaron* is a single, continuous, Gospel narrative which eliminates duplications, harmonizes parallel passages and reconciles contradictions.

Docetic/Docetism The school of thought in which adherents claimed that Jesus was not fully human (but had existed only in a spiritual body) and did not, therefore, really suffer and die.

Ebionites From the Hebrew root meaning "the poor". May have referred to the earliest communities of Jesus people in and around Jerusalem. In his letter to the Galatians, Paul referred to these groups as "the poor". There is no question, however, that "Ebionites" was one name used to identify early Jewish-Christians.By the early part of the second century, however, Jewish-Christianity fell into disfavor, and Jewish-Christians—Ebionites in particular—were condemned as heretics by the Church.

Elohim Plural form of the word El, a Canaanite term for God that was appropriated by the Hebrews when they conquered Palestine.

Emmaus A town in Palestine mentioned only in Luke 24:13. Supposedly seven miles from Jerusalem, the existence of such a town has never been substantiated.

Enlightenment As used in this text, the state of consciousness in which the ego identity dissolves and is replaced by the consciousness of being one with all things.

Epiphany In Christian usage, refers to the recognition of a manifestation of a supernatural being.

Eschaton/Eschatology Greek word meaning the "end times". Eschatology is the set of beliefs having to do with events that will lead up to the end of time.

Essenes Along with Pharisees and Sadducees, the Essenes were one of three major Jewish sects during, and previous to, the first century C.E. The Essenes were devoted to holiness, strict observance of Torah, or Law, and separation from society. Scholars still debate whether or not the Qumran Community—which produced the Dead Sea Scrolls—was actually an Essene community.

Eusebius A contemporary and friend of Constantine, Eusebius was a fourth century bishop of Caesarea, a scholar, theologian, and the Church's first "historian" who wrote the famous *Ecclesiastical History* of early Christianity. As an "historian", Eusebius would have made a better apologist and mythologist since many of his claims are historically inaccurate,and are often based on nothing more than hearsay and tradition.

Exegete A person skilled at exegesis, or critical interpretation of scripture.

Extant Refers to literary works that are still in existence.

Galatians, Galacia At the time of Jesus and Paul, Galacia was a large Roman province in Asia Minor consisting of many cities. Paul's letter to the Galatians suggests that he founded more than one church in this region.

Gospel of Q, The "Q" is short for the German word, "quell", meaning "source". Also known as the Synoptic Sayings Source. New Testament scholars believe that they have identified a separate source document that was used by the authors of Matthew's and Luke's Gospels. While there are no extant remains of "Q" to prove its existence, scholars argue that the Gospel is embedded in these two Gospels. Scholars divide "Q" material into Q^1, Q^2 and Q^3—which represent three separate stages of transmission within the early Jesus movement, Q^1 being the most primitive.

Gnosis/Gnostic Greek word meaning, "to know". Refers to spiritual knowledge, intuition and enlightenment, rather than to intellectual knowledge. While there were Gnostic Christians, there were also Jewish Gnostics and a more generalized and larger movement which was neither. Scholars still cannot agree as to whether or not Gnosticism predated Christianity.

Gregory the Great Sixth century pope who famously delivered a homily in which he combined Mary Magdalene, Mary of Bethany, and the sinful woman of *Luke* 7:37, into a single person.

Hellenism Greek philosophy and culture.

Hasid/Hasidic A person who follows the teachings of Jewish mysticism—especially those found in the *Kabala*, a book of esoteric interpretations of scripture.

Hebrew *Bible*, The Texts officially accepted by rabbinic Judaism. Known to Christians as the Old Testament, the Hebrew *Bible* includes such sections as the Pentateuch, or five books of Moses, the Psalms, and the Prophets. Apocryphal books written before the first century C.E. are often included in modern versions of the *Bible*.

Heresiologist In early orthodox Christianity, one who spoke or wrote against Christian heresies.

Hippolytus Third century C.E. Roman Church father, philosopher, martyr and defender of the faith who wrote the extensive *Refutation of All Heresies*.

Ignatius Early second century Church father and bishop of Antioch in Syria.

James the Just Jesus' half-brother, and Nazirite priest, was a well known leader of the early Jesus movement centered in Jerusalem. James' holiness is attested to by numerous early writers, and he was loved and respected as a teacher throughout the Jewish community. In 62 C.E., by order of the high priest of the Temple, James was murdered. First thrown to the ground from a high Temple wall, he was then beaten to death with a laundry club. James was so popular and revered that many blamed the first Jewish/Roman war of 66-70 C.E. on his assassination. James was probably martyred for the same reason Jesus was: he protested against the Temple cult which believed that God could be appeased through the practice of animal sacrifice.

James, The (first) *Apocalypse of* Discovered at Nag Hammadi, *James* is a revelation dialogue between Jesus and his brother, James—although this text suggests that James is the *spiritual*, not physical, brother of the Lord. With its specific interest in James the Just, allusions to the fall of Jerusalem, and certain tenants of Jewish-Christian origin, *James* was probably written no later than the first half of the second century.

Jesus Movement Early traditions founded on the teachings of historical Jesus. Some within this movement may have become Christians. The Jesus movement ceased to exist as such after the Jewish/Roman wars of 66-70 C.E., although many scholars believe that remnants of these communities may have survived in various locations outside Palestine.

Josephus A Galilean, Josephus was a revolutionary leader against the Romans during the early days of the first Jewish/Roman war (66-70 C.E.). After his capture, however, he changed sides and became an historian for the Romans—writing Jewish history that covered a period just before and just after the time in which Jesus had lived. His two massive works were titled *The Jewish War* and *The Jewish Antiquities*.

John, The Gospel of Attributed to the disciple John, brother of James and son of Zebedee. Parts of *John* may be based on very early traditions, but the final version of this Gospel (having been redacted several times) was probably composed around the end of the first century C.E., making it roughly contemporary with the Gospels of *Matthew* and *Luke*—from which it differs greatly. Most scholars believe that *The Gospel of John* was produced by a Johannine school or community—referred to by Raymond Brown as The Community of the Beloved Disciple

Judeans Refers to Jews of the second temple period (520 B.C.E.-70 C.E.).

Justin Martyr Second century Church father and apologist who was martyred between the years 163-167 C.E.

Kingdom of God/Kingdom of Heaven/Son of Man Many early Christians believed that the "kingdom" Jesus spoke of was a world to come, and would be ushered in after an apocalypse had cleansed the Earth of evil doers. Jesus, however, did not use the term in an apocalyptic sense, but considered "the kingdom" to be a present reality that could be recognized by those who were spiritually astute. The terms "kingdom of God" and "kingdom of heaven" are often used interchangeably in the New Testament, and mean the same thing. In the *Gospel of Mary*, the term "Son of Man" is used to refer to the same present reality and state of consciousness.

Lacuna A blank spot in a manuscript caused by damage.

Luke, The Gospel of Like the author of *The Gospel of Matthew*, the anonymous author of *Luke* used at least two source documents (see *Mark* below) in the construction of his narrative, then added additional material—either of his own making, or drawn from yet another unknown source. The same author wrote *Acts of the Apostles*—or at least the first half of that work. Scholars believe that *Luke/Acts* was originally a single work. The usual dating for *Luke/Acts* is around 90 C.E. Some scholars now propose, however, that the document(s) may have been written as late as 120 C.E.

Mark, The Gospel of *Mark* is considered to be the first narrative Gospel, written around 70 C.E. The anonymous author of *Mark* probably used written sources and oral traditions as a basis for his mostly fictional narrative (which was copied by the authors of *Matthew* and *Luke*) about the life of Jesus. Mark's outlook was apocalyptic, and favors the patriarchal tradition of Simon Peter. Other versions of Mark's Gospel may have once existed (see ***Secret Mark*** below).

Matthew, The Gospel of This Gospel was written sometime after the end of the first Jewish/Roman war in 70 C.E.—most probably around 85 C.E. Like all of the Gospels, its author is anonymous—although the work was attributed to the disciple, Matthew. At least two source documents were used by the author: *The Gospel of Mark* and *The Gospel of Q*.

Mary and Martha of Bethany Mary and Martha were sisters of Lazarus who, in John's Gospel, Jesus raised from the dead. The two sisters and their brother were disciples and friends of Jesus, and lived in the town of Bethany which was located just outside Jerusalem.

Naassenes A heretical sect mentioned by the Church father, Hippolytus. Robert Eisenman believes that there is a direct link between the Naassenes and the Essenes, both of which may also be linked to the Ebionites, or "poor ones".

Nag Hammadi Now a town in Egypt near the site where the Christian Gnostic works—known as the Nag Hammadi Library—were discovered in 1945.

Nazirite A Jew who made certain vows that set him apart from regular Jewish society. Nazirites did not drink wine, were vegetarians, and did not cut their hair. Famous Nazirites were Samson, John the Baptist, James the Just and, perhaps, Jesus himself.

Nazoreans, Nazarenes, Nazirites A Jewish sect. There may be some linguistic connection between all of these appellations according to Robert Eisenman in *James the Brother of Jesus*. There may also be a connection with the heretical Naassenes.

Nicene/Nicea, and the Council of The Council of Nicea (325 C.E.) was called by Constantine on behalf of Catholic bishops in order to deal with the "Arian heresy". Arius, a priest of the church of Baucalis had—some years before—come into conflict with his bishop by denying the eternity and divine nature of the Word. Arius taught that Christ, the "Son" of God, was not co-substantial with the Father. In essence, Arius denied the strict Trinitarian concept of the Christian Godhead, and left the door open for Christian polytheism. While Arius gained wide support for his thesis, he was ultimately anathematized by the Council (which was attended by only a fraction of bishops worldwide—few of them Arians). As a response to the Arian heresy, the Council of Nicea produced what has been known ever since as The Nicene Creed—which contains the words, "We believe in one Lord, Jesus Christ, the only Son of God, eternally begotten of the Father . . . begotten not made, being of one substance with the Father. . ."

Nicodemus Nicodemus, who appears only in John's Gospel, was a member of the Sanhedrin, or Jewish high council. A Pharisee, Nicodemus had come to Jesus at night to learn about his teachings concerning the kingdom of heaven. After Jesus was crucified, Nicodemus—along with Joseph of Arimathea—received the body of Jesus and prepared it for burial.

Nicolaitans/Nicolaus A heretical Gnostic Christian sect (mentioned in the *Book of Revelations*). The founder of this movement, supposedly, was Nicolaus—one of the seven men elected as deacons of the Jerusalem church according to *Acts of the Apostles*.

Origen Perhaps the most brilliant early philosopher of Christianity, Origen of Alexandria lived during the early part of the third century and was an apologist for Christianity. Far more broadminded than those who came before and after him, Origen was a mystic, believed in reincarnation—and, if we are to believe the rumors, castrated himself in order to banish his sexual desires. Origen was a prolific writer and popular teacher, but for all of his troubles, the Church—long after his death—anathematized him as a heretic.

Oxyrhynchus A village in Egypt where numerous papyrus fragments of ancient Christian texts have been discovered.

Papyrus A bog plant found along the Nile river in Egypt. In ancient times, Papyrus was harvested to make writing material. The reed-like stalks of the plant were first cut open, then pounded flat. These flat pieces were then criss-crossed to form long sheets, and dried in the sun. Once dried, the material would be cut into individual pages, or in long strips used for scrolls.

Parable A vivid narrative containing metaphor and simile—never to be taken literally. The listener is left in doubt as to the exact meaning of the narrative, forcing him or her to think deeply and use intuitive powers of the mind.

Parousia Greek word for "presence". In Christianity, refers to the coming of the Messiah and/or the second coming of Christ.

Passion Generally refers to the last two days of Jesus' life, from his arrest to his burial.

Paul, the Apostle Originally Saul of Tarsus, Paul claimed to have been a Pharisee in his younger years and a zealous follower of the Torah, or Law. He also admitted having persecuted members of the Jesus movement after the crucifixion of Jesus. At some point Paul had a mystical experience in which he claimed that "God's son had been revealed to him". From that point on, Paul declared himself an apostle of Christ. Paul was a traveler and founded many churches along the rim of the Mediterranean Sea. He preached freedom from the Law and believed that salvation came as a result of God's grace through faith in Jesus Christ. Paul's letters to his churches make up the only written documents from an eyewitness to events during the early Christian period. Many consider Paul to be the true founder of Christianity.

Peter, The Gospel of A fragment of this Gospel (which may have been written around the end of the first century C.E.) was discovered during the 19th century in Egypt. It contains a passion and resurrection story that greatly embellishes similar traditions in the canonical Gospels.

Pharisees One of three principal sects of first century Judaism (along with the Sadducees and Essenes). The Pharisees were theologically liberal, but politically conservative (chafing against Roman occupation). They insisted on strict adherence to Torah (the Law of Moses), believed in an afterlife, and were often Messianists who expected a coming apocalypse. The Pharisees were roundly criticized in the canonical Gospels, but most scholars believe that these criticisms reflect a later time period when early Christianity was in conflict with Jewish synagogues. Ultimately the Pharisaic party became rabbinic Judaism after the destruction of Jerusalem in 70 C.E.

Philip, the Gospel of Discovered as part of the *Nag Hammadi Library*, Philip is not actually a "gospel" in any sense of the term. It is more of a sermon and a catechesis. *Philip* represents the philosophy of Valentinian gnosis, and was possibly written as late as the second half of the 3rd century C.E.

Pistis Sophia **(Faith Wisdom)** Also known as the Askew Codex, the *Pistis Sophia* was discovered in a London bookstore during the latter part of the 18th century. It is a long work containing, variously, 4-5 "books". Because most of the questions asked of the Savior in this work are attributed to Mary Magdalene, earlier scholars believed, erroneously, that the *Pistis Sophia* was the lost *Questions of Mary*.

Pseudo-Clementines Third century writings falsely attributed to Clement, the early second century bishop of Rome.

Pseudo-Mark Verses 9 through 20 which were added to the end of the original version of the *Gospel of Mark*, probably sometime during the second century.

Realized Eschatology The belief that by becoming a Christian one has already been resurrected in Christ.

Redactor One who reworks a text for a particular purpose. Redaction can include adding or subtracting material, substituting material, rearranging, etc.

Sadducees One of three principal Jewish sects of first century Judaism, along with the Pharisees and Essenes. The Sadducees were theologically conservative, still believed in ritual sacrifice, but not in an afterlife. In contrast to the Pharisees, they were politically liberal and were willing to work with their Roman occupiers. Since virtually all of the Temple priests were Sadducees, when the Temple and

Jerusalem were destroyed by the Romans in 70 C.E., the Sadducees ceased to exist.

Sanhedrin The Greek term for the Jewish high council. Led by the high priest of the Temple, this council decided on matters religious and political. Under Roman occupation, however, the high council had limited political authority. According to the canonical Gospels, the Sanhedrin condemned Jesus to death. This is fiction, however, since the Romans did not allow Jews to pass death sentences.

Secret Gospel of Mark, The An earlier version of *The Gospel According to Mark*, of which only a few passages remain. These were discovered embedded in a letter from Clement of Alexandria.

Simon Magus Simon the Magician, the protagonist of Simon Peter mentioned in *Acts of the Apostles*. The works of Simon and stories about his life are narrated in the Pseudo-Clementines, as well as many other early texts. Calling himself "the Standing One", Simon considered himself to be divine, performed great feats, and traveled with a consort, Helena. Simon is traditionally considered to have been the founder of Gnosticism, although this is unlikely.

Salome Not to be confused with Salome, niece of King Herod, who asked for the head of John the Baptist. Salome is mentioned only in the *Gospel of Mark* as a companion of Mary Magdalene, and a witness to the crucifixion and resurrection of Jesus. The name of Salome early on became associated with Gnostic Christians, which probably explains why she is not mentioned in any of the later canonical Gospels.

Son of Man Earlier scholars considered this self-referential term used often by Jesus to mean the one who would usher in the apocalypse. Certainly the authors of the canonical Gospel often gave this sense to those words they put into Jesus' mouth. Many contemporary scholars, however, explain that if Jesus used this term at all, he was merely identifying himself as a human being (son of Adam).

Sophia Ancient Greek word meaning "wisdom". Sophia is often personified as a divine feminine figure in Judaism as well as in Gnostic Christian literature.

Sophia of Jesus Christ, The This work was discovered, first, as part of the Berlin Codex, during the nineteenth century. That codex also included *The Gospel of Mary, The Apocryphon of John*, and *The Act of Peter*. A second manuscript of *Sophia* was also discovered at Nag Hammadi in 1945. A revelation dialogue, *The Sophia of Jesus Christ* is also a Christian reworking of a non-Christian text called

Eugnostos the Blessed. The Sophia may have been written as early
as the second half of the 1ˢᵗ century.

Synoptic   From two Greek words meaning "to see together". *The
Gospels of Matthew, Mark*, and *Luke* are considered synoptic
Gospels because, when they are laid side by side in columns, it
becomes obvious that there are direct narrative parallels between
al three Gospels. Nearly all scholars agree that Matthew and Luke
copied Mark's Gospel almost word for word, then added their own
separate source material and fictional stories before and after Mark's
verses.

Syzgies   According to Gnostic Christians, God manifested all of
creation in pairs of opposites: night and day, black and white, male
and female, good and evil, positive and negative, etc. Unlike in Taoist
philosophy where yin and yang are equal forces in the Universe, the
philosophy of the syzgies maintains that one in each pair of opposites
is ultimately weaker than the other.

Tao/Taoism   Chinese philosophical system founded on principals
attributed to Lao Tzu who is credited as the author of the *Tao Te
Ching* (Way of life) which was written around 1,000 B.C.E. The
Tao, or Way, is composed of two polar opposite—but constantly
interchanging—cosmic principals called yin and yang.

Tertullian   Abrasive second century Church apologist and polemicist,
Tertullian was a convert from Carthage in North Africa.

Thomas the Contender   A text found at Nag Hammadi, and attributed
to the disciple, Thomas. In Gnostic Christianity Thomas was revered
as a special disciple who, like Mary Magdalene, had great spiritual
insight. "Contender", often translated as "athlete", refers to one who
works at gaining mastery over his or her desires and physical urges.

Thomas, The Gospel of   Three fragments of *The Gospel of Thomas*,
written in Greek, were discovered At Oxyrhynchus, Egypt, near the
end of the nineteenth century. Then, in 1945, a complete copy of
Thomas, written in Coptic, was discovered at Nag Hammadi. The
Gospel is a "sayings" gospel, not a narrative. It consists of 114 logia
("words"), or sayings of Jesus. Some of these sayings can be traced
to the historical Jesus, and do not appear in any of the canonical
Gospels. Still other sayings, which parallel sayings found in the
canonicals, represent more primitive (that is, more authentic) versions.
These parts of *Thomas* have been dated to 50 C.E. A second layer
of sayings was added to *Thomas* sometime around the end of the
first century, and shows a definite Gnostic influence. Like *Thomas*

the Contender, the *Gospel of Thomas* is attributed to the disciple, Thomas, and probably originated out of a Thomasian community.

Torah Divine Law in Judaism, also known as the "Law of Moses". Torah is also often identified with the entire Pentateuch—the first five books of the Hebrew *Bible*.

Uios Greek word for "son"—often used in a non-gendered sense.

Valentinian Texts produced by the second century school of Gnostic Christianity founded by Valentinus.

Subject Index

A

Achmim: iii-iv; and *The Gospel of Mary* 21

Acta Thaddaei: Mary Magdalene replaced in 234

Acts of the Apostles: as misrepresenting Paul's relationship with the Jesus movement 99; and the disappearance of Peter 135, 140; its representation of Simon Magus 144-146

Acts of John: 215

Acts of Philip: Mary Magdalene's role in 107-108, 233-234

Adam: as victim of Eve's deception 43, 71-72; as physical source of Eve's existence 71

Alexandria, Egypt: as seat of the Church's power in the East 18

Alexandria, Library of: the Christian destruction of 35

Ananias and Sapphira: as condemned by Peter 143

Anastasis (see Goddess)

Androgyny: as a Gnostic metaphor 11; and the Canaanite God, El 75; as spiritual ideal 111

Antioch: as site of showdown between Peter and Paul 99, 140; as center of the Christ cult 136

Apocryphon of John, The: viii, 215

Apostle: legitimate and "false" 31, definition of 54; women as the first apostles 54, 78; Mary commissioned as 54; women as 57; Hippolytus' support for women as 78; Paul and "false" apostles 88-90; Paul rejected as apostle by Corinthians and Galatians 87-89; Paul rejected as an apostle by James the Just 87; women denied apostolic succession 151

Arsinoe: as one of four primary female disciples of Jesus in *The (first) Apocalypse of James* 28

Asherah: as Yahweh's consort 76

Askew Codex (See *Pistis Sophia*)

Athanasius: as ordering the elimination of heretics in the East iv, 259

Augustine: and his rhetoric against women 70; and sexual innuendos about Mary Magdalene 79; his words as the basis for Pope Gregory's sermon 79; and gender bias 81

B

Bartholomew: the Coptic literature of 107; Mary replaced in 235

Beloved Disciple: 216-217, 219, 253-254; community of 215-216; 223, 254; Mary as 216-218, 253-254

Berlin Codex: discovery of i, 21; contents of 21-22 (see also *The Gospel of Mary*)

Book of the Resurrection of Jesus Christ: Mary replaced in 235

Book of Revelations: 215

P

Paul the Apostle: his silence on Mary as a witness to the resurrection 37-38, 44, 85-86, 90-91, 95-96, 163, 167-168; as a resurrection witness 46; his credentials as an apostle 38, 87-88; and Junia 57; his disinterest in the historical Jesus 87; as a Baptist 149; his gender bias 38, 42; as a misogynist 38, 42, 44 ; his anti-feminist rhetoric 44, 46, 87, 91; his policy on women 37-38, 41-42, 44-46, 53, 86-87; in relation to the Corinthian women prophets 38, 41-42, 44-46, 49, 57, 85-101, 122-123; and Eve 89; seeing himself as special 47-48; retaining the belief that God demands sacrifice 157; as a disciplinarian 44-45, 92-93, 96, 144; his gospel 48, 87, 89-90; and patriarchal authority 49, 93; and the "pillars" of Jerusalem 65, 99-100; his relationship with Peter 136-137; as a persecutor of the Jesus movement 87-88, 100; as an enemy of the Jesus movement 90, 99-100; as rejected by the Jesus movement 87, 91, 94, 97, 99; and false apostles 48, 88-89, 90, 136; and heretics 44-45; his journeys to Jerusalem 136; his Christ cult 136-137; and the risen Christ 45, 94; and the general resurrection 47, 94-95; his list of those to whom the risen Jesus had appeared 37, 168; description of Jesus' appearance to Paul 169; and the apocalypse 121, 123; as Luke's mentor 38,

70, 82; In *I Corinthians* 41, 44-45, 86-88, 120, 123, 144, 168; in *II Corinthians* 88; in *Acts of the Apostles* 113; and the Galatians 87, 89, 168, 238; and sister-wives 120; as celibate 120-121, 128; on celibacy 121-123; his policy on marital duties 46; and the God of Jesus 77

Parousia: 95

Pentecost: in *Acts of the Apostles* 65-66; as Luke's commissioning story 66

Peter (Simon Peter/Cephas): of history 133; as a subject for myth-making 34; as a disciple of John the Baptist 146, 149-150; named by Paul as having seen the risen Jesus 37; as a hypocrite 137, 139; compared to Satan by Jesus 137; as a denier of Jesus 137, 154, 232-233; and the arrest of Jesus 140-142; as a denier of the resurrection 195, 233; as ill tempered 20, 52; as negative, vacillating and dense 137; as spiritually undeveloped 156; as a rock of faith 138; as having visions of the risen Jesus 37, 85, 150-151, 212; as having a wife 120-121; as related to others 133; as one of the "pillars" of the Jerusalem church 65, 93; in Paul's first letter to the Corinthians 37, 168; in Paul's letter to the Galatians 85; his relationship with Paul 136, 139-140; his first meeting with Paul 136; his meeting with Paul at Antioch 137; accused by Paul as a Judaizer 137; his disappearance from the Jerusalem church 135,

R

Resurrection event: originally identified with Mary Magdalene 166-167; as a transformative experience for Peter 138; as taking place over a long period of time 167; as understood by Gnostic Christians 190-191

S

Sadducees: their rejection of the afterlife 94

Salome: In the *Pistis Sophia* 20; in *The (first) Apocalypse of James* 28; in *Mark* 169-170, 177, 187; in *Secret Mark* 181-182, 185, 187; associated with heretical sects 200, edited out of *Matthew* 200, 206; as the sister of James and John 216

Shaman: Jesus as 180, 185-187

Simon Peter (see Peter)

Simon Magus: 16, 144-146

Sister-wives: 119-121

Sophia: as the Hebrew Goddess 76; and the wisdom teachings of Jesus 76; in Gnosticism 10, 76; and the divine couple 76; as a victim of patriarchal monotheism 76; as the divine Mother 112; Mary as 10, 27, 109, as the facilitator of the Savior's resurrection 112

Sophia of Jesus Christ, The: discovery of viii, 25; as part of the Berlin Codex 22; as part of *The Nag Hammadi Library* 22; as a revised version of *Eugnostos the Blessed* 22; and the seven female disciples of Jesus 25; theology of 25; Mary as important disciple in 25; its ending compared to the ending of Pseudo-Mark 193

Soul: in Gnostic theology 12

Synoptic Sayings Source (see *The Gospel of Q*)

Syzgies: compared to yin and yang 11; as described in the Pseudo-Clementines 188

T

Temple, Jerusalem: its destruction and relationship to James the Just 99-100

Tertullian: his sermon on the sin of Eve 70-71; as orthodox heresiologist 13; his rhetoric against women 70-71; and Genesis creation myth 77-78; his parroting of Paul 78; on celibacy 129; and the physical resurrection 196

Thomas, The Gospel of: attributed to James the Just 28, 98; its multiple discoveries 28; as the "fifth" Gospel 29; and formerly unknown sayings of the historical Jesus 29; its construction and dates of composition 30; in relation to *The Gospel of Q* 30; its lack of interest in the death and resurrection of Jesus 30, 169, 238; as portraying a non-apocalyptic Jesus 30; its disinterest in Jesus as the Messiah 138, or as a savior from sin 138, 244; its representation of Simon Peter 149-150; and Peter's attack on Mary Magdalene 30; compared

The Primary Texts in which Mary Magdalene Appears

THE GOSPEL ACCORDING TO MARK

70 C.E.

Sources: oral tradition

Mark identifies Mary as a follower of Jesus in Galilee, and a witness to his crucifixion (along with "Mary the mother of James and Joses, and Salome").

Mark connects Mary Magdalene to the earliest empty tomb tradition.

Mary and the other women are given an apostolic commission ("go and tell his disciples") by a "young man".

The original ending of Mark's Gospel is lost, so the earliest extant version of *Mark* provides no evidence that the women ever made contact with the male disciples.

"Pseudo-Mark": This second century appended ending to Mark's Gospel (16:9-20) identifies Mary as once having been possessed by seven demons (an entry probably borrowed from *The Gospel of Luke*); also that Jesus appeared to Mary after his crucifixion. In Pseudo-Mark, Mary reports her experiences to the male disciples, but her report is rejected.

THE GOSPEL ACCORDING TO PETER (fragment)

70-120 C.E.

Sources: oral tradition.

Although *Peter's* empty tomb tradition underwent a later embellishment, the original author of *Peter* accessed the same early tradition about Mary Magdalene as the author of *Mark*. While the women at the empty tomb in *Peter* are denied an apostolic commission, this part of the empty tomb story was probably reworked by a later redactor for the purpose of diminishing the importance of the female witnesses to the resurrection.

Peter provides no evidence that women witnesses to the resurrection made contact with the male disciples.

THE GOSPEL ACCORDING TO JOHN

50-100 C.E.

Sources: oral tradition and the *Signs Gospel*.

Although the final redaction of John's Gospel was completed near the end of the first century, the original author seems to have accessed a very early tradition about Mary Magdalene. While Mary is accompanied by other women at the crucifixion of Jesus, she alone witnesses his resurrection. When Jesus appears to Mary, he commissions her, specifically, to be his apostle to the other apostles.

In *John* 20:2-10 Mary reports finding Jesus' tomb empty to Simon Peter and "the disciple whom Jesus loved". However, these verses are a later scribal addition and not part of the original story. In *John* 20:18, Mary reports to the male disciples as a group and makes a statement of faith: "I have seen the Lord".

The resurrection narrative in which Jesus appears to Mary is also an ascension story. Jesus sends Mary to the male disciples (to create resurrection faith) precisely because he will be making no other appearances. Subsequent stories in John Gospel's in which Jesus appears to male disciples are, therefore, redactions to the original text.

THE SOPHIA OF JESUS CHRIST

50-100 C.E.

Source: A non-Christian work known as *Eugnostos the Blessed*.

A post-resurrection revelation dialogue Gospel, *Sophia* names Mary Magdalene as one of a group of seven women disciples of Jesus, although no other women are named.

Mary is named along with four male disciples: Matthew, Philip, Thomas and Bartholomew. If the *Sophia* can be dated to the second half of the first century, as some scholars propose, then the name of Mary Magdalene became identified with Gnostic-Christian theology prior to the beginning of the second century.

THE GOSPEL ACCORDING TO MATTHEW

80-90 C.E.

Sources: *The Gospel of "Q"* and *The Gospel of Mark*.

Matthew reports that Mary Magdalene witnessed the crucifixion of Jesus along with "many" women who had followed him in Galilee. Two other women are named: Mary the mother of James and Joseph, and the mother of the sons of Zebedee.

Mary Magdalene and "the other Mary" witness the empty tomb of Jesus, experience an earthquake, and are greeted by an angel who tells them to "go quickly and tell his disciples that he has risen from the dead, and behold he is going before you to Galilee."

As the women "run" to carry out these instructions, Jesus himself meets them on the way. He tells them to "go and tell my *brethren* to go to Galilee, and there they will see me." But there is nothing in *Matthew* that suggests that the women actually made contact with the male disciples.

These two commissioning stories in *Matthew* represent two different resurrection traditions involving Mary Magdalene. The first (Angelophany) parallels the tradition found in *Peter* and *Mark*, while the second (Christophany) parallels the tradition in *John* and in pseudo-Mark.

THE GOSPEL ACCORDING TO THOMAS

Earliest layer: 50 C.E. Second layer: 90–100 C.E.
Sources: oral tradition.

Thomas contains two references to Mary Magdalene, both of which are probably the work of a redactor who wrote near the end of the first century C.E.

Thomas represents Mary Magdalene as a prominent member of Jesus' inner circle. Only five disciples are named: Mary, Matthew, Simon Peter, Thomas and Salome. Peter is represented in this Gospel as Mary's protagonist.

THE GOSPEL ACCORDING TO LUKE

90-120 C.E.
Sources: *The Gospel of Q* and *The Gospel According to Mark*.

In an attempt to diminish Mary's credibility as a witness to Jesus' resurrection, the author of *Luke* invented Mary's "seven demons", refused to identify her by name as a witness to the crucifixion, subordinated her authority to that of the male disciples and denied her an apostolic commission. The author of *Luke* represents the earliest attempt by an orthodox Christian evangelist to substantially alter the original tradition about Mary Magdalene through inference and innuendo.

DIALOGUE OF THE SAVIOR

50-100 C.E., with a final redaction sometime during second century.
Sources: none.

As in *Thomas*, *The Sophia of Jesus Christ*, and the *Pistis Sophia*, Mary is featured as one of just a few prominent disciples of Jesus. Only Matthew and Judas (Judas-Thomas) join Mary in making statements and asking questions of Jesus. At one point Mary states: "I want to understand things just as they are". After another of her statements the author says of Mary: "She uttered this as a woman who understood completely."

THE GOSPEL ACCORDING TO MARY (fragment)

125 C.E.
Sources: unknown

In this Gospel attributed to Mary Magdalene, Mary plays the role of teacher, comforter, woman of great faith, and Jesus' most worthy and beloved disciple. Mary comforts and strengthens the grieving disciples who fear for their own lives. Peter asks Mary to share Jesus' secret teachings with him and the other disciples. After she does so, however, Peter and his brother, Andrew, accuse Mary of lying, and of teaching "strange" ideas. They also argue that Jesus would not have passed on his secret teachings to a woman! Levi comes to Mary's defense, and states that Jesus chose Mary as a confidant because of her spiritual maturity.

THE EPISTULA APOSTOLORUM

150 C.E.
Sources: one, or all, of the canonical Gospels.

In this "Letter of the Apostles", the author retells the crucifixion story, but does not mention any witnesses. "Three women" go to the tomb of Jesus on Easter morning where they mourn and weep. The Ethiopic manuscript names Mary Magdalene, Martha and Sarah. The Coptic manuscript names Mary Magdalene, an unidentified Mary, and the daughter of Martha.

Just as the women discover the empty tomb they are met by Jesus, who sends one of them to his "brothers" to inform them that he has risen. The Ethiopic text names Mary as the emissary, but the Coptic text replaces Mary with Martha. In both versions, the male disciples do not believe the women.

THE (first) APOCALYPSE OF JAMES

180-250 C.E.

Sources: possibly Jewish-Christian Gospels such as *The Gospel of the Hebrews* and *The Gospel of the Ebionites*

Not a true apocalypse, this work is a dialogue between the risen Jesus and his brother, James the Just. Mary Magdalene (Miriam) is identified as one of four female disciples (out of a group of seven) who are given names. The others are Salome, Martha and Arsinoe. Jesus specifically instructs James to encourage the teaching of these four women, and James expresses amazement at how these seemingly powerless women have become strong by the "perception that is within them."

THE GOSPEL ACCORDING TO PHILIP

250-300 C.E.

Sources: none.

Philip is not actually a gospel, but a compilation of theological teachings by the author. He names Mary Magdalene in two different sections of the text. In the first, he tells his audience that Mary Magdalene was one of three women who always walked with the Lord (together with Mary his mother, and her sister). The second reference to Mary compares her to Sophia, or Wisdom, and names her as Jesus' "companion". As in *The Gospel of Mary*, the *Pistis Sophia*, and *The Gospel of Thomas*, Mary Magdalene elicits the jealousy of the other disciples because she is favored by Jesus. Jesus explains that he favors Mary because she—alone among the disciples—has the ability to recognize "the Light".

THE *PISTIS SOPHIA*

250-300 C.E.

Sources: none.

In this very long work, Jesus continues to discourse with his disciples for eleven years after his resurrection. Mary Magdalene asks thirty-nine of the forty-six questions posed to Jesus. But rather than just asking questions, Mary also interprets, explains and otherwise earns her stripes as a teacher in this work. Other disciples named are Mary, the mother of Jesus, Martha, Salome, Philip, James, Peter, Andrew, Bartholomew, Matthew and Thomas.

Mary is singled out, along with John "the virgin", as one of the two disciples who will surpass all the others in spiritual understanding, qualifying them to receive the "mysteries in the Ineffable". Because of their spiritual abilities, Jesus promises that Mary and John will sit on his right and left hands, and states, "I am they and they are I".

The *Pistis Sophia*, like *The Gospel of Thomas* and *The Gospel of Mary* represent Simon Peter as Mary's protagonist.

THE EVOLUTION OF CHRISTIANITY

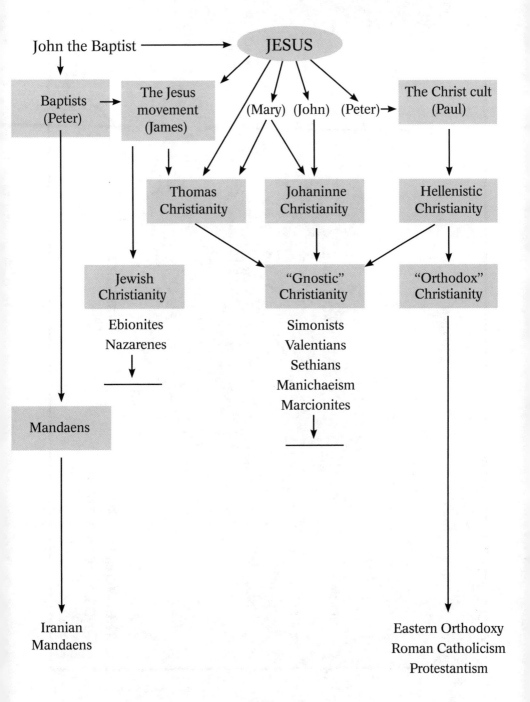

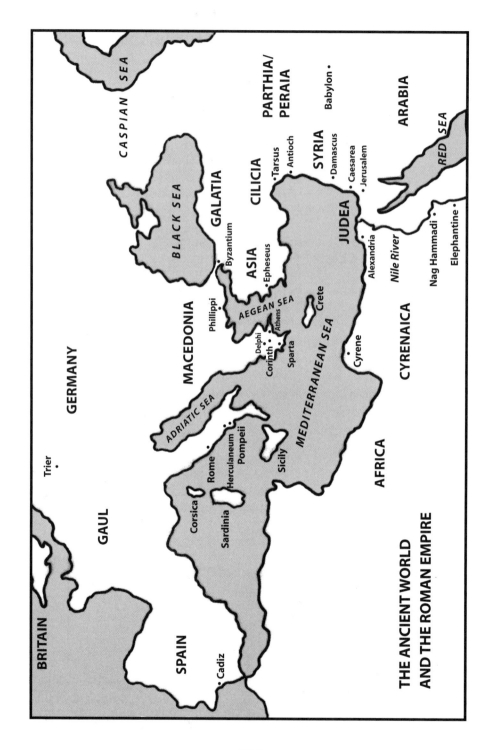

THE ANCIENT WORLD
AND THE ROMAN EMPIRE

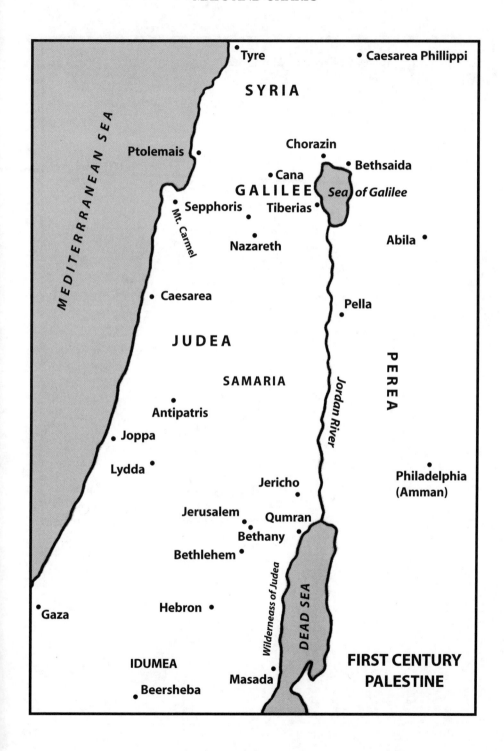

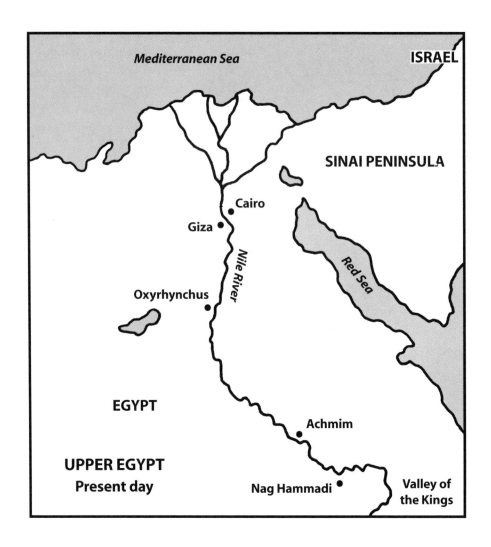

About the author

Richard Hooper received his Bachelor of Arts degree in the Philosophy of Religion from San Francisco State University in 1966, and his Master of Divinity degree from Pacific Lutheran Theological Seminary in 1970. He was ordained by the American Lutheran Church in 1971, and for the following eight years conducted a specialized ministry to the counter culture on the Monterey Peninsula in California. In 1978, Richard left the ministry to become a nature recordist and radio commentator. He subsequently founded the Nature Recordings© and World Disc Music© record labels, and was CEO of World Disc Productions© for many years. Throughout his business career, the author has maintained his interest in the continuing "quest for the historical Jesus", and his studies in the field of Gnostic Christianity and the early Church.

Also available by Richard Hooper:

The Gospel of the Unknown Jesus: His Secret Teachings from the Apocryphal and Gnostic Gospels

For further information, contact: info@sanctuarypublications.com

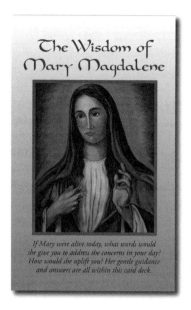

The Wisdom of
Mary Magdalene

*If Mary were alive today, what words would
she give you to address the concerns in your day?
How would she uplift you? Her gentle guidance
and answers are all within this card deck.*

NOTES

NOTES